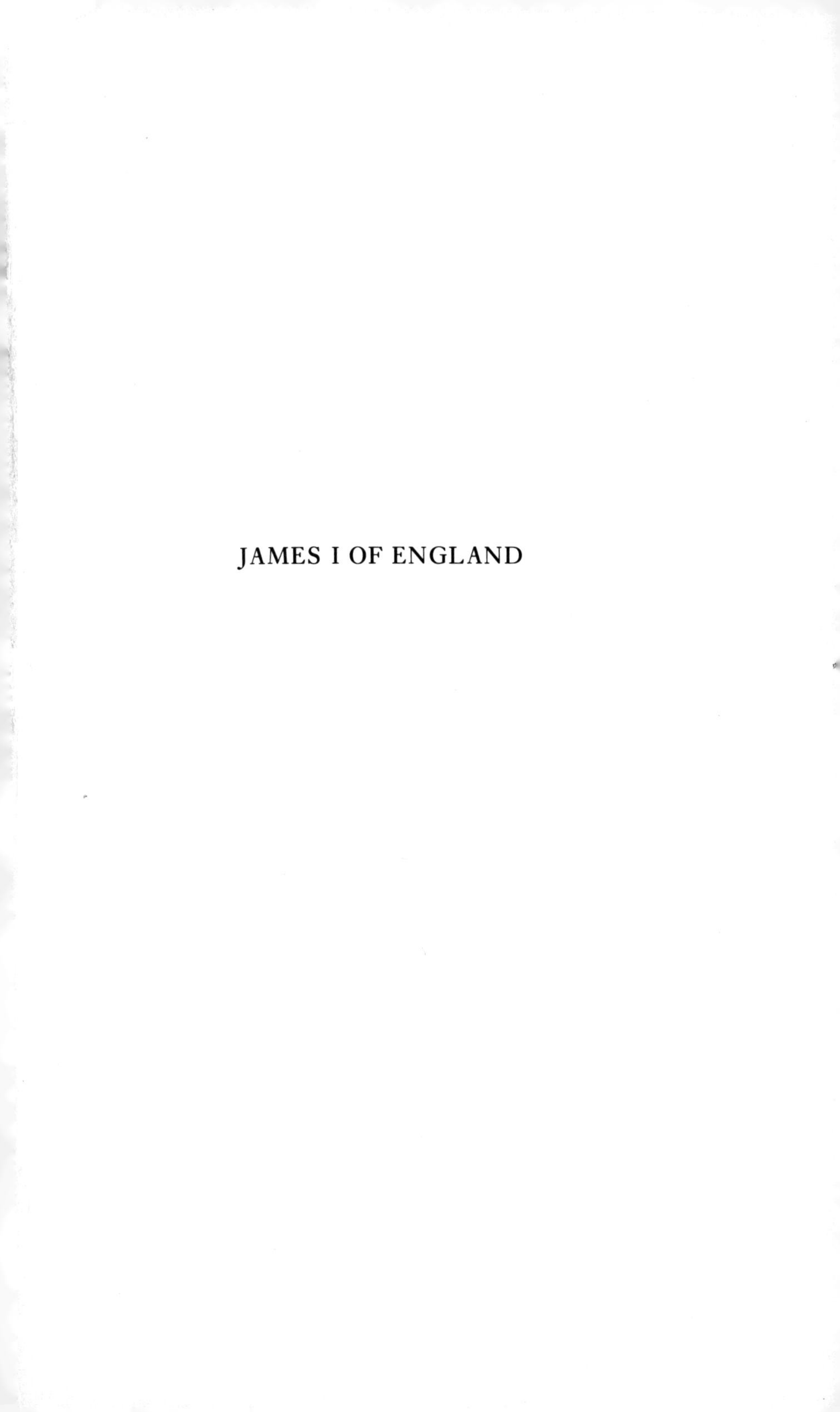

JAMES I OF ENGLAND

BY THE SAME AUTHOR

The Making of a King:
The Early Years of James VI *and* I

James V, *King of Scots*

The Life and Times of Edward II

The Stewart Kingdom of Scotland, 1371–1603

The Kings and Queens of Scotland

The Crowned Lions:
The Early Plantagenet Kings

James VI *of Scotland*

Anthology

The Voice of the Lion:
Caroline Bingham's Choice
of Scottish Historical Verse

JAMES I

OF ENGLAND

Caroline Bingham

WEIDENFELD AND NICOLSON
London

To

my parents

Cedric and Muriel Worsdell

First published in Great Britain by
George Weidenfeld and Nicolson Ltd
91 Clapham High St, London SW4 7TA
1981

ISBN 0 297 77889 7

Printed in Great Britain by
Butler & Tanner Ltd
Frome and London

Contents

Illustrations

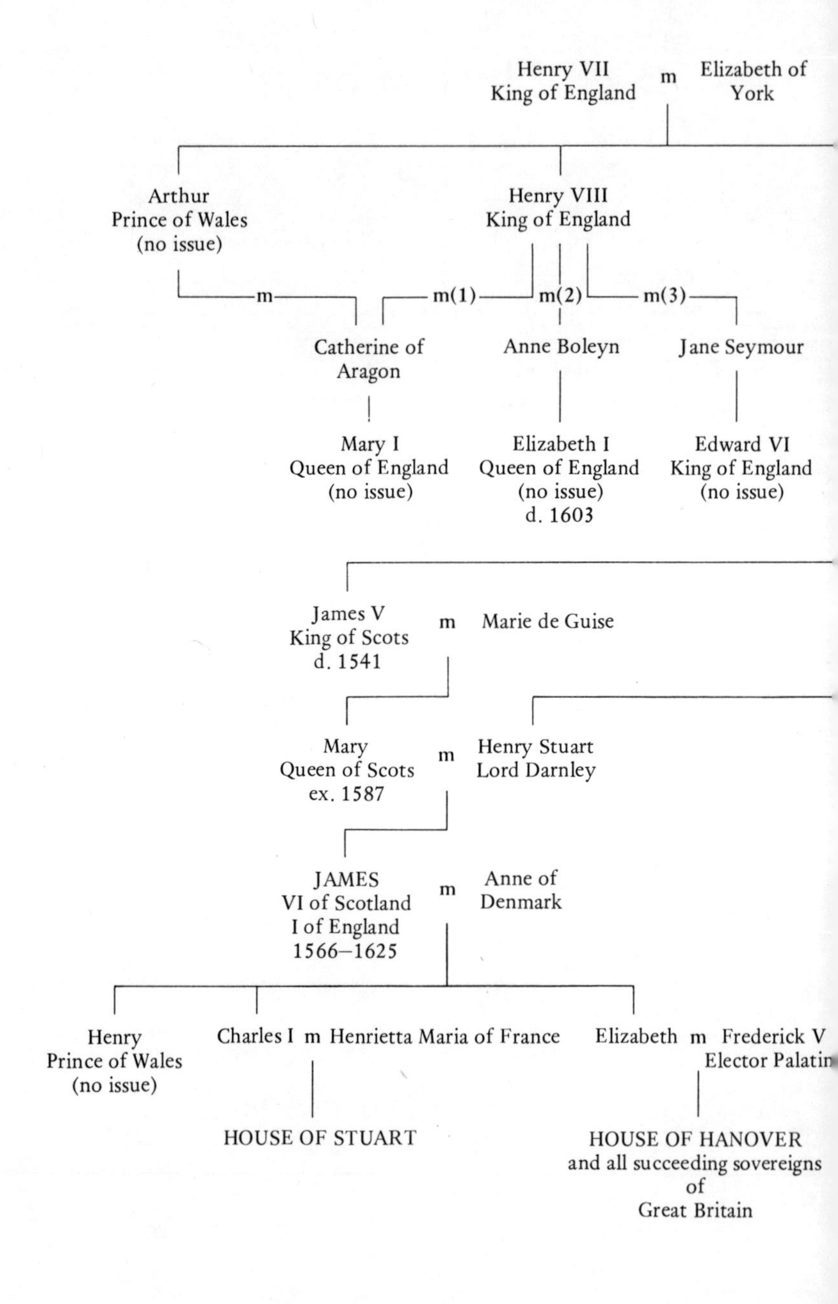
Henry VII
King of England
m
Elizabeth of
York
Arthur
Prince of Wales
(no issue)
Henry VIII
King of England
m
m(1)
m(2)
m(3)
Catherine of
Aragon
Anne Boleyn
Jane Seymour
Mary I
Queen of England
(no issue)
Elizabeth I
Queen of England
(no issue)
d. 1603
Edward VI
King of England
(no issue)
James V
King of Scots
d. 1541
m
Marie de Guise
Mary
Queen of Scots
ex. 1587
m
Henry Stuart
Lord Darnley
JAMES
VI of Scotland
I of England
1566–1625
m
Anne of
Denmark
Henry
Prince of Wales
(no issue)
Charles I m Henrietta Maria of France
Elizabeth m Frederick V
Elector Palatin
HOUSE OF STUART
HOUSE OF HANOVER
and all succeeding sovereigns
of
Great Britain

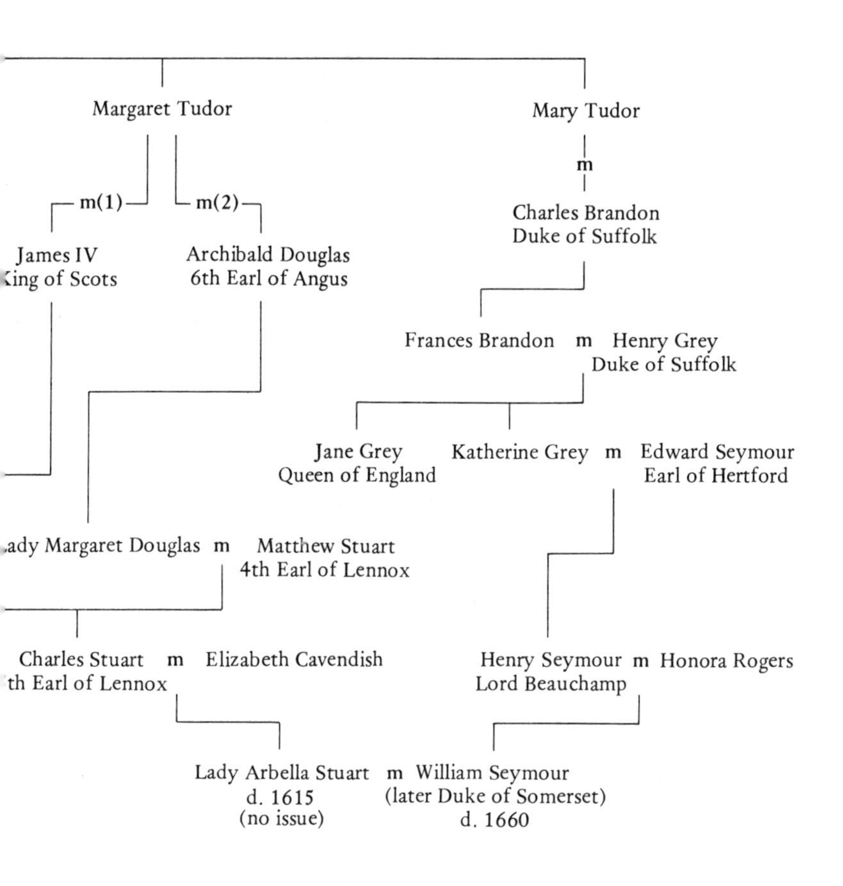

King James VI and I, his family and relations, and the succession to the throne of Great Britain

Author's Note

James I of England is the sequel to *James VI of Scotland*, in which the story of the King's life was recounted from his birth to his thirty-seventh year. Readers of this book who have not read the preceding volume will find a résumé of its contents in the Prologue. Readers who are already familiar with those events may prefer to begin at Chapter One.

I would like to take the opportunity of paying the debts of gratitude incurred in the writing and preparation of this book.

In the first place, I am particularly grateful to Dr Roger Lockyer, who with great generosity lent me the manuscript of his forthcoming biography of George Villiers, Duke of Buckingham. My evaluation of Villiers's character owes much to Dr Lockyer's research, and individual statements are acknowledged in the text and in the notes.

So far as illustrations are concerned, I would like to thank Mr Michael Farr of Warwickshire County Record Office for being kind enough to allow the reproduction of illustration number 10, and Mr Richard Chamberlain-Brothers, who showed me this manuscript and a number of others connected with King James I also in the possession of the Record Office.

Miss Elspeth Evans of the National Portrait Gallery gave me the benefit of her help and advice, and I would like to thank the Gallery for permission to reproduce illustrations nos 1, 4, 5, 7, 8, 9, 11, 12, 13, 14, 16 and 17. The National Portrait Gallery provided the reproduction of number 9, but the present location of this picture remains undiscovered.

The Trustees of the British Museum have kindly given their permission for the reproduction of illustrations nos 2 and 3; nos 6 and 15 are reproduced by courtesy of the Parham Park Collection.

Finally I would like to thank Miss Alex MacCormick of Weidenfeld & Nicolson, the editor of this book, for her sensitive and meticulous assistance, and also Mrs Sheila Collins, who has been typing my manuscripts for a decade.

CAROLINE BINGHAM
October 1980

PROLOGUE

The King of Scots

I was alone, without father or mother, sister or brother, King of this realm and heir apparent of England.

James VI of Scotland, 1589

IN THE SMALL hours of 10 February 1567 the city of Edinburgh was roused by a violent explosion. Before morning the strange story of what had happened was on the lips of everyone: the old house known as Kirk O'Field on the outskirts of Edinburgh had been blown up by a massive quantity of gunpowder. Dead in the garden lay Henry Stuart, Lord Darnley, consort and cousin of Mary, Queen of Scots; but the destruction of the house in which he had slept had left him uninjured, and he had died of strangulation.

The death of Darnley remains one of the unsolved murders of history, but the principal suspect, both to his contemporaries and to posterity, was James Hepburn, fourth Earl of Bothwell. Suspicions concerning the Queen's complicity in her consort's death received apparent substantiation when Bothwell was tried for the murder and acquitted by a transparent travesty of justice, after which the Queen married him, on 15 May. Her downfall followed swiftly. A rebellion against her, led by her half-brother, James Stewart, Earl of Moray, triumphed on the battlefield of Carberry Hill, near Musselburgh, exactly one month later. The Queen of Scots was imprisoned in Lochleven Castle, and forced to abdicate in favour of her infant son, Prince James.

The only son of Mary, Queen of Scots and Lord Darnley had been born on 19 June 1566; he was crowned as King James VI in the Church of the Holy Rude at Stirling, on 29 July 1567. The coronation of the thirteen-month-old King by newly-devised Protestant rites completed a process begun in 1560 when the Reformation rebellion successfully established the Protestant religion in Scotland. The rebellion of 1567 illustrated that the reign of the

Catholic Mary, Queen of Scots, had been no more than an interlude in the progress of the Reformation. The leaders of the successful regime resolved to consolidate their victory by educating the new King to become the exemplar of Reformation rulers.

Before this educational experiment was begun, a diversion was caused by the escape of Queen Mary from Lochleven, on 2 May 1568. But on 13 May her hastily collected army of supporters was defeated by the forces of the Earl of Moray, at the battle of Langside, near Glasgow. Queen Mary, in the disastrously mistaken belief that she would receive help from her cousin Elizabeth I of England, sought refuge south of the Border, where her hopes were rewarded with the hospitality of a cage. For the remainder of her life, nearly nineteen years, Mary was detained as a prisoner in England.

King James VI spent his early years in Scotland almost as closely confined, for his own safety, in Stirling Castle, where he received a formidable education from the classical scholar and reformer George Buchanan, who taught him Greek, Latin, History and Calvinist Theology, and endeavoured to indoctrinate him with *avant garde* political theories concerning the rights of the subject against a tyrannous king. James, who proved to be a clever and obstinate pupil, absorbed the scholarship of Buchanan, but repudiated his political theories. The Stirling schoolroom was probably the incubator for James's own celebrated contribution to political theory: vigorous expositions of the Divine Right of Kings, in two books, *The Trew Law of Free Monarchies* (1598) and *Basilikon Doron* (1599), which stressed the king's responsibility to God alone and his subjects' duty of obedience.

James grew to be a precociously intellectual boy, with a passionate love for horses and hounds, and a deep-seated fear of violence. Most of the time he was safe enough in Stirling Castle, but outside the sheltering walls his kingdom was in turmoil while his adherents fought a civil war with the remaining supporters of his mother. Occasional incursions of violence into his little world left him with a neurotic terror of naked weapons which he was never able to overcome.

Four regents ruled Scotland for James VI: his uncle the Earl of Moray, who was assassinated in 1570; his paternal grandfather the Earl of Lennox, who was killed in an affray in 1571; his guardian the Earl of Mar, who probably died of natural causes, though poison was rumoured, in 1572; and his second cousin the Earl of Morton, who ruled successfully and authoritatively for some years.

The King experienced the first happiness of his life when he fell in love with his Franco-Scottish cousin, Esmé Stuart d'Aubigny, who visited Scotland in 1579. The charm of this sophisticated man, who encouraged and may have exploited James's affection, won him the dukedom of Lennox, created for him in 1581. Lennox and his ruthless henchman Captain James Stewart arranged the downfall of Morton, by accusing him of participation in the murder of the King's father. Morton denied participation, but admitted foreknowledge, for which he was executed. Lennox, who was a Catholic, was deeply suspect to the Protestant Kirk and nobility, who imagined that he had come to Scotland to plot the restoration of Queen Mary. Despite his efforts to obviate suspicion by religious conversion, Lennox's influence was ended in 1582 by a *coup d'état*, in which the King was seized and held captive by the Earl of Gowrie and other Protestant lords. Lennox was forced to leave Scotland, and he died in France the following year. The grief-stricken James remained a prisoner for ten months, but at the age of seventeen he was ambitious to assert his authority over his kingdom. In June 1583 he escaped from his captors and began to reign independently, assisted by Captain James Stewart, whom he created Earl of Arran.

From the beginning of his personal rule James revealed the preoccupation which obsessed him increasingly during the ensuing years: his claim to the English throne (see Genealogical Table). In the hope of inducing Queen Elizabeth I to grant him official recognition as heir apparent, from 1584 onwards he began to cultivate closer relations with England. Elizabeth, who distrusted Arran as a self-seeking adventurer, encouraged the coup by which he fell from power in 1585. James then formed an administration in which most shades of political and religious opinion were represented. With the wise advice of his Chancellor, John Maitland of Thirlestane, James VI began to emerge as the 'Universal King' which he aspired to be.

In 1586 a formal alliance with England was concluded, and though Elizabeth steadfastly refused to recognize James as her heir, she began to pay him a pension of £4,000 a year, and led him to understand that his prospects of succeeding her were improving. This delicately balanced situation was almost immediately threatened by the revelation of Mary, Queen of Scots' peripheral complicity in Anthony Babington's conspiracy to dethrone and assassinate Elizabeth.

James was placed in an appalling dilemma. His attitude to his mother was inevitably dichotomized. He had tried not to believe Buchanan's story that she was an adulteress and a murderess; but he had never known her, and he could not love her. So long as she lived he could not feel secure, either as King of Scots or as prospective heir of England: in Scotland there remained a remote possibility that the international situation might favour her restoration; in England her claim to the throne preceded his own. Nonetheless, James sent Elizabeth a forceful protest against her trial and condemnation to death. In the end, although he threatened to sever diplomatic relations with England, he did not do so; he could not bring himself to jeopardize his own future by taking the only action which might have saved his mother's life.

James's ambition to gain the English throne also dictated his attitude to the Spanish Armada of 1588. Friendly neutrality was the policy towards England which he endeavoured to maintain, though at the last moment he promised Elizabeth his support, in return for extravagant inducements offered by the English ambassador. However, James knew that his Catholic lords, led by the Earl of Huntly, for whom he had a warm affection, were in communication with Philip II of Spain. In the event of a Spanish victory, he hoped that his favour to Huntly and the latter's co-religionists might give him a chance of survival. The crisis was averted by the defeat of the Armada before James was driven to show his hand, and relations with England were unimpaired.

In 1589 James left the British Isles for the only time in his life when he sailed to Oslo to bring home his bride, Anne of Denmark. After the death of his first love, Esmé, Duke of Lennox, James had remained susceptible to the charms of handsome men; but he was not wholly uninterested in women, and he had willingly initiated negotiations for his marriage. He returned to Scotland with his sixteen-year-old Queen on May Day 1590. Briefly he was ardently in love with the golden-haired Anne, to whom he addressed some charming, if conventional. love poems. Anne's intelligence was no match for her husband's, and their relationship failed to deepen with the passage of time. Intrigues and quarrels caused a period of domestic discord, which in turn gave way to an agreeable though attenuated *camaraderie*. Dynastically the marriage served its purpose, for Anne bore James a total of seven children, of whom three – Prince Henry, Princess Elizabeth, and Prince Charles – survived the perils of infancy.

During the later years of James's reign in Scotland he had three principal preoccupations: the regulating of relations between Church and State; the imposing of law and order; and the securing of the English succession.

Under the leadership of Andrew Melvill, a disciple of Calvin, the Scottish Kirk imitated the church of Calvinist Geneva, and claimed to be a theocratic organization empowered to direct the secular head of state, in accordance with the will of God. James counter-attacked by stressing the Divine Right of Kings, and by adroitly infiltrating the Presbyterian structure of the Kirk with a reinstated episcopacy as the channel of royal authority. When Andrew Melvill declared that the King was 'God's sillie vassal' (i.e. God's simple servant), and James pronounced his well-known dictum 'No Bishop, no King', both men were equally successful in crystallizing their views in a single phrase. In his own lifetime James was victorious, for Melvill was exiled to end his life as Professor of Theology at the University of Sedan, while James's Scottish Bishops became servants of the Crown, instrumental in the King's task of imposing law and order in the remote areas of his kingdom.

The problems of re-establishing public order and of administering justice, especially in the Highlands and the Isles, after the convulsions of the Reformation period and the disorders of his own minority, might have appeared to James to be insuperable. But gradually his continuous labours to implement the rule of law and to make life less violent and hazardous for his subjects were rewarded with success. Certain dramatic incidents – such as the mysterious 'Gowrie Plot' of 1600, which may have involved an unsuccessful attempt upon James's life – serve to highlight his difficulties. But this drama, and others, were mere interruptions of the process which, after he had become King of England, enabled James to write: 'This I may say for Scotland, and may truly vaunt it: here I sit and govern it with my pen. I write and it is done, and by a Clerk of the Council I govern Scotland now, which others could not do by the sword.' James's boast did less than justice to the achievements of his mediaeval ancestors; but if he were comparing himself only to post-Reformation rulers and regents, his words were true enough.

Elizabeth I died on Thursday, 24 March 1603. For the previous two years James had been in secret correspondence with her principal Secretary of State, Sir Robert Cecil, who had assured him that his accession to the English throne would be secured peacefully. News of the Queen's death was brought to James by an unofficial messenger, Sir Robert Carey, who rode at breakneck speed from London to Edinburgh, to arrive at Holyroodhouse 'be-bloodied with great falls and bruises' late on Saturday night, and to hail King James VI by his new titles of 'King of England, France and Ireland'. The title to France was an anachronistic fiction; the others represented the fulfilment of his ambitions.

CHAPTER ONE

'The Augmentation'

The augmentation ... is but in cares and heavy burdens.

James VI and I to his son
Prince Henry, April 1603

KING JAMES VI of Scotland was three months short of his thirty-seventh birthday when he became King of England, but already he was a consciously paternal figure. In *The Trew Law of Free Monarchies* he had written 'the style of *Pater Patriae* [the father of his country] was ever, and is commonly, used to Kings'; and as he had been described in adolescence as 'an old young man', he may well have appeared a convincing *Pater Patriae* when he reached the threshold of middle age.

An Italian diplomat who saw him soon after his arrival in England found his appearance impressive: 'The King has a handsome, noble and jovial countenance. His colouring is pale, his hair rather fair, his beard square-cut and longish. He has a small mouth, blue eyes, and a straight, well-formed nose. He is a man in the full vigour of life, neither fat nor thin, in height [he is] tall rather than short.'[1] This description makes it clear that James's hair was no longer the pale red which it had been when he was a boy, and that his colouring in general was fairer than it appears in the portraits which show him in maturity. The historian Arthur Wilson, who saw him in later life, remembered that he was 'of a ruddy complexion, his hair, of a light brown in his full perfection, had at last a tincture of white'.[2] These contemporary impressions are necessary correctives to the misleading patina with which time has darkened his portraits.

On Sunday, 3 April 1603, when he had been officially King of England for eight days, James attended morning service in the High Kirk of St Giles, in Edinburgh. After the sermon he rose to take a formal farewell of his subjects, or of the appropriately representative cross-section of them which had squeezed itself into the church. He made 'a most learned, but more loving oration', in which he exhorted his subjects to continue in 'obedience to him, and agreement amongst themselves'.[3] He made a public promise that he would return to Scotland every three years, but in fact he made the return journey only once, in 1617. No doubt James made his promise in good faith, without envisaging the difficulties which frequent journeys would involve. Uppermost in his mind was Sir Robert Carey's recent ride from London to Edinburgh in the record time of three days. Before that event, and throughout James's reign in Scotland, messengers had ridden to and fro, the speed of their travel varying with the urgency of their business, the quality of their horses, and the conditions of the weather and the road. Ambassadors had ridden north and south, moving more slowly as ambassadorial dignity demanded. But there had been constant coming and going, and James had no reason to suppose that the King could not come and go as freely as any other. It was by his commands that others set out on their travels, and his personal wishes had certainly as much force as his commands. In later years he discovered that his wishes were frequently subject to the exigencies of financial necessity; but as he prepared to enter the rich inheritance of his English kingdom, he did not imagine that necessity would ever curtail the actions of England's king.

James's hasty preparations to leave Scotland seemed far more necessary at the time than they appear in retrospect. His peaceful accession had been the work of Sir Robert Cecil, supported on the Queen's death by the English Privy Council; to the last Elizabeth had made no public acknowledgement of James as her heir. Until the solemn proclamations of James's accession were read in the cities and towns of England, the English people continued in fear of invasion or insurrection; and until the King had taken possession of his kingdom, there could be no public certainty that neither of these interruptions of the peaceful course of events would occur. With the knowledge of how uneventful was the transition from the Elizabethan to the Jacobean age, it is difficult to remember that, for those who were living at the time, tranquil continuity was not guaranteed.

Under these circumstances, it was not surprising that James decided to leave behind in Scotland his wife, who was pregnant, and his three children, whose lives assured dynastic security in both kingdoms.

Prince Henry, now nine years old and heir to two thrones, was being educated in the care of the Erskine family in Stirling Castle. The fact that James had wished to continue the tradition of royal fosterage, and to have his eldest son brought up as and where he himself had been, had remained a cause of lasting resentment to Queen Anne. Though Anne herself had spent part of her childhood in fosterage, the royal family of Denmark had maintained a closeness and a strong bond of affection which naturally Anne would have hoped to recreate with her own children. However, James's decision, for reasons of security, was inflexible, and contact between mother and son was too infrequent to content the Queen.

Before he left Scotland James wrote to Prince Henry:

> My son,
>
> That I see you not before my parting, impute it to this great occasion wherein time is so precious, but that shall, by God's grace, be recompensed by your coming to me shortly, and continual residence with me ever after. Let not this news make you proud or insolent, for a King's son and heir was ye before, and no more are ye yet. The augmentation that is hereby like to fall unto you is but in cares and heavy burdens; be therefore merry but not insolent.... Look upon all Englishmen that shall come to visit you as upon your loving subjects, not with that ceremony as towards strangers, and yet with such heartiness as at this time they deserve....
>
> Your loving father,
>
> James R[4]

This affectionate and sensible letter contained a prescient observation which, in the ensuing weeks, it became increasingly difficult for James himself to keep in mind: that the 'augmentation' of his kingdoms would be 'but in cares and heavy burdens'. From the moment of his entry into England, his southward journey was a sustained triumphal procession. As he rode towards London such a chorus of rejoicing, praise and adulation greeted and accompanied him that with some justification he might have begun to believe that the prospect before him offered no cares or burdens at all. A contemporary observer, Sir Roger Wilbraham, was moved to write: 'I pray unfeignedly that his most gracious disposition and heroic mind be not depraved with ill-counsel, and that neither the wealth and peace of England make him forget God, nor the painted flattery of the court cause him to forget himself.'[5]

The style of 'painted flattery' offered to the new King derived directly from the previous reign. Elizabeth I had skilfully nourished the cult of her own personality. Symbolically personified as a virgin goddess – variously named Gloriana, Belphoebe, Astraea, Cynthia, Diana – Elizabeth had received poetic worship. Not only poets but sober statesmen had observed the convention of addressing the Queen as though she were indeed a goddess. A remarkable example of this exalted style is provided in a letter written by Sir Robert Cecil to the Queen in 1592:

> The comfort I receive of those sacred lines [i.e. assurances of favour written him by the Queen] is best expressed in silence, but I have written them anew in my heart and adjoined them unto the rest of my admiring thoughts, which always travailing from wonder to wonder spend themselves in contemplation, being absent and present, in reading secretly the story of marvels in that more than human perfection.[6]

The easy metamorphosis of Elizabethans into Jacobeans ensured that James inherited uninterrupted the cult of the monarch which his predecessor had developed. As he journeyed through England he heard, in a repetitious series of panegyrics, words which accorded with the theories of kingship that he himself had expressed in *The Trew Law of Free Monarchies* and *Basilikon Doron.* In his prefatory sonnet to the latter, James had written,

> God gives not Kings the style of gods in vain
> For on His throne His sceptre do they sway....

How exalting he must have found it, therefore, to hear himself greeted with the words,

> Hail, mortal god, England's true joy, great King![7]

James travelled south 'all his way to London entertained with great solemnity and state, all men rejoicing that his lot and their lot had fallen in so good a ground. He was met with great troops of horse and waited on by the sheriff and gentlemen of each shire, in their limits; joyfully received in every city and town; presented with orations and gifts; entertained royally all the way by noblemen and gentlemen at their houses....'[8]

On 16 April he reached York, which, as the seat of the Council of the North, still enjoyed the status of the northern capital of England. The following day '... being Sunday, his Majesty passed towards York Minster, being one of the goodliest minsters in all the land.... To this minster the King passed to hear the sermon; and at the gate [i.e. of the King's Manor, where he was lodging] a coach was offered to his Highness, but he graciously answered "I will have no coach, for the people are desirous to see a King, and so they shall, for they shall as well see his body as his face." So to the great comfort of the people he went on foot to church.'[9]

On Monday, 18 April, he extended a gracious and grateful welcome to Sir Robert Cecil, who had hastened to York to establish with the new King the relationship of mutual trust on which Cecil's whole future career would depend. James was not unmindful of how much he owed to him. He confirmed Cecil's tenure of office, and assured him of his future favour with joviality and benevolence. A few days later Cecil thankfully recorded: '... his virtues are so eminent as by my six days kneeling at his feet I have made so sufficient a discovery of his royal perfection as I contemplate greater felicity to this isle than ever it enjoyed.'[10]

James's response to Cecil's well-judged veneration was marked by that slightly heartless playfulness which, in an age that still had a place for court dwarfs, was the unenviable portion of men of small stature. Cecil was hunchbacked, and no more than five feet three inches in height. His great intellect and high position saved him from the crueller treatment offered to the low-born who were similarly disadvantaged. However, in 1588 he had written to his father words as close to criticism of Queen Elizabeth as anyone might have dared to approach: 'I received from her Majesty ... a gracious message under her sporting name of Pygmy ... though I may not find fault with the name she gives me, yet seem I only not to mislike it because she gives it....'[11]

This benign brutality, which Cecil had been obliged to endure with a smile, was less cruelly offered by James, who spontaneously nicknamed him 'Little Beagle'. A king who loved sporting dogs probably bestowed this 'sporting name' without an unkind thought; but Cecil might well have sighed with weary acceptance, and perhaps remembered a line from a popular play: 'Little again? Nothing but low and little?' He rode south once more to attend Queen Elizabeth's funeral on 28 April, leaving James to follow at the leisurely pace of a royal progress.

From York James rode to Doncaster, where he lodged at an inn, the Bear, 'giving the host of the house, for his good entertainment, a lease of a manor-house, in reversion, of good value'.[12] By the 21st James had reached Newark, where he lodged in the castle in which King John had died. It is seldom forgotten by any historian that at Newark James ordered the summary execution of a cut-purse who had travelled with the royal entourage and preyed upon it *en route*; but it is seldom remembered that he also ordered a general amnesty 'to all the other poor and wretched prisoners, clearing the castle of them all'.[13]

On 23 April James was received at Burghley House, the seat of Thomas Cecil, second Lord Burghley, Sir Robert Cecil's elder half-brother, who in 1605 James was to create Earl of Exeter. Burghley House, according to a lyrical chronicler of the King's journey, seemed 'so rich as if it had been furnished at the charges of an Emperor. Well, it was all too little, his Majesty being worthy much more, being now the greatest Christian Monarch of himself as absolute.'[14]

The imperial theme was stated with equal hyperbole when King James was entertained at Sir John Harington's house of Burghley-Harington.[15] Here he was obliged to listen to the seventy-three verses of Samuel Daniel's *Panegyric Congratulatory*, which began:

Lo, here the glory of a greater day
  Than England ever heretofore could see
In all her days! When she did most display
  The ensigns of her pow'r; or when as she
Did spread herself the most, and most did sway
  Her state abroad: yet could she never be
Thus bless'd at home, nor e'er to come to grow
  To be entire in her full orb till now.

And now she is, and now in peace; therefore
  Shake hands with Union, O thou mighty State!

Now thou art all Great Britain and no more;
No Scot, no English now, nor no debate:
No borders but the Ocean and the shore;
No wall of Adrian serves to separate
Our mutual love, nor our obedience
Being subjects all to one Imperial Prince.

As it turned out, Daniel was a century premature in hailing the Union, which so far was only a Union of Crowns; but the project of a complete Union was dear to James, and no doubt Daniel's reference to it gave him as much pleasure as did the poet's reference to the imperial status of Great Britain. Daniel went on to prophesy that greater gifts would be bestowed through the King's personal qualities:

Glory of men! this hast thou brought to us
And yet hast brought us more than this by far:
Religion comes with thee, Peace, Righteousness,
Judgment and Justice; which more glorious are
Than all thy kingdoms....

Perhaps the sharp spring air, the smell of horses and hounds, and a hard fall from his horse while he was hunting with Sir John Harington served to remind James that he was mortal. On 26 April, the day after his fall, he returned to Burghley House in a coach. He was reported to be in great pain, but the next day, none the worse, he resumed his journey, and reached Hinchingbrooke in Huntingdonshire. Here it was said that he received 'the greatest feast that had ever been given to a King by a subject'.

The prodigal owner of Hinchingbrooke was Sir Oliver Cromwell, an inappropriately-named host for a Stuart sovereign. He was the uncle of the future Lord Protector, whose career he lived to witness with heart-felt disgust. The elder Sir Oliver had married the widow of the immensely rich Italian-born financier, Sir Horatio Palavicino, and he won great popularity by his generous spending of his wife's wealth. It was said that his lavish entertainment of James led the latter to exclaim: 'Morry, mon, thou hast treated me better than any since I left Edinburgh!'[16] If the story is not apocryphal, this cheerful tribute might have given the King's previous hosts considerable offence.

At Hinchingbrooke James was presented with a volume of poems entitled *Sorrow's Joy*, a book which perfectly illustrates the transfer of monarch-worship from Elizabeth to James. Most of the poems contributed to *Sorrow's Joy* have little intrinsic merit, and are of greater interest for their content than for their quality. Thomas Cecil, Lord Burghley, offered a typical contribution:

> Now is my muse clad like a parasite
> In partie-coloured robes of black and white:
> Grieving and joying both, both these together,
> But grieves or joys she more, I know not whether ...
> Eliza's dead, – that rends my heart in twain,
> And James proclaimed – this makes me well again.
> If hopes fail not (and if they do 'tis strange),
> The loss is but as when the Moon doth change;
> Or when as Phoenix dies; Phoenix is dead,
> And so a Phoenix follows in her stead....
> Whilst April showers do teach us how to weep
> The Sun betwixt two watery clouds doth peep,
> And bids us cheerly sing our tears among:
> Consent to different notes must tune our song.

The theme was best summed up by Henry Campion in a single line:

> For Phoebe dead, a Phoebus now doth shine.

In his youth at the court of Scotland James had presided over a coterie of courtly poets to whom he was 'the royal Apollo'.[17] Campion may have been aware that he was recalling a previous personification, but for the most part English poets sought new symbolic metaphors to personify James. The death of a monarch and the succession of another inevitably suggested the allegory of the Phoenix, since the unique bird of mythology could only propagate its kind in death. Other personifications were Solomon, 'England's Caesar', and King Arthur (since Arthur, in English folklore, had been, like James, King of all Britain).

Despite the fears which Sir Roger Wilbraham expressed that the 'painted flattery' offered to James might cause him to 'forget himself', in the long run it was remarkably unefficacious in corrupting him. His own views of the exalted nature of kingship led him to accept language which to the ears of later centuries sounded narrowly distinguishable from blasphemy as merely his due. He also accepted the cult of the monarch as an ingredient of the court life of England, though he grew impatient of its public manifestations, and refused to play the god before his people as Elizabeth had played the goddess. It is a frequently repeated story that, sick and tired of the attentions of a crowd which he was told desired to gaze upon his face, he exclaimed 'God's wounds! I will pull down my breeches and they shall also see my arse!' If adulation ever led James to forget himself, he did so in reacting against it.

The effect upon him of a single aspect of the 'wealth and peace of England' was more profound, in the sense of being more deleterious to his performance as a ruler.

Many pleasant descriptions have been written of James riding through springtime England, amazed at the lushness of his new kingdom by comparison with the barrenness of Scotland, astonished by the evidences of abundance on every side, in contrast to the harsh poverty which he had left behind. This traditional picture requires modification.

The countryside through which James's journey lay, the north-east and the east midlands of England, presents not a sudden but a gradual contrast to southern Scotland. The landscape for the most part is flat and sometimes bleak, the land is fertile enough but not noticeably rich until the home counties are reached.

At the beginning of the seventeenth century England was still largely open country with great tracts of marsh and heath. Here and there areas of natural forest still remained, year by year eroded for timber and fuel. Slowly the wild landscape was tamed by enclosure, and the patchwork of fields which came to characterize the English countryside took its place. The transformation of England had been in progress for only a century when King James rode south; wildness, not cultivation, surrounded him for much of his journey.

As the first Stuart King traversed this kingdom it would not have appeared to him to have been flowing with milk and honey. The series of poor harvests which had extended through the 1590s would have left its mark in the form of visible poverty, and James would have ridden past many poor cottages and even more wretched hovels, the dwellings of people at or below subsistence level. The contrast between Scotland and England which impressed itself upon him was not general but specific; it was the contrast between the lifestyles of the Scottish and English nobility.

James was well acquainted with the mediaeval strongholds of his Scottish lords, some of which had renaissance improvements, and with the new tower-houses which lords and lairds (gentry) had been building during the later years of his reign. The style of the new buildings was still defensible, the structures were massively walled, several storeys high, and crowned with conically-roofed turrets. Indoors, the bold and colourful decoration of painted ceilings extended above rooms which for the most part aspired to a modest standard of comfort and contained few articles of luxury.[18]

As he journeyed through England James found the greatest among his new subjects living in a far more elaborate manner. Old strongholds and fortified manor-houses were still in use, but the newer Elizabethan great houses were not built for defence. They were monuments to the worldly success of their builders, and in the exact sense of the words they were 'stately homes': they were intended not only to house the families and servants of their owners, but to receive royal and noble guests. Burghley House had been used to entertain Queen Elizabeth, though the first Lord Burghley had seldom enjoyed the leisure to occupy it. It was 'set down uncompromisingly in the fields to the south of Stamford' in rambling and ostentatious splendour.[19]

James was offered an even greater revelation of magnificence at the other Cecil house of Theobalds, which he reached on 3 May. Theobalds was old Lord Burghley's second monument to his own success, and the inheritance of his second son; but while Burghley House remains, not one of Theobalds' rose-bed bricks stands upon another. However, a synthesis of contemporary descriptions enables the reader's inward eye to see what the King saw as he approached it:

Before him stood the entrace door of the great house, flanked by magnificent stretches of mullioned windows. On either side of the broad façade rose square towers, three storeys high, more glass than wall in their stretches of window. From each tower rose four turrets, surmounted each with a golden lion holding a golden vane shining brightly in the sun above the rich red brickwork of the building below.[20]

In front of the entrace stood the small, dignified figure of Sir Robert Cecil, with the English Privy Councillors grouped around him, waiting to offer their official welcome to the King. When the ceremonial presentations were over, Cecil led the King into his house.

Here wonders were to be seen. There was a hall whose ceiling was a kind of planetarium with the signs of the zodiac, the stars shining by night, and the sun performing its course by ingenious mechanism by day. Flanking the walls were trees with natural bark attached, with birds' nests and leaves and fruit so natural in appearance that when the steward opened the windows overlooking the pleasure gardens outside birds flew in and, perching on the trees, sang.[21]

James was entranced by the elegance and impressed by the opulence of Theobalds. The glorious house, which he not only admired but immediately coveted, was the culminating example which he encountered of the lavishness of the English nobleman's life. The impression which remained with him was that if a subject could live in such a style as a king might envy, then he must be the subject of a king of almost incredible wealth. In fact, the King of England must be as rich as Croesus. Recurrent financial crises may have disabused James of this erroneous opinion in the end; in the beginning it caused him to forget such financial caution as he had ever possessed.

From Theobalds James rode the last stage of his journey to London. He was met 'four miles from London by the Lord Mayor and such unspeakable number of citizens as the like number was never seen to issue out upon any cause before'.[22] Ever since James had left Scotland a steady stream of Englishmen had been pouring north to meet him. John Chamberlain, whose correspondence vividly illuminates the Jacobean scene, had written as early as 30 March: 'many run thither of their own errands, as if it were nothing but first come first served or that preferment [i.e. advancement] were a goal to be got by footmanship.' It seemed that he was not far wrong, for 'in every county it pleased his Majesty to knight the chief gentlemen ... commended to him by the noblemen and favourites about him.... In his Majesty's passage to his own house [probably the reference is to Whitehall Palace] there were three hundred knights at the least made, never known but by report to his Majesty.'[23] The total by far surpassed this contemporary estimate, for in the first four months of his reign James created 906 knights. His prodigality in bestowing knighthoods aroused amazement, which was chiefly critical except in the recipients, for during the forty-five years of Elizabeth's reign only 878 men had been knighted, not all of them by the Queen herself, or in accordance with her wishes.[24] Before he became aware of what he did, James changed the character of English knighthood by making it a badge of status, in contrast to the policy of Elizabeth, who had intended that it should be a mark of personal prowess or merit.

A brief cessation of the process which historians have labelled 'the inflation of honours' occurred after the King's arrival in London:

> ... It seemed the King, misliking out of his royal heart that either the unworthy should receive his favours, or that the worthy should come to favour by unworthy means, removed from the Tower [of London] to Greenwich, and there published that such as expected knighthood should attend [wait] till the coronation; whereby the throng at Court ... was suddenly abated ... so as his Majesty to his just contentment had time to see his houses, castles, forests and chases within twenty miles of London, and therein took high delight, especially to see such store of deer and game in his parks for hunting, which is the sport he preferreth above all worldly delights....[25]

In London, besides the Tower, which was seldom used as a royal lodging except by tradition immediately before the coronation. James acquired St James's Palace, the remains of the mediaeval Palace of Westminster, and the rambling Tudor Palace of Whitehall, the headquarters of the royal household, which stretched along the north bank of the Thames, between Westminster and Charing Cross. The ancient importance of these palaces is recalled today by the formal expression 'the Court of St James's' and the informal use of the words 'Westminster' and 'Whitehall' to denote the seats of government and bureaucracy. Beyond London lay the outer circle of royal residences, which James, like Elizabeth before him, occupied on progress: Greenwich, Richmond, Hampton Court, Windsor, Nonsuch and Oatlands. In 1607 he would add Theobalds, which Cecil was persuaded to give him in exchange for the old royal manor of Hatfield.

James had another reason than his desire for the pleasures of the chase, or for peace and quiet after his journey, which led him to leave London and acquaint himself with the properties of the Crown. During the summer of 1603 London suffered the worst visitation of the plague which overcrowding and insanitary conditions had hitherto invited. At the beginning of the seventeenth century the population of the mediaeval city and its newer and ever-growing suburbs was between a quarter of a million and 300,000, of which in a single summer 30,000 died of the plague.

Despite the overshadowing presence of death, which almost silenced the rejoicing that had greeted the King's accession, it was decided that the coronation should be held on 25 July, appropriate as the feast of St James the Great. In the intervening weeks James awaited the arrival of his wife with their two older children.

No sooner had James left Scotland than Queen Anne had taken advantage of his absence to demand the custody of Prince Henry from his guardian, John Erskine, second Earl of Mar. But to the Queen's fury Mar stood firm in his obedience to James, and refused to hand over the Prince without his father's consent. Anne wrote James a letter of bitter complaint, in which she far exceeded the bounds of truth or justice, accusing James of preferring Mar to herself and of slighting her royalty in refusing her the custody of her son. Despite the injustice of her accusation, it is very easy to understand Anne's sentiments. The fact that her pregnancy ended in a miscarriage at about this time may have done more to bring about James's sympathetic reaction to her wishes than did her own violent expression of them.

Once James was safely in possession of the throne of England it was no longer important that Prince Henry should be kept securely at Stirling. James gave Mar permission to allow the Prince to be united with his mother, and he wrote Anne a pleasant and reasonable answer to her tirade:

My Heart,

Immediately before the receipt of your letter I was purposed to have written unto you, and that without any great occasion ... but now your letter has given me more matter to write, although I take small delight to meddle in so unpleasant a process....

... I thank God I carry that love and respect unto you which, by the law of God and nature, I ought to do to my wife and mother of my children, but not for that ye are a King's daughter, for whether ye were a King's or a cook's daughter, ye must be all alike to me, being once my wife. For the respect of your honourable birth and descent I married you; but the love and respect I now bear you is because ye are my married wife, and so partaker of my honour as of my other fortunes. I beseech you excuse my rude plainness in this; for casting up of your birth is a needless impertinent argument to me. God is my witness I ever preferred you to all my bairns, much more than to any subject; but if you will ever give place to the reports of every flattering sycophant that will persuade you that when I account well of an honest and wise servant for his true faithful service to me, that it is to compare or prefer him to you, then will neither ye or I be ever at rest [or] at peace....

... Praying God, my Heart, to preserve you and all the bairns, and send me a blyth meeting with you, and a couple of them.

Your own,

James R.[26]

A much mollified Anne set out to join her husband, accompanied by Prince Henry, and his delightful seven-year-old sister, Princess Elizabeth. The three-year-old Prince Charles was considered as yet too frail to undertake the journey. The southward progress of James's family was scarcely less magnificent than his own, and it aroused almost equal enthusiasm. Queen Anne pleased her new subjects by her gracious response to their greetings; the royal children began as they were to continue, Prince Henry by inspiring admiration and Princess Elizabeth by winning all hearts.

James rode some way north to meet them, and the family reunion took place at Althorp in Northamptonshire. Here the entertainment offered was a masque by Ben Jonson, the first of many which enchanted the Jacobean court. Later the collaboration between Ben Jonson and Inigo Jones brought exquisite poetry and visual splendour together to enact the most sophisticated celebrations of the cult of monarchy which England ever witnessed.

In the charming foretaste presented at Althorp, Queen Anne was hailed with a song which admitted her to the post-Elizabethan monarch-worship in which James was already experienced:

> This is she, this is she
> In whose world of grace
> Every season, person, place,
> That receives her happy be;
> For with no less
> Than a kingdom's happiness
> Doth she private Lares* bless,
> And ours above the rest
> By how much we deserve it least.
> Long live Oriana
> T'exceed whom she succeeds, our late Diana†.

On 25 July, in the plague-stricken capital, the King and Queen were crowned. In the words of a contemporary chronicler: 'By reason of God's visitation for our sins, the plague and pestilence there reigning in the city of London ... the King rode not from the Tower through the city in royal manner as had been accustomed ...' The pageants which had been prepared were postponed until the new year, and the citizens were forbidden to crowd around Westminster Abbey. Archbishop Whitgift of Canterbury crowned and anointed the King and Queen, and the fact that Anne, a Catholic convert, refused to receive Holy Communion according to the Anglican rite aroused surprisingly little notice, as a result of the truncated splendours of the occasion.

After the sombre coronation, the euphoria which had attended James's accession and lasted throughout the spring faded and died away. James of Scotland and Anne of Denmark found themselves King and Queen of an England which was still an unknown kingdom, its lineaments and characteristics to be learnt at leisure; its cares and heavy burdens, which James had foreseen and perhaps forgotten in the interim, yet to be discovered.

* Household gods.
† i.e. Elizabeth I.

CHAPTER TWO

'Hellish Spiders'

Oh, barbarous! ... Do you bring the words of these hellish spiders ... against me?'

Sir Walter Raleigh
at his trial, 1603

AMONG THE MANY Englishmen who rode north to meet King James as he entered his new kingdom was Sir Walter Raleigh. He was fifty years old, a dark and saturnine man, whose pointed beard curled outward from his chin, a feature which advertised the provocative aspect of his character. His pride was proverbial and detested. His many enemies called him a 'Machiavellian' and an 'Atheist' – vague terms of abuse which had nothing to do with his political or religious views. He had 'that swagger which, when displayed by a man of middle age, was quite repugnant to the Scottish sovereign'.[1] Moreover, Sir Robert Cecil and Lord Henry Howard, in their correspondence with James before his accession, had successfully poisoned his mind against Raleigh. When Raleigh presented himself before the King at Burghley House, his poor reception was predictable to them if not to himself.

On 15 April 1603 Raleigh was dismissed from the Captaincy of the Royal Guard, and his appointment was given to Sir Thomas Erskine of Gogar, younger brother of the Earl of Mar, who was later raised to the peerage as Viscount Fenton. It was natural that James should have wished to transfer the responsibility for the safety of his person from the hands of a suspect Englishman to those of a fellow-countryman whose loyalty was above suspicion. Other Scots were also given positions of honour and responsibility in England. Mar himself was appointed to the English Privy Council, and so were the king's kinsmen Ludovic Stuart, Duke of Lennox, James Elphinstone, Lord Balmerino, Edward Bruce, Lord Kinloss,[2] and Sir George Home, later Earl of Dunbar.

Adverse English reaction to James's favour towards his Scottish subjects was less than justified for, with the Union of Crowns, Scotland had lost its royal court and with it the whole spectrum of court preferment to which Scotsmen had previously aspired. It was therefore both just and reasonable that some Scots should receive preferment at the English court, which was now the cynosure of ambition to men of both nations.

Favour to incoming Scotsmen was, however, balanced by favour to Englishmen who had assisted in securing the succession, and who represented continuity with the Elizabethan establishment. Highest in favour stood Sir Robert Cecil, who (as previously mentioned) retained his position as principal Secretary of State. Within weeks of the King's accession he was created Lord Cecil of Essendon; in 1605 he would become Earl of Salisbury. Lord Henry Howard, who had successfully insinuated himself into James's favour by his serpentine and sycophantic letters, was also appointed to the Privy Council, and was soon created Earl of Northampton. His cousin, Charles Howard, Earl of Nottingham, who as Lord Howard of Effingham had commanded the English fleet which did battle with the Armada, retained his office as Lord Steward of the Household. The Lord Chamberlain, George Carey, Lord Hunsdon, the elder brother of Sir Robert Carey, who had independently endeavoured to ingratiate himself with the King by his dramatic delivery of the news of Queen Elizabeth's death, was displaced from his office in favour of another member of the Howard family, Lord Thomas Howard, who was shortly afterwards created Earl of Suffolk.

The titular head of the Howards was the eighteen-year-old Thomas Howard, Lord Maltravers, the grandson of Thomas, Duke of Norfolk, who had been executed in 1572 for his intrigue to marry Mary, Queen of Scots. King James consummated his favour to the Howards by restoring to Lord Maltravers his father's forfeited earldom of Arundel, though he did not crown the young man's ambition by the restoration of his grandfather's dukedom. For the present the Duke of Lennox remained the only Duke in either of James's kingdoms. Nonetheless, it was clear that the Howards were the most favoured of the noble families of England. The tragic connection with Mary, Queen of Scots, received a long-delayed reward.

Besides Sir Robert Cecil and various of the Howards, other holders of high office in the previous reign retained their appointments under the new administration, or received further advancement. Edward Somerset, Earl of Worcester remained Master of the Horse, an appointment of importance in the court, though not of significance in the government. Thomas Sackville, Lord Buckhurst, tragedian and poet in his youth and statesman in his maturity, retained the post of Lord Treasurer and was created Earl of Dorset. Sir Thomas Edgerton retained the office of Lord Keeper of the Great Seal, and was also appointed Lord Chancellor of England and created Lord Ellesmere. Sir Edward Coke continued in office as Attorney General, and became successively Chief Justice of Common Pleas and of King's Bench. Almost immediately after James's accession he played a dramatic part in the downfall of Sir Walter Raleigh.

No sovereign can fulfil the hopes of all his subjects. Inevitably, those whose hopes James had disappointed became malcontents, either passive or active, according to the influence of character or circumstances. Raleigh was not a man inclined by nature to passivity. Furthermore, he was goaded by the extent of his misfortunes. He lost not only the Captaincy of the Royal Guard but the Governorship of Jersey, the appointment of Lord Warden of the Stannaries, the monopoly on the sale of sweet wines, and his London residence of Durham House, which, after twenty years' possession, he was required to restore to the Bishop of Durham.

'Raleigh may have been at certain times dishonourable,' as Archbishop Mathew had written, 'but his mind was lucid. There had to be a serious reason behind all his actions.'[3] The difficulty of describing his downfall is that the precise action which he took eludes discovery. His action was connected with those obscure episodes the 'Bye' and 'Main' plots; the serious reason behind it was the necessity of repairing his ruined fortunes.

The 'Bye' plot has been dismissed as 'an abortive plot whose intentions it is at this date hardly possible to decipher'.[4] It seems to have had its origin in the disappointment of William Watson, a secular priest who had visited James in Scotland on the eve of his journey into England, and who believed that James had promised sympathetic treatment for the English Catholics. While

James had so far abstained from levying the recusancy fines since his arrival in England, he had taken no legal steps to improve the position of the Catholics, who remained still subject to the Elizabethan penal laws, which were 'designed to ruin their finances, inhibit Catholic worship, destroy their priesthood, and arrest proselytization'.[5] It was undeniable that James had wooed European and English Catholics with smooth words before his succession to the English throne was assured, and as a result, he inevitably reaped the consequences of having disappointed the hopes of the latter afterwards.

Watson and another priest named Clarke, and Sir Griffin Markham, a relative of Anthony Babington, whose conspiracy had led directly to the death of Mary, Queen of Scots, plotted with George Brooke, the brother of Lord Cobham, and Lord Grey de Wilton, to kidnap the King and exert some form of coercion upon him to relieve the disabilities of his Catholic subjects. The plotters appear to have envisaged, as a result of this compulsion, the acquisition of various government appointments for themselves. The plot was discovered while it was still in gestation, and Watson, Clarke and Brooke were executed.

The 'Bye' plot and the more serious though scarcely more realistic 'Main' plot were later described by Sir Edward Coke as 'Treasons ... like Samson's foxes, which were joined in their tails, though their heads were severed'.[6] The 'tails' in question were George Brooke and Lord Cobham, who was the prime mover of the 'Main' plot.

The purpose of the 'Main' plot emerged more clearly. It was that Lord Cobham should persuade Count d'Aremberg, the ambassador of the Spanish Netherlands, to arrange and finance the landing of a Spanish force in Britain. 'The King and his cubs' were to be murdered, and Lady Arbella Stuart placed upon the throne and married in accordance with the directives of the Catholic sovereigns of Spain and Austria.

If James and his children were indeed eliminated, Arbella Stuart stood next in the succession. She was the daughter of James's uncle, Lord Charles Stuart, and his wife Elizabeth Cavendish, the daughter of Elizabeth, Countess of Shrewsbury, the famous and formidable 'Bess of Hardwick'. Arbella, left parentless early in life, had been brought up by her grandmother in the grandeur and seclusion of Hardwick Hall in Derbyshire. She was described by Bishop Goodman as 'a very virtuous and good-natured lady, and of great intellectuals'.[7] She was a classical scholar whose learning was reputed to extend to an acquaintance with Hebrew; yet her pleasure in study did not preclude a taste for finery and jewels, and a longing for love and marriage. Outwardly she was gentle and diffident, but she possessed an underlying obstinacy which would cost her the King's favour when she crossed the royal will in her choice of a husband. Early in the reign, however, she was in high favour with James, who had earlier written: 'Nature enforces me to love her as the creature living nearest kin to me, next to my own children.'[8]

Lord Cobham decided that Arbella should write letters promising peace between England and Spain, toleration for the English Catholics, and the Catholic marriage which the plot envisaged. Arbella, however, was a loyal subject to her kinsman, and entirely without ambition to occupy his throne. Furthermore, she was a firm Protestant. She gave the first and only letter which Lord Cobham wrote her to the King. With an unconsenting figurehead the plot lacked any kind of substance, but this did not alter the fact that its intentions were treasonable.

Lord Cobham, who was the brother of Sir Robert Cecil's long-dead wife, was a busy-minded man, frustrated in his hopes of advancement, and utterly lacking in practicality. He was closely associated with Sir Walter Raleigh, who while despising him, admitted him to an apparently intimate friendship. When the 'Main' plot was exposed, Raleigh, together with Cobham, faced the accusation of treason.

It seems almost incredible that Raleigh, whose career had been heroically anti-Spanish during the late Queen's reign, should have changed so much under the exigencies of his own misfortunes as to participate in a pro-Spanish plot. The words with which he strove to refute the prosecution of Sir Edward Coke, when he stood his trial at Winchester in November 1603, seem to have the ring of truth about them (it is easy to imagine them delivered in the rich accent of Devon which Raleigh spoke all his life): 'Oh, barbarous! ... I was never any plotter with them against my country, I was never false to the Crown of England. I have spent 4,000 pounds of my own against the Spanish faction for the good of my country. Do you bring the words of these hellish spiders Clarke, Watson and others against me?'[9]

Coke answered coldly: 'Thou hast a Spanish heart, and thyself art a Spider of Hell; for thou confessest the King to be a most sweet and gracious prince, and yet thou hast conspired against him.'[10]

The reputation of Coke, who has been so greatly admired as the champion and exponent of the English Common Law, has suffered severely for his remorseless prosecution of Raleigh at Winchester. However, there was circumstantial evidence against Raleigh, even if the legal evidence against him was extremely weak, and Coke's prosecution was entirely in the tradition of his times, in which a state trial was held not to examine an accusation against a man in order to arrive at a true verdict, but to exhibit publicly the process by which the verdict of 'guilty' had been reached. The verdict in this instance was unconvincing, and even Coke's violent attacks could not conceal the fact.

Yet, though he was obviously the victim of injustice at his trial, Raleigh's involvement with Cobham was quite clearly to be seen within the context of the 'Main' plot, a context which was self-evidently uncharacteristic of the man. Archbishop Mathew has offered a plausible hypothesis for the purpose of this involvement: 'It is my suggestion that when everything had been neatly tied up, Raleigh would have handed over Cobham to the government. Surely such an action would content the King and Raleigh would be restored to partial favour.'[11] Upon this hypothesis, Raleigh's action was certainly dishonourable towards Cobham, but in no respect was it treasonable towards the Crown of England; that the plot was divulged prematurely masked, unhappily for him, his ultimate intention, and completed his downfall.

Apart from the question of the nature of Raleigh's involvement, the most interesting aspect of the whole tortuous episode of the 'Bye' and 'Main' plots is King James's reaction. He did not display undue alarm at the revelations that he had been in danger of compulsion under threat, and assassination. Probably he did not accord the plots more seriousness than they deserved. However, the intention of the plotters to commit treason had led to three executions and four sentences of death. While Lord Grey de Wilton, Lord Cobham, Sir

Griffin Markham and Sir Walter Raleigh remained under sentence, James studied the evidence which had led to the verdicts of guilty against them. With him lay the decision as to whether or not the sentences were carried out. He reprieved all four men: Grey, Cobham and Markham on the scaffold; Raleigh without having subjected him to the preliminaries of execution.

James probably hoped that further information concerning the plots would emerge in the speeches of men face to face with death. If he had such hopes, they were disappointed. But undoubtedly he intended to create a strong public impression that he was a just and yet a merciful prince. In this, he was probably successful. According to his lights James was a just man, and in the context of his time he was an exceptionally merciful ruler. No subject of the Tudors would have hesitated to give him his due in the latter respect.

Ironically, if James had been sufficiently lacking in justice and mercy to have executed Sir Walter Raleigh in 1603, then the quintessential Elizabethan hero would have died unmourned by most of his contemporaries, and therefore probably by posterity. Though the virulence of Coke's prosecution aroused a wave of sympathy for him, it would probably have been short-lived; he was widely hated for his arrogance, and could have been executed without emotional repercussions. The fact that he endured long years of imprisonment, during which he wrote his famous *History of the World*, and was eventually executed after he had suffered yet more flagrant injustice, left a greater stain upon James's reputation than any other personal action or public act of his reign.

James's clemency in 1603 gave Raleigh the opportunity to amend men's opinion of him, and by his conduct after he was released to make nonsense of the verdict of the court at Winchester. It also allowed him the chance to have the last word in some deeply moving lines of poetry, in which he looked forward to the justice of the 'bribeless judgment hall' of Heaven, where he would find

> No conscience molten into gold;
> No forger accuser bought or sold;
> No cause deferred, no vain-spent journey;
> For there Christ is the King's Attorney.

CHAPTER THREE

'No Novel Device'

'It is no novel device, but according to the example of all Christian princes, for Kings to take the first course for the establishing of the Church both in doctrine and policy.'

James VI and I, at the Hampton
Court Conference, 1604

AFTER THE DISRUPTIONS of the 'Bye' and the 'Main' plots, King James I took up the task of ruling with the seriousness which his reputation would have led his subjects to expect. The King had arrived in England with a dual reputation: that of a successful and intellectual king, and that of a foreigner. His achievements as a successful ruler were self-evident; his intellectualism was well attested by his writings. At the time of his accession to the English throne his published works comprised two volumes of verse, and two volumes of religious meditations,[1] his well-known book on witchcraft and Satanism, *Daemonologie*, and his two recently-republished books on political theory, *The Trew Law of Free Monarchies* and *Basilikon Doron*. His books were creditable examples of their various *genres*, the more so in view of his recommendation to Prince Henry, at the conclusion of *Basilikon Doron*: 'Being content to let others excel in other things, let it be your chiefest earthly glory, to excel in your own craft' (i.e. the craft of ruling).[2]

King James's intellectualism was an undoubted asset in the eyes of his new subjects. That he was both a king and an author was unusual and impressive in itself, and his tendency to didacticism accorded suitably with the paternal character of his kingship. His foreignness was an equally undoubted liability, for in England prejudice against the Scots, who had for so long been the national enemy, was slow to die. The rejoicing which had greeted James's accession had been offered him as the personification of assured peace and not as a Scottish sovereign.

During the later years of his reign in Scotland James's vocabulary and orthography had grown noticeably more anglicized;* but his accent remained uncompromisingly Scots, and his speech sufficiently adorned with Scotticisms for his subjects constantly to be made aware of his nationality. The xenophobic tendencies of early seventeenth-century Englishmen might have made James's foreignness a far more serious disadvantage than in fact it proved to be; fortunately for him, the 'great and manifold' blessings of his rule went far to neutralize that disadvantage. These blessings were not merely the personal qualities and achievements which had created a good first impression upon the English, nor even the gifts of 'inward' and 'outward' peace, which James was to point out to his first Parliament as the gifts of his accession: to his new subjects the greatest blessing which James could bestow was to guarantee the continuance of the Protestant religion in a form which was widely acceptable, as 'that inestimable treasure which excelleth all the riches of the earth . . . and disposeth men unto that eternal happiness which is above in heaven'.[3]

James's foreignness had least relevance in the all-important context of religion. Paradoxically, no more suitable head of the English church could have been found than the 'regal Calvinist'[4] who had ruled in Scotland.

The Church of England alone among the Protestant Churches claimed to have an episcopate which had retained the apostolic succession from St Peter. It also retained a hierarchy based upon the Roman model, and a liturgy which was largely translated from the Latin liturgy of the Roman Church. But resemblance to the Church of Rome extended no further. The majority of the Bishops and clergy held theological views characteristic of extreme Calvinism, and they recorded their acceptance of the doctrines of predestination and election in the Lambeth Articles of 1595, promulgated by Archbishop Whitgift. This collective clerical attitude was re-stated in 1618 when England gave official approval to the edicts of the

* Quotations from James's letters, proclamations, books and speeches have been anglicized in this book and in the preceding volume, *James VI of Scotland*, for the convenience of the reader, and therefore the immediate impression of James's foreignness has been sacrificed. However, the gradual anglicization of his language can be followed to some extent in the quotations from his poems, in both the preceding and the present volumes, in which the original orthography has been retained.

Synod of Dort. Theologically the Church of England could be defined as Calvinist.

James was undoubtedly gratified that the English Church possessed bishops (since he was still in the process of imposing episcopacy upon the Scottish Kirk), and that it supported the doctrines in which he himself had been educated, and which he was to profess throughout his life. But, satisfactory as these advantages were, James had no intention of exercising his headship of the Church without undertaking a thorough examination of it, and of the discontented Puritan element within it.

Puritanism, which eludes a brief definition, was not at the beginning of James's reign represented by a religio-political party opposed to King, Court or Church, though later it came to embody so many forms of opposition to the Establishment that the great historian of the period, S.R. Gardiner, labelled the convulsions of the mid-century 'The Puritan Revolution', a term which has not wholly fallen into desuetude. Early in the seventeenth century Puritanism was the climate of opinion of the clergy and laity who desired to see the Church of England purified of the ceremonies and usages which appeared to them redolent of the Church of Rome. They were characterized by their distaste for vestments and surplices, for the sign of the Cross, and even for the use of the wedding ring. James had been made aware of their numerical strength when on his journey into England he was presented with the 'Millenary Petition', so-called because it was supposed to represent the views of one thousand Puritan clergymen.

Whether he had received the Millenary Petition or not, James would probably have summoned some form of ecclesiastical conference at the beginning of his reign. Ever since Henry VIII had broken with Rome, his successors had used their power as Supreme Head or Governor of the Church to redefine the religious foundations of the reign by a solemn act of state which served to make national the sovereign's personal religion. Accordingly, James summoned the Hampton Court Conference, which was attended by Archbishop Whitgift of Canterbury, Bishop Bancroft of London, Bishop Mathew of Durham, Bishop Bilson of Winchester, Bishop Babington of Worcester, Bishop Rudd of St David's, Bishop Watson of Chichester, Bishop Robinson of Carlisle and Bishop Dove of Peterborough, with eight deans, and the Lords of the Privy Council who were present as spectators.

The first session of the conference, on 14 January 1604, constituted the 'solemn act of state' by which the Head of the Church would establish the religious foundations of the reign. The second and third sessions provided discussions with representatives of Puritan opinion, with the intention of securing conformity throughout the Church.

The bishops who listened to James's opening speech on the first day must have found it deeply reassuring:

> It is no novel device, [he said] but according to the example of all Christian princes, for Kings to take the first course for the establishing of the Church both in doctrine and policy. To this the very heathen related in their proverb *a Jove principium*. Particularly in this land, King Henry VIII towards the end of his reign altered much, King Edward VI more, Queen Mary reversed all, and lastly Queen Elizabeth (of famous memory) settled religion as it now standeth. Herein I am happier than they, because they were fain to alter all things they found established, whereas I see yet no such cause to change as confirm what I find settled already.

James went on to make a complimentary reference to the English churchmen who were present, and an unfriendly one to the Scottish ministers who had caused him trouble in the past: 'For blessed be God's gracious goodness, who hath brought me into the Promised Land where religion is purely professed, where I sit among grave, learned and revered men, not as before, elsewhere, a King without state, without honour, where beardless boys would brave us to the face.'

This sentence has been frequently quoted out of context as a generalized contrast between Scotland and England, to the disfavour of the former. But it is evident that James was referring specifically to the unreverent conduct towards him of Scottish divines, and to the impudent speech of one young minister in particular; for later in the course of the Hampton Court Conference he said: 'Mr John Black, a beardless boy ... told me at the last conference in Scotland [December 1602] that he would "hold conformity with his Majesty in matters of doctrine, but every man for ceremonies was to be left to his own liberty". But I will have none of that....'[5]

The King's opening speech reverted to his disinclination to introduce any changes into the Church of England, and concluded with the assurance that if anything was amiss in the Church he intended to see it put right:

... I assure you we have not called this assembly for any innovation, for we acknowledge the government ecclesiastical as it now is, to have been approved by manifold blessings from God himself, both for the increase of the Gospel, and with a most happy and glorious peace. Yet because nothing can be so absolutely ordered, but something may be added thereunto, and corruption in any state (as in the body of man) will insensibly grow, either through time or persons, and because we have received many complaints, since our first entrance into this kingdom, of many disorders, and much disobedience to the laws, with a great falling away to popery; our purpose therefore is, like a good physician, to examine and try the complaints, and fully to remove the occasions thereof, if scandalous; cure them, if dangerous; and take knowledge of them, if but frivolous, thereby to cast a sop into Cerberus's mouth that he bark no more....[6]

The reiterated reassurances of this speech can have done nothing to prepare the bishops for the inquisitorial questioning which followed, in which the King demanded information on the Church of England's use of Excommunication, Absolution, Confirmation and Baptism (with particular reference to private Baptism, and Baptism by lay-persons and women). The bishops showed an almost desperate determination to convince the King that the usages of the English Church were entirely in conformity with the views of 'Mr Calvin'.[7]

The debate on Baptism was of special interest, as the King gave a full expression of his own opinion, which revealed that his personal belief was deeply felt, but without any element of fanaticism. Archbishop Whitgift introduced the topic with the words: 'To the point of Private Baptism, the administration thereof by women and lay persons is not allowed in the practice of the Church, but enquired of, and censured by Bishops in their visitations.'

James, reading the rubric in the Book of Common Prayer, replied: 'The words of the Book cannot but intend a permission of women and private persons to baptize.'

'The doubtful words may be pressed to that meaning,' admitted

Babington of Worcester, 'yet the compilers of the Book did not so intend them, as appeareth by their contrary practice....'

Bishop Bancroft added: 'Those reverend men intended not by ambiguous terms to deceive any, but thereby intended a permission of private persons to baptize in case of necessity....' (It was reported that 'Here he spake long and earnestly about the necessity of Baptism.')

The King, who throughout the Conference neither interrupted any speaker, nor permitted one to interrupt another, heard him out, and answered: '... I maintain the necessity of Baptism, and always thought that the place *John* iii 5 "Except one be born again of water" etc was meant thereof. It may seem strange to you, my lords, that I think you in England give too much to Baptism, seeing fourteen months ago in Scotland, I argued with my divines there, for attributing too little unto it. Insomuch that a pert minister asked me if I thought Baptism so necessary that, if omitted, the child should be damned. I answered, "No: but if you, called to baptize a child, though privately, refuse to come, I think you shall be damned." But, this necessity of Baptism, so I understand ... is necessary to be had if lawfully to be had, that is, ministered by lawful ministers ... though I utterly dislike all re-baptization on those whom women or laics have baptized.'

Bishop Bilson of Winchester conceded; 'To deny private persons to baptize in case of necessity, were to cross all antiquity.'[8]

The debate continued, and James revealed himself not only as a king thoroughly well versed in theology, but as a 'crafty, patient, voluble man, who was almost undefeatable in face to face negotiation'.[9] The bishops must have been intensely relieved that the purpose of the debate was to establish agreement, which proved to be possible chiefly through deference to the works of 'Mr Calvin' and to the usages of the primitive church.

A source much relied upon for accounts of the Hampton Court Conference is *The Summe and Substance of the Conference* by William Barlow, Dean of Chester, who was present as one of the supporters of the episcopal delegation. His anti-Puritan bias led him to overstress both the blandness of the discussion between the King and the bishops and the abrasiveness of that between the King and the

Puritans. On the whole, towards the Puritan divines who attended the second and third sessions of the Conference, James showed an affability of manner and a readiness to make concessions for which he has not received due credit.

The second session took place on 16 January, with only Bishops Bancroft and Bilson present to represent the episcopate, but with Prince Henry and Patrick Galloway, the King's Scottish Chaplain, added to the audience. James repeated his opening speech for the benefit of the four Puritan delegates, and concluded with some complimentary remarks to the effect that he believed them to be 'the most grave, learned and modest of the aggrieved sort'. He expressed himself 'ready to hear at large what they could object'.[10]

The four Puritans – Dr Reynolds, Dr Sparks, Mr Chaderton and Mr Knewstubbs – shared the academic background of the bishops, most of whom had come to the episcopal bench by way of University appointments.[11] Dr John Reynolds was President of Corpus Christi College, Oxford, and Laurence Chaderton was Master of Emmanuel College, Cambridge. They represented the views of the signatories of the 'Millenary Petition', who declared themselves to be acting 'neither as factious men affecting a popular parity in the Church, nor as schismatics aiming at the dissolution of the state ecclesiastical, but as faithful servants of Christ and loyal subjects'.[12]

Unfortunately Bishop Bancroft was deeply suspicious of the Puritans. He obviously believed that their 'grave, learned and modest exteriors' concealed a latent religious fanaticism, entirely inconsistent with the moderation of the 'Millenary Petition'. In this view he was not altogether to blame, for the word 'puritan' was current as a term of casual abuse, and it had been applied to the radical, anti-episcopalian, religious malcontents of the previous reign. He was on his guard as Dr Reynolds began his enumeration of the moderate Puritans' requests: 'That the doctrine of the Church might be preserved in purity, according to God's word; that good pastors might be planted in all churches to preach the same; that the Church government might be sincerely ministered according to God's word; that the Book of Common Prayer might be fitted to more increase of piety....'[13]

As soon as Reynolds began to elaborate upon this outline, Bancroft interrupted him: 'May your Majesty be pleased that the ancient canon may be remembered, *Schismatici contra episcopos non sunt audiendi*?' (Schismatics are not to be listened to against bishops.) He expostulated to this effect at some length before James put him firmly in his place: 'My lord Bishop ... I mislike your sudden interruption of Dr Reynolds, whom you should have suffered to have taken his liberty [i.e. to speak]. For there is no order, nor can be any effectual issue of disputation, if each party be not suffered, without chopping, to speak at large.'[14]

Some of the ensuing exchanges between James and Reynolds were sympathetic and notably fruitful. The best-known concerns the desirability of a new translation of the Bible. To Reynold's proposal that one should be made, Bancroft sourly replied, 'If every man's humour might be followed, there would be no end of translating.'

But James responded with enthusiasm: 'I profess I could never yet see a Bible well translated in English.... I wish some special pains were taken for an uniform translation, which should be done by the best learned in both universities, then reviewed by the Bishops, presented to the Privy Council, lastly ratified by royal authority, to be read in the whole Church, and no other.'[15]

This speech of the King, in response to the Puritan academic, was the origin of the 'Authorized' or 'King James' version of the Bible, which has been justly characterized as 'the glory of his reign'.[16]

Less memorably to posterity, but tactfully at the time, James dealt with various Puritan prejudices.

'Would that the Cross [i.e. the Sign of the Cross],' said Dr Reynolds, 'being superstitiously abused in popery, were abandoned, as the brazen serpent was stamped to powder by Hezekias, because abused to idolatry.'

'Inasmuch as the Cross was abused to superstition in time of popery,' James replied, 'it doth plainly imply that it was well used before. I detest their courses who peremptorily disallow of all things which have been abused in popery, and know not how to answer the objections of papists, when they charge us with novelties, but by telling them we retain the primitive use of things, and only forsake their novel corruptions.... Material crosses, to which people fell down in time of popery (as the idolatrous Jews to the Brazen Serpent), are already demolished as you desire.'

He made a humorous response to Reynolds' objection to the words 'with my body I thee worship', in the marriage service. 'I was made believe', James admitted, 'the phrase imported no less than divine adoration, but find it an usual English term, as when we say "a gentleman of worship", and it agreeth with the Scriptures, "giving honour to the wife". As for you, Dr Reynolds, many men speak of Robin Hood who never shot in his bow.' (This the King spake smiling.) 'If you had a good wife yourself, you would think all worship and honour you could do her were well bestowed on her.'

'Some', said the Dean of Salisbury, provocatively, 'take exception to the ring in marriage.'

'I approve it well enough,' replied Dr Reynolds, mildly.

James rejoined, 'I was married with a ring, and think others scarce well married without it.'[17]

Unfortunately the harmony of these exchanges was abruptly broken when Reynolds suggested that '... according to certain provincial constitutions the clergy may have meetings every three weeks', and referred to the desirability of remitting any disagreements which might arise at these meetings to an 'Episcopal Synod'.

'Synod' was an emotive word which Reynolds used ill-advisedly. To James it carried the disturbing suggestion that English Puritans might hanker after the ecclesiastical polity of the presbyterian Kirk of Scotland, with its hierarchy of ecclesiastical courts, the Kirk Sessions, Presbyteries, Synods and General Assembly.

> If you aim at a Scottish Presbytery, [he exclaimed wrathfully] it agreeth as well with monarchy as God and the Devil! Then Jack and Tom and Will and Dick shall meet and censure me and my Council.... Stay, I pray you, for one seven years, before you demand [that of me], and then if you find me grow pursy and fat, I may perhaps hearken unto you....
>
> I will tell you a tale: after that the religion restored by King Edward VI was soon overthrown by Queen Mary here in England, we in Scotland

felt the effect of it. For thereupon Mr Knox wrote to the Queen Regent* (a virtuous and moderate lady) telling her that she was supreme head of the Church; and charged her ... to take care of Christ his evangel, in suppressing the popish prelates who withstood the same; but how long trow you did this continue? Even till, by her authority, the popish prelates were repressed, and Knox with his adherents being brought in, made strong enough.... My Lords the Bishops ... if once you were out and they in, I know what would become of my supremacy, for *No Bishop, no King*.... I will make them conform themselves, or else I will harry them out of the land, or else do worse.[18]

However, James was reacting to a threat which was not inherent in moderate Puritanism, and once his irrational blaze of anger had burned itself out, he seems to have recognized the fact. His hot words have often been quoted in support of the statement that he was intolerant of Puritanism, but they did not result in action. The third and last session of the Hampton Court Conference ended on a note of compromise.

James accepted the Puritans' representations that a 'preaching ministry' was desirable, and that the abuses of pluralism and non-residence should be rooted out. He had enthusiastically espoused the scheme for a new translation of the Bible; he also agreed to the improvement and simplification of the Catechism, and accepted suggestions for some minor changes in the Book of Common Prayer. For instance, Confirmation was to be called 'Confirmation, or further examination of the children's faith', a definition which would satisfy Puritan opinion by stressing the educational aspect of the rite at the expense of the sacramental concept. All this amounted to something more substantial than an effort 'to cast a sop into Cerberus's mouth that he bark no more'.

In return the King requested the Puritan delegates to do their best to ensure that Puritans in general conformed themselves to the doctrine, liturgy and usages of the established Church. This they promised to do, disappointed perhaps that the King's willingness to grant concessions had extended no further, but thankful at least that he had shown some sympathy with their views, and that his anger had not led to irretrievable misunderstanding.

* Marie de Guise, widow of King James V and mother of Mary, Queen of Scots.

The bishops, though they offered the King fulsome thanks for his support of the *status quo*, regretted that he had thought it desirable to offer the Puritans any concessions at all. In consequence, the Hampton Court Conference gained less for the Puritans in practice than in principle, since unfortunately the bishops in many instances avoided implementing the reforms which the King had intended to see carried out, and James paid less attention to the aftermath of the Hampton Court Conference than he should have done. Though James entrusted the bishops both with the promulgation of the intended reforms and with the enforcement of conformity within the Church, and thereafter failed to pay sufficient attention to their actions, they did not requite him with the complete disobedience which their passive resistance to the reforms appeared to threaten.

In February Archbishop Whitgift died, whispering last words which epitomized the dedication of a lifetime: '*Pro ecclesia Dei*, *pro ecclesia Dei*. . . .' He was succeeded by Bancroft, whose reputation as an anti-Puritan primate has been greatly exaggerated. If Bancroft quietly forgot to grant the Puritans most of James's agreed concessions, he was conscientious in acting upon James's requirement that conformity should be enforced with a gentle hand. In consequence, of the nine thousand incumbents who were obliged to conform themselves to the usages of the Church of England as defined by the Canons of 1604, only ninety resisted and suffered deprivation of their benefices. Furthermore, there were many who failed to conform but were none the less allowed to remain, while Bancroft and his bishops attempted to induce the recalcitrants to make some gesture which would suffice to prevent their deprivation.

The result of this studied moderation was that only a small minority of Puritans was forced to adopt a separatist position, while the great majority was successfully contained within the established Church. This is not to say that the moderate Puritans who conformed were satisfied; indeed, grumbling continued throughout Bancroft's primacy. Significantly, the Commons' Petition on Religion, which voiced the discontent of the laity represented by the Puritan gentry in Parliament, was presented in 1610, the year before Bancroft's death. In 1611 James appointed as his successor George Abbot, whose personal Calvinism made him conciliatory towards the Puritans. Thereafter the grumbling died away into silence until 1628, and those who seek to trace the development of Puritanism as a continuous process throughout the reign of James I have little evidence for their argument.

CHAPTER FOUR

Prince and State

I am the head, and it is my body; I am the shepherd, and it is my flock....

Speech of James I
to Parliament, 1604

ALMOST EXACTLY A month after the Hampton Court Conference, on 15 March 1604, the long-delayed coronation procession at last took place. Two days beforehand the King, the Queen and Prince Henry went to lodge at the Tower, in readiness for the traditional ride through the City to Whitehall. The prisoners, including Raleigh, had been removed to the prisons of the Gatehouse and Marshalsea to make way for the royal family; and the apartments of the Tower had been decorated with borrowed finery. Though privileged state prisoners were permitted to make themselves as comfortable as they could afford, it cannot have been easy to recreate the cheerful splendours of Whitehall Palace within the walls of the grim stronghold which had witnessed the last hours of saints and queens, and innocent victims of the purposes of state, as well as of conspirators and traitors.[1] The sinister reputation of the Tower was already well established. In lodging there, James and his wife and son obeyed the dictates of tradition, but it is unlikely that the visit was congenial.

The King was welcomed by William Hubbocke, 'Preacher in the Tower', who delivered a fulsome Latin oration, in which he referred to the heraldic Lions Couchant of England bowing down before the Scottish Lion Rampant. He went on to extol the Union of the Kingdoms:

Christ ... doth command 'Let no man separate that which God hath joined together'. The partition wall between these two kingdoms, by the finger of God at your coming to the crown, is gone ... no more two peoples, nor two kings, nor two pastors, nor two flocks ... nor two regions, nor two religions. One King, one people, one law, and as it was in the beginning, one land of Albion. All things in one heavenly God alone; all things in one earthly God ('For I have styled you Gods' as the Scripture speaketh), one. ...[2]

This speech was admirably suited to please the King. It mirrored his own sentiments exactly, and it prefigured the speech which he intended to make to the first Parliament of his reign on the 19th of the month. Perhaps he was turning it over in his mind as he retired to his lodgings; perhaps it was already written, for his speeches were highly elaborate and personal, evidently the products of careful composition.

Next day James and Anne were given a tour of the Tower Mint, 'where both the King and the Queen coined money, and gave to divers persons there present'.[3] Then they went to see the lions in the royal menagerie. Somebody, by way of conversation, remarked to the King that although England bred no lions, it bred a beast of 'as great a courage as the lion, namely the mastiff dog ...'. James's empirical curiosity immediately led him to send for three of the mastiffs which were used for bear-baiting in the Paris Garden, south of the Thames. One of the lions was separated from the rest, and when the dogs arrived an impromptu lion-baiting was held. The mastiffs were pitted against the lion in turn, and they acquitted themselves with the utmost valour. All three dogs were savagely bitten and mauled before the lion decided that he had had enough, and slunk back to his den. Victory, however, was difficult to attribute, for while two of the unfortunate dogs died of their wounds, the lion retired from the fray. The surviving dog was claimed by Prince Henry, who showed a fine instinct for a regal gesture, 'saying, he that had fought with the King of Beasts should never after fight with any inferior creature'.[4] As the mastiff was taken into the Prince's household, with instructions to 'make much of him', it may be assumed that he ended his days in well-deserved comfort.

Prince Henry, who was bold, forthright and impatient for adulthood, never failed to draw the public eye. He was a boy of striking appearance, with auburn hair, vivid blue eyes, and an expressive face which he learned to use with an actor's skill. His 'gracious' smile and 'terrible' frown were considered very princely attributes.

His popularity with the English people soon outstripped his father's, and James's love for his promising son became unhappily alloyed with jealousy.

The 15th of March was the sort of occasion in which Prince Henry delighted. To James it was a protracted ordeal. Arthur Wilson's uncharitable comment was that 'he endured this day's brunt with patience, being assured that he should never have such another'.[5] It was a day on which nothing was permitted to be innocent of symbolism. James rode from the Tower mounted on a white horse, symbolic of sovereignty. At intervals along his route through the City seven symbolically-decorated triumphal arches had been set up. The first and second bestrode Fenchurch St and Gracechurch St, and had been built at the expense of the Italian and Dutch resident merchants respectively. The remaining five had been commissioned by the City Companies of London. One arch towered over Cornhill, beside the Royal Exchange, two straddled Cheapside and another Fleet Street. The last, representing the Temple of Janus, stood at Temple Bar.

The arches, fifty to sixty feet in height, were constructed of carved and painted wood, decorated with inscriptions, *imprese*, and statues, all of which the King was expected to study with minute attention. Probably his eye would have caught the familiar lines which he himself had quoted from Virgil at the conclusion of *Basilikon Doron*, flatteringly adapted on the triumphal arch, so that they appeared to be addressed to him in person:

> *Tu regere imperio populos, Jacobe, memento,*
> (*Hae tibi erunt artes*), *pacisque imponere morem,*
> *Parcere subiectis, et debellare superbos.*
> (Remember, James, these be thy arts,
> to rule over the nations, and impose the laws of peace,
> to spare the conquered, and to subjugate the proud.*)[6]

In the niches of the first archway stood figures representing the British Monarchy, Divine Wisdom, the Genius of the City, the Counsel of the City and the River Thames, besides such less readily identifiable personages as Gladness, Veneration, Promptitude, Vigilance, Loving Affection and Unanimity. The Genius of the City

* The original contained the word 'Romane' in place of 'Jacobe'.

and the River Thames turned out to be real people, who greeted the King with loyal addresses.

At each archway James was expected to watch a pageant illustrating the benefits of his rule, and to listen to a speech, a verse panegyric or a song of welcome. Seven times he paused, reined in his white horse, and gave the best attention that he could muster, before riding on to encounter a bewildering succession of personified abstractions: Pleasantness, Accord and Flourishing, Fame and Circumspection, *Eirene* and *Euphoria* (alias Peace and Plenty).... No wonder he sometimes anticipated the conclusion, and moved forward, leaving some orator or singer disappointed.

Once, as he paused in Cheapside, the monotony of the symbolic pageantry was transmuted into magic by an exquisite song. Two choristers of St Paul's sang 'in sweet and ravishing voice' that London – poetically called 'Troynovant' or 'New Troy' – was no longer a city, but the bridal chamber of James's united kingdoms:

> Troynovant is now a bridal chamber,
> Whose roofe is gold, floore is of amber
>   By virtue of that holy light
>   That burns in Hymen's hand more bright
>   Than the silver moone,
>   Or the torch of noone,
>   Harke, what the ecchoes say
>   Brittaine till now nere kept a holiday!
> For Jove dwells here; and 'tis no pittie
> If Troynovant be now no more a cittie.[7]

This charming conceit proved too much for the understanding of some onlookers, who objected to the idea that London was 'no more a city'. Thomas Dekker, who wrote a pamphlet describing the festivities, explained somewhat contemptuously that London had suffered no permanent diminution of dignity, but that she had ceased to be a city only while her merchants had put aside their commercial concerns to become courtiers for a day.[8]

His explanation had a broader significance than this single application. The majority of the Englishmen whom James had met since his accession had become courtiers for a day, or for the time that they spent in his presence. The exceptions, the 'Bye' and 'Main' plotters, had been executed or imprisoned. The aggrieved Puritans had shown themselves flatteringly deferential. For the rest, James had encountered no opposition, heard no overt criticism. His dearest project, the union of his kingdoms, was spoken of by poets and orators as though it were an accomplished fact. James must have assumed that the necessary legislation was a matter of form; and he would have had some justification for believing that all his plans were destined to come to untroubled fruition. His first year's experience as England's king had left him wholly unprepared for the difficulties which he was to encounter with the English Parliament.

Under the King, England was ruled not by Parliament but by the Privy Council. There were a dozen councillors at the beginning of the reign, and thirty-five by the end of it. The expansion of the Council had a transforming effect upon it. From being a small group of statesmen which collectively advised the monarch, it became a loose association of politicians, bureaucrats and courtiers, which, for efficient functioning, divided into committees. This was the natural result, first of James's need to appoint additional councillors at the beginning of the reign, and second of his preference for consulting the men in his confidence one or two at a time. He liked to consult in private and then to delegate; lengthy sessions of the Council tried his patience, which decreased with the passage of the years.

As a result of James's enlargement of the Council there came to be two distinct types of councillors, the functional and the honorific. The former participated in the daily routine of government, the latter did not. For example, the Earl of Salisbury, Lord Chancellor Ellesmere and the Earl of Northampton seldom missed a Council meeting, whereas the Duke of Lennox and Viscount Fenton seldom attended one.

The Council, as the principal working organ of government, had three functions: consultative, administrative and judicial. In its consultative capacity, the Council was intended to offer advice to the King, though, more frequently, having been formally consulted by him, it was expected to bear the responsibility for decisions which he knew in advance would be unpopular. In its administrative capacity, it dealt with a vast range of business, from the most important to the most trivial: the collection of taxes, the enforcement of the laws against recusants, the condition of roads, the granting of passports, the petitions of private persons upon every subject under the sun. In its judicial capacity, the Council, with the addition of some of the judges, sat as the Court of Star Chamber, taking its name from the place of its meeting at Westminster: 'The place is called the Star Chamber,' explained John Stow, 'because the roof thereof is decked with the likeness of stars gilt. There be [com-] plaints heard of riots, routs and other misdemeanors. . . .'[9] The Court of Star Chamber in fact heard cases relating to a vast variety of misdemeanours: abduction, blasphemy, conspiracy, fraud, poaching, suspected poisoning and rape.

With so comprehensive a range of responsibility, it was necessary that the Council should meet at least once a week (the sessions of the Court of Star Chamber took place only during the Law Terms). At the beginning of the reign the ordinary meetings of the Council were on Sunday morning, after Divine Service. From the Council Chamber in Whitehall Palace the councillors adjourned to dine with the Court. But by 1605 the volume of business had grown so demanding that extra meetings on Wednesday afternoons were instituted, and this innovation may have served initially to divide the functional from the honorific members.

If the King were absent, the Archbishop of Canterbury automatically presided over the Council. Archbishop Abbot was to prove himself a particularly assiduous attender.[10] However, during the early years of the reign, it was Salisbury who managed the Council's business, and thereby a great part of the government of the realm.

When James had been a young man in Scotland he had been criticized for leaving too much of the routine of government in the hands of his ministers, while he himself spent hours a day in the hunting field.[11] Gradually this criticism had become less true as James applied himself more determinedly to the task of ruling, and after the death of his Scottish Chancellor, Maitland of Thirlestane, in 1595, James probably worked harder than at any time before that date or after 1603. But, after his accession to the English throne, having found a minister as addicted to work as Salisbury, James began once again to delegate those aspects of government which did not appear to him to fall within his definition of 'kingcraft'. All that concerned the application of his political theories, all that concerned the interaction of Church and State, all that concerned the political decisions which laid the foundations of diplomacy, he regarded as the peculiar responsibilities of the King. Administration, as a whole, fell within the province of the Council.

By comparison with the omnicompetence of the Council, the significance of Parliament might have appeared to be very slight. While the Council met twice a week for the greater part of the reign, Parliament met for only a few weeks during the year. Nor did it meet by any means every year.[12] However, Parliament possessed two functions which no other institution could perform in its place: it could grant or withhold taxation, and it could legislate by statute.

Because these two particular functions were not imperatively required of it at the outset of the reign, Professor J. P. Kenyon recently made the initially surprising statement that 'there was no obvious reason why Parliament should be summoned at all in 1604'. He went on to explain: 'There was no immediate grant of taxation to be expected ... and the act confirming James's accession was not an urgent political necessity, as was the similar act of 1485 confirming Henry VII's accession....'[13]

The previous Parliament had granted four 'subsidies' to Elizabeth I, and these were still being collected in 1605, which was why James could not expect an immediate grant of taxation. However, he was actually benefiting from the previous grant to an appreciable extent, for a subsidy was a levy of 4 s in the £ on land and 2 s 8 d. in the £ on personal property. One subsidy was reckoned to produce £80,000, so that £320,000 was the sum to be expected from a grant of four subsidies. Nonetheless, between expectation and collection lay a large area of uncertainty: a subsidy might bring in £10,000 less – or more – than the original assessment.

So far as the Act of Succession was concerned, James himself would have taken a view very different from that of a modern historian. If it was not imperative to see the act on the Statute Book as quickly as possible, as in the case of Henry VII, whose accession was the result of his recent victory at Bosworth, it was at least highly desirable, for the act was the legal definition of the hereditary right to which James had long and patiently laid claim.

But James had other reasons for wanting to meet the English Parliament. The first was a gracious desire to thank the representative assembly of his subjects for the euphoric welcome which England had given him. 'Shall it ever be blotted out of my mind', he demanded rhetorically, in his opening speech to Parliament on 19 March, 'how at my first entry into this kingdom the people of all sorts rid [rode] and ran, nay rather flew to meet me, their eyes flaming nothing but sparkles of affection, their mouths and tongues uttering nothing but sounds of joy? . . .'[14]

This handsome expression of gratitude was a mere preamble to the presentation of James's second and stronger reason for summoning Parliament – his desire for the formal enactment of the union of his kingdoms. He presented the case for it persuasively:

> Hath not God first united these two Kingdoms both in language, religion and similitude of manners? Yea, hath He not made us all one island, encompassed with one sea, and of itself by nature so indivisible as almost those that were borderers themselves on the late Borders, cannot distinguish, nor know, or discern their own limits? These two countries being separated neither by sea, nor great river, mountain, nor other strength of nature, but only by little small brooks, or demolished little walls, so as rather they were divided in apprehension than in effect; and now in the end and fullness of time united, the right and title of both in my person, alike lineally descended of both crowns, whereby it is now become like a little world within itself, being entrenched and fortified round about with a natural and yet admirable strong pond or ditch, whereby all the former fears of this nation are quite cut off.[15]

He continued by reminding his hearers that troubles with Scotland in the past had been 'the greatest hinderance and let that ever my predecessors of this nation gat in disturbing them from their many famous and glorious conquests abroad'.[16]

While James himself had no desire for conquests, he was right in sensing that internecine strife was a natural hindrance to it. Indeed, his observation was instinct with unconscious prophecy, for the great expansion of later British Imperialism only followed the Anglo-Scottish Union of 1707. James's unimperialistic desire for the unification of his kingdoms was based on his belief that it was the natural fruition of the Union of Crowns. He expressed this belief in the familiar Scriptural imagery which had clothed numerous speeches of welcome addressed to him.

> What God hath conjoined, then let no man separate. I am the husband, and the whole isle is my lawful wife; I am the head and it is my body; I am the shepherd and it is my flock. I hope, therefore, that no man will be so unreasonable as to think that I, that am a Christian King under the Gospel, should be a polygamist and husband to two wives; that I, being the head, should have a divided and monstrous body; or that being the shepherd of so fair a flock (whose fold hath no wall to hedge it but the four seas) should have my flock parted in two. But ... I am assured that no honest subject of whatever degree within my whole dominions, is less glad of this joyful union than I am....[17]

James may have been correct in his belief that the union should have been the natural outcome of his accession; for had it occurred in 1603, there would have been no appearance of Scotland's being devoured by England, as to many Scots there seemed to be in 1707.[18] Indeed, the fear that Scotland would take over England as the result of the accession of a Scottish king was an influential ingredient in the English Parliament's resistance to James's arguments. For though James may have been right in his belief concerning the appropriateness of the union, he was wrong in his assessment of the sentiments of the members of Parliament.

James had assumed too much, upon too little knowledge of the English Parliament. As a basic misapprehension, he may have assumed that it had more in common with the Scottish Parliament than was in fact the case.

The Scottish Parliament was unicameral, and had originally contained representatives of the three Estates: nobility, clergy and commons. After the Reformation the clerical estate had come to be made up of 'Commendators' or laymen who took their titles from the bishoprics, abbacies and priories which had come into their possession. With the conversion of these 'commendams' into temporal lordships, known as 'Lordships of Erection', the clerical estate had ceased to exist. Very recently, James had reintroduced clerics into the Scottish Parliament, as part of his adroit programme to strengthen Scottish episcopacy, by nominating some ministers of the Kirk to 'Parliamentary Bishoprics'.[19] This measure itself is symptomatic of the control which the Kings of Scots had gained over their Parliament. James had brought to a fine art the managerial system of his predecessors: a nominated committee, the 'Lords of the Articles', presented ready-prepared legislation to Parliament, which then legislated without argument. The system functioned smoothly and caused minimal delay and expense to the representatives of the Estates, who had travelled to Edinburgh often by difficult roads, and who had no wish to be detained there longer than necessary.

James's efficient dealings with his Scottish Parliament may have led him to suppose that the English Parliament would prove as biddable. But a bicameral Parliament was an institution for which his previous experience had not prepared him. So far as the House of Lords was concerned, he had no problems to face; the temper of the House of Commons was less predictable.

The classic description of the early Stuart Commons by G. M. Trevelyan suggests that they possessed a unanimity of outlook, an insularity of vision, and a superhuman standard of integrity, which would have made them very predictable indeed.

> The pick of the country gentlemen sent up by far distant communities [he wrote] came to Westminster uncorrupted by previous contact with Vanity Fair. Except the lawyers resident at the Inns of Court, the members knew no more of London than that the merchants were honest men, and no more of Whitehall than that the courtiers were false knaves. ... But this homely ignorance of the great world, while it fortified their characters as men, limited their outlook as politicians.... Fortunately what the time required of them was not an alternative national policy, but the protection of national liberties; for that task the English squires were fitted by their birth, their traditions, and the freshness of mind with which they came to each new Parliament from hunting deer ... marked by a directness of intention and simplicity of mind, the inheritance of modest generations of rural life, but informed by Elizabethan culture and inspired by Puritan religion.[20]

To a later generation of historians it appears a naïve supposition that 478 individuals should have been infused by such extraordinary unanimity, and a more realistic assumption that men of limited experience and strong prejudices would have been as likely to have acted wrong-headedly as high-mindedly. In fact, the Jacobean

House of Commons was neither so unanimous in outlook nor so homogeneous in composition as it was once believed to have been.

There was certainly a preponderance of country gentry: the landed classes were, and long remained, over-represented in the House of Commons, while mercantile interests continued absurdly under-represented in proportion to their growing influence in the community. However, there was a small leavening of lawyers and a surprisingly large group whose affiliations belonged to the Court rather than to the localities. In the first Parliament of James's reign sat Sir Roger Aston, Gentleman of the Bedchamber, Sir Richard Levison and Sir Edward Hoby, Gentlemen of the Privy Chamber, Sir Lewis Lewkenor, Master of Ceremonies, Sir Robert Mansell, Treasurer of the Navy, and many other holders of minor offices, together with cadets of the great courtly families, including two Cecils, two Howards and one Sackville.[21]

James may not have realized that the English House of Commons required as much managing as the Scottish Estates, and possibly even more; but he sacrificed his best potential method of management when he ennobled his leading Privy Councillors. Sir Robert Cecil, before his rapid progression to an earldom, had been at once a statesman, a Crown servant, and a seasoned parliamentarian. The peerage conferred upon Sir Thomas Egerton also removed another wise and experienced regalian from the Commons, and left only two Privy Councillors, Sir John Herbert and Sir John Stanhope, neither of whom possessed much influence, to take their seats in the Lower House. The most brilliant mind at the King's disposal, whether in the Commons or elsewhere, belonged to Sir Francis Bacon. Unhappily, the rivalry between Bacon and his cousin the Earl of Salisbury prevented the King having full access to Bacon's services until after Salisbury's death in 1612. Salisbury could be very generous to his mental or social inferiors; a potential competitor such as Bacon experienced his influence only in the form of discouragement.

James, therefore, encountered a House of Commons which the government had taken no effective steps to control, but which he had as yet no reason to believe either desired or was equipped to oppose him. However, certain events of the previous reign, of which he was inevitably aware, might have led him to approach the English

Parliament with less confidence. Elizabeth I had encountered sufficient unanimity of anti-Catholic prejudice to oblige her to accept the enactment of the penal laws against Catholics, which were contrary to her own more advanced views on freedom of conscience, and to force her to agree to the execution of Mary, Queen of Scots, which was deeply repugnant to her belief in the sacred character of monarchy. But she had successfully resisted Parliamentary pressure, which had been exerted upon her for so long as it was relevant, to marry; and she had steadfastly refused to allow her Parliaments to intervene in her conduct of foreign affairs. The fact that Parliamentary debate had continually trenched upon matters which the Queen had regarded as pertaining to the sovereign alone might have served to highlight the fact that Parliament was as much interested in the extension of its powers as in the defence of its privileges.

James soon discovered that the Commons who assembled in the first Parliament of his reign brought with them the attitudes of their predecessors. They detested Catholics and Spaniards, which made the rescinding of the penal laws impossible, and the impending peace with Spain unpopular. (In fact the Peace Treaty was signed in August 1604, and James followed Elizabeth in formulating his foreign policy without recourse to Parliament.)

If he could have concluded the Union of Scotland and England without consulting Parliament, no doubt he would have done so, for he was rapidly made aware that the English Commons viewed the Scots with a cold dislike which was a hangover from the Anglo-Scottish enmity of the Middle Ages. Though they treated the King himself with respect, and did not forget that his peaceful accession had been an unmitigated blessing, their attitude to his countrymen led to the ultimate rejection of the Union although debates concerning it continued until 1607. In the meantime James assumed the title of King of Great Britain without Parliamentary sanction.

Possibly both Elizabeth and James would have been justified in imagining, in allegorical terms, that the ambitious Commons resembled a flock of crows which aspired to invade the nest of the Phoenix. But the more politically aware members of Parliament were equally justified in their belief that their House needed to be upon its guard, for the power of parallel institutions in other countries – the Etats-Généraux of France, the Diet of the Empire, the Cortes of Spain – was dwindling to the point of vanishment. They did not want to see the renowned Parliament of England follow the same course. In consequence they were frightened by the paternalistic language in which James addressed them, even though he used it to assure them that he was a conscientious ruler, with an almost mystical awareness of his responsibility to God for his good government.

An alarmed committee of the Commons began to put together a document known as *The Form of Apology and Satisfaction to be Presented to His Majesty*, which was once regarded as 'a lecture to a foreign King on the constitutional customs of the realm which he had come to govern, but which he so imperfectly understood'.[22] In fact the *Apology* was never seen by the King, for the large committee – which eventually numbered over seventy members – was troubled by internecine disagreements: 'The Apology was never presented to the King because it was never accepted by the House . . . the Commons not only never got around to endorsing the draft; they may in all fairness be said to have deliberately rejected it.' But James heard about it, and apparently made an oblique reference to it in the speech with which he prorogued Parliament on 7 July 1605: 'The best Apology-maker of you all, for all his eloquence, cannot make all good. . . .'

James had hoped to 'make all good' in his first encounter with the English Parliament. He did not understand, either then or later, why his paternalistic, didactic and well-intentioned speeches were destined always to receive a cold response.

CHAPTER FIVE

'A Train of Gunpowder'

A King shall be better entreated and more mildly dealt withal ... if at a siege of some city he be blown up with a mine, than by ... a train of gunpowder laid under his Palace of Parliament House in time of peace...

James I, *A Remonstrance for the Rights of Kings*, 1615

KING JAMES I was a confident man. Upon his arrival in England he acted authoritatively; he did not condescend to feel his way. At the Hampton Court Conference he showed tactical skill in his negotiations with the Puritans, and his attitude to the bishops was one of favour tempered with firmness. Probably he expected that in dealing with the other outstanding religio-political question – that of the official attitude to be adopted towards the English Catholics – he would be equally free to act upon his own initiative.

In Scotland co-existence with the surviving Catholic minority had not been one of the King's greatest problems. The situation in England was different, and the difference resulted from the divergent religious histories of the two kingdoms. While the Scottish Reformation had taken the form of a rebellion against Marie de Guise, Regent for her daughter the infant Catholic sovereign, Mary, Queen of Scots, the English Reformation had been the sustained policy of an adult, apostasizing sovereign, Henry VIII, against the Papal supremacy.

When James VI was crowned as a Protestant King of Scots, his regency government set him upon the throne of his Catholic mother, whose restoration remained feasible, at least as a diplomatic fiction, until her execution in 1587. After her death, the Papacy and Catholic Europe continued to regard James as a possible convert, an erroneous impression which he encouraged.

Elizabeth I of England, on the other hand, was forced to adopt an overtly anti-Catholic position, because in Catholic eyes she was illegitimate, and so debarred from the succession. When she succeeded her half-sister, the Catholic Mary I, she was obliged to reverse the latter's policy, and to become Head of the Church of England. She herself was a true *politique*, and inclined to toleration, but her situation obliged her to acquiesce in the passing of the first penal laws against her Catholic subjects in 1559. In 1570 she was excommunicated by Pope Pius V, and the English Catholics were absolved from their natural allegiance to her. Thus, in England, loyal Catholics were forced into a potentially treasonable position, and the Jesuit mission to England exacerbated their unhappy condition. After 1585 any Catholic priest caught in England was liable to be executed as a traitor. As a result, many admirable missionaries, who had no politically subversive intentions, and some lay people who succoured them suffered execution. Some of them were among the recently canonized 'Forty Martyrs of England and Wales'.

In Scotland the situation was greatly eased by the fact that the practice of Catholicism was dying out. The pre-Reformation monks and nuns who had been allowed to go on living in their dilapidated monasteries and convents though forbidden to live the religious life, were dying too.[1] There were no secular clergy working secretly among the people, and there was no Jesuit mission to Scotland. A few Jesuits came and went as observers, but without danger to their lives. In 1585 Andrew Melvill was ordered to go to the north of Scotland to look for Jesuits, and 'travail to reduce them to the true and Christian religion';[2] and in 1588 James himself held a polite, public disputation with the Jesuit Father James Gordon, uncle to the Earl of Huntly.

James showed no desire to initiate persecution. Indeed he alarmed the Kirk by his leniency to the remaining Catholic noblemen, especially to Huntly, who was married to a proselytizing Catholic wife, Lady Henriette Stuart, the daughter of James's favourite, Esmé, Duke of Lennox.

Unlike Elizabeth I, James did nothing to provoke excommunication. Rather, his diplomacy in the last decade of the sixteenth century was designed to woo the support of both English and European Catholics. He even turned the conversion of his wife (who may have been a convert of Lady Huntly) to good use, by inducing her to write to the Pope on his behalf, using a form of address appropriate to the Supreme Pontiff from a Catholic sovereign, and employing the royal plural, so that it appeared as though Anne were speaking both for herself and James. The English Catholics thought that they had excellent reasons for optimism when they contrasted the attitudes of the English and Scottish governments. It was not surprising that they ardently looked forward to the day when the King of Scots would reign over them, and that they entertained extravagant hopes of him.

Undoubtedly James was disingenuous in his dealings with the Papacy and with the powers of Catholic Europe; but it is almost equally undoubted that he did not intend to double-cross the English Catholics once he had gained the English throne. There is no reason to suppose that he did not intend to rescind the Elizabethan penal laws, for they remained largely unenforced during the first year of his reign. In his opening speech to his first Parliament he tried to draw embattled extremists towards harmony with ecumenical sentiments, which were ill-received:

> ... I would wish from may heart that it would please God to make me one of the members of such a general Christian union in religion, as laying wilfulness aside on both hands, we might meet in the middest, which is the centre and perfection of all things. For if they [the Catholics] would leave, and be ashamed of, such new and gross corruptions of theirs as themselves cannot maintain ... I would for my own part be content to meet them in the midway, so that all novelties might be renounced on either side. For as my faith is the true, ancient, Catholic and Apostolic faith, grounded upon the Scriptures and express word of God, so will I ever yield all reverence to antiquity, in the points of ecclesiastical policy....[3]

James, like Elizabeth before him, was driven to recognize that his audience was more prejudiced than logical, and that it rejected the policy of toleration which both he and his predecessor would have preferred, and demanded persecution. Reluctantly, James accepted the necessity of re-enacting the penal laws, and understandably the English Catholics were bitterly disappointed that their high hopes had been answered by apparent betrayal. The best that James could do to soften the cruel blow was to leave the re-enacted legislation so far as possible a dead letter on the statute book. But, inadvertently, he had lit the fuse which led to the gunpowder 'under his Palace of Parliament House'.

William Parker, Lord Monteagle, had a pleasant house with a small garden and orchard, at Hoxton, outside London. He had acquired it through his marriage to a daughter of the rich and eccentric Catholic squire, Sir Thomas Tresham, whose surviving fame results from his building the Triangular Lodge at Rushton in Northamptonshire, 'a mathematical fantasy of bewildering complication, fashioned of variations on the figure 3',[4] in honour of the Holy Trinity, to whom Sir Thomas had a special devotion.

Lord Monteagle was thirty, and he had led an eventful and troubled life. He had been married when he was seventeen, was later involved in the Essex Conspiracy, sent to the Tower, and released after paying a fine of £8,000. He was nominally a Catholic, which was perhaps a prerequisite of marriage into the Tresham family; but recently he had sought to ingratiate himself in the royal favour by writing to the King, and announcing his conversion to the state religion. This discreet apostasy may be the key to the strange events of the late autumn of 1605.

On 26 October Monteagle was about to sit down to supper in his house at Hoxton, which he rarely used, when one of his servants came in bringing a letter which he said had been handed to him outside by a stranger. Lord Monteagle's response was curious: he gave the letter to one of his gentlemen, Thomas Warde, and told him to read it.

My Lord, [the letter ran] out of the love that I bear to some of your friends, I have a care of your preservation. Therefore I would advise you, as you tender your life, to devise some excuse to shift off your attendance at this Parliament. For God and man have concurred to punish the wickedness of this time. And think not slightly of this advertisement [information], but retire yourself into your country, where you may expect the event in safety. For though there be no appearance of any stir, yet I say, they shall receive a terrible blow this Parliament, and yet they shall not see who hurts them. This counsel is not to be contemned, because it may do you good, and can do you no harm, for the danger is past so soon as you have burnt the letter. And I hope God will give you the grace to make good use of it: to whose holy protection I commend you.[5]

The letter was unsigned, but its author is widely believed to have been Francis Tresham, Monteagle's brother-in-law.[6] Old Sir Thomas Tresham had died in September, and after his death his son, who had been described as 'a wild and unstayed man', had joined the band of Catholic desperadoes whose plot to blow up King, Lords and Commons when Parliament met on 5 November the anonymous letter revealed.

Assuming that Francis Tresham was indeed the author of the letter, his motive in writing it may have been precisely that of saving his brother-in-law, who would have been taking his seat in the Lords. But if, as is possible, Tresham like Monteagle was seeking to establish himself in government favour, and had joined the plotters for purposes of counter-espionage, then he did not intend that Monteagle should read the letter privately and burn it, but 'make good use of it' to expose the plot.

The possibility that Monteagle was playing a pre-planned role is suggested by his paying a rare visit to Hoxton, conveniently to receive the letter. The impression that he knew its contents without the necessity of studying it is conveyed by his action of handing it to Thomas Warde to read. The conspirators were closely connected with Monteagle; his showing the letter to Warde was a means of warning them that their secret was about to be disclosed. Conjecturally, his intention was to give his friends, relations, and erstwhile co-religionists a last chance to save themselves, before he used the letter to assist his chosen means of self-advancement. Abandoning his supper, he set out to ride to Whitehall to place the letter in the hands of the Earl of Salisbury. Salisbury read the letter, which, if Monteagle and Tresham were acting as double agents, would not have been his first intimation of the existence of the plot. However, he acted as though it were. He sent for the inner circle of the Privy Council, the Earls of Northampton, Suffolk and Worcester. They studied the letter, and decided upon watchful inaction. It was nine days till the opening of Parliament, and the King was hunting at Royston.

Lately, James had absented himself more and more frequently

from London, for his southern capital had never endeared itself to him. He liked to ride fast and far over the Essex countryside, where the clear air, if not as keen and invigorating as the cold winds of Fife, blew the pollution of the city from his lungs. On 1 November he returned to Whitehall, and Salisbury presented the Monteagle letter without comment, and waited in respectful silence for James to decipher it. He read its message without difficulty, for the language was essentially not obscure. Its purpose was revelation. James, however, congratulated himself that he had discerned the meaning when others apparently had failed, and Salisbury and the rest duly marvelled at his perspicacity.

Next year, the statute which declared 5 November a day of national thanksgiving assured the people of England that the intended destruction would have taken place 'had it not pleased Almighty God, by inspiring the King's most excellent Majesty with a divine spirit, to interpret some dark phrases of a letter showed his Majesty, above and beyond all ordinary construction'.[7] These rituals of the cult of monarchy cannot fail to irritate posterity by the rankness of their sycophancy, or to display the King to poor advantage, as the victim of a relatively transparent deception concerning the superiority of his mental powers. Yet despite such 'clouds of incense as the censers swung before the King continually',[8] James's practical good sense did not desert him. He did not over-react to the fear of assassination. He ordered that the vaults beneath the Houses of Parliament should be searched on the night of 4 November, within a few hours of the intended perpetration of the crime.

That search revealed a man standing guard over thirty-six barrels of gunpowder, criss-crossed with iron bars to increase the force of the explosion, and concealed beneath a stack of firewood. He told the Justice of the Peace for Westminster, Sir Thomas Knyvett, who arrested him, that he was called John Johnson. Later he admitted that his real name was Guy Fawkes. He was taken to the Tower, to be tortured until he named his accomplices and revealed the full extent of their intentions.

Throughout the night he maintained a resolute silence, 'like Mutius Scaevola',[9] the King observed, with a trace of admiration for the villain's courage. When they took him to the rack perhaps he was sustained by the thought that the longer was his silence, the longer was the distance that his friends might ride; for they had delayed to act on the warnings of Thomas Warde, and had waited in London, hoping against hope that their plot might yet succeed. Guy Fawkes knew that they would certainly flee when the news of his arrest came out; they might be far away by the time he reached the limit of endurance and spoke their names. Those names would have meant more to Salisbury, who had long sat like a spider at the centre of the web of English society, than to the King. But James would have learned from him that the 'Powder Treason', as the Jacobeans came to call it, was the plan of a close circle of men, most of them linked by kinship or marriage, almost a family affair, like certain of the conspiracies of Scotland.[10]

The leader and organizer of the plot was Robert Catesby, one of the turbulent gallants who had been linked with the Essex conspiracy. At that time he had been one of Lord Monteagle's greatest friends, and he was also first cousin to Francis Tresham. He is said to have been a man of dominating personality and powerful charm, one who could talk anybody into anything. Archbishop Mathew, with his great knowledge of the varicoloured fabric of seventeenth-century Catholicism, described him as characterized by 'that swordsman's piety which was found among the officers of the League and of the Spanish *Tercios*'.[11] If, as has been surmised, he was a convert, he had a typical convert's passion for his faith. He had an ill-conceived ardour which made him as willing to murder for the Church as to die for it.

Catesby won to his way of thinking his two second cousins, Robert and Thomas Winter, and their brother-in-law John Grant; his friend Thomas Percy, who was a cousin of the Earl of Northumberland, and Percy's two brothers-in-law, John and Christopher Wright, with their friend Robert Keyes. These men were all well-connected malcontents, who felt themselves to be undeservedly at odds with fortune. The remaining conspirators were of a type less likely to be found in a rebels' camp: Francis Tresham had means and position which did not rely upon connections, and so did the young Suffolk squire Ambrose Rookwood, and the handsome and accomplished Sir Everard Digby. The odd man out was John Bates,

Catesby's servant, who was probably made privy to the plot for Catesby's convenience and whose loyalty to his master cost him his life.

These were the names at last extracted from Guy Fawkes, in the extremity of torture. Fawkes himself was a mercenary soldier, born in York, who had served with other renegade English Catholics in the armies of Spain. He was a man of courage and resource, whose part in the plot, the firing of the powder, was the most dangerous of all. Had he lit the fuse and made good his escape, he was to have found a boat at Wapping, which was waiting to take him to Gravelines.

The whole concept of the Powder Treason had a monstrous simplicity. Robert Catesby believed that he would end the persecution of the English Catholics by blowing up the whole of the heretical government; he would then summon the English Catholic gentry to arms, sublimely confident that they would rise in his cause; and he would set upon the throne, as the puppet of a Catholic government, the Princess Elizabeth, who would not be present in Parliament to share her father's end. The two Princes, Henry and Charles, he assumed, would be there to die with the King. It was the plot of a simple, fanatical man, wholly lacking in a politician's sense of the limitations of the possible. This fanatical lack of practicality led Catesby and his fellow plotters onward to attempt the second phase of the plot although the first had failed. On the morning after Guy Fawkes's arrest, the plotters rode hard for their rendezvous on Dunsmore Heath, to which Sir Everard Digby had invited a large hunting party of Catholic gentry. Digby's guests must have viewed with amazement his precipitate arrival with his raffish friends; but amazement turned to utter consternation when preliminary greetings were followed by Catesby's call to arms.

Every man who was not already a party to the plot refused to have anything to do with it. The Catholics of England might face financial ruin, and they might risk their lives if they helped or hid their priests; but so long as they lay low, and the penal laws remained dormant or minimally enforced, they could achieve a *modus vivendi*. Furthermore, they had been commanded by the Pope to endure their disabilities with patience. Catesby and his friends were urging them not only to commit treason against the King but also to disobey the spiritual authority of the Pope. The final condemnation of the plotters is that 'these Catholics were behaving like Protestants inasmuch as they thought that they knew better than the Church'.[12]

The refusal of the Catholic gentry to rise in arms spelt the doom of the Powder Treason in letters clear enough even for the sanguine Catesby to read. The plotters fled from Dunsmore, to be refused refuge by one Catholic house after another. At last they found shelter at Holbeach House, the home of a Catholic squire, Humphrey Littleton. There disaster struck them. It had been a day of heavy rain, and they spread out their own stock of gunpowder to dry before a fire. A flying spark ignited it, inflicting upon them burns and injuries which they believed must be the punishment of God for their intended treason. On 8 November the High Sheriff of Worcestershire, Sir Richard Walsh, came to take them with a force of two hundred men. They resisted arrest with the tenacity of desperation, and the knowledge of what the consequences of capture would be. Robert Catesby was a fortunate man, for he was shot dead in the attack on Holbeach House. Thomas Percy and John and Christopher Wright were almost equally lucky to die soon afterwards of their wounds. The rest were taken alive, and transported to London, to stand their trial and die the traitor's death.

The words describing the sentence are easily written or read: it was to be 'hanged, drawn and quartered'. It comprised semi-strangulation, which did not lead to loss of consciousness, followed by castration, disembowelment and dismemberment. In the hands of a skilled executioner the victim could be kept conscious until a very late stage of the proceedings. The sentence was sometimes commuted to death by hanging, and the barbarities were inflicted upon the corpse. But this mercy was not extended to the surviving conspirators. Guy Fawkes, John Grant, Robert and Thomas Winter, Ambrose Rookwood, Sir Everard Digby, Robert Keyes and John Bates were tried on 27 January 1606, and executed in accordance with the full rigours of the law.

Francis Tresham, who had been in poor health before he joined the conspiracy, had died in the Tower on the preceding 22 December. His part in the conspiracy has never been fully explained. Neither has that of Lord Monteagle, whose reception and revelation of the famous letter made him the hero of the hour.

King and Parliament met and enjoyed the heightened sense of mutual appreciation which people sometimes experience after a danger shared and averted. The King made a heartfelt speech of thanksgiving: '*Misericordia Dei supra omnia opera eius* [the mercy of God is above all His works]. For Almighty God did not furnish so great matter to His Glory by the creation of this great world, as He did by the redemption of the same....'[13] He elaborated the parallel between the redemption of mankind and the miraculous preservation of the King, his posterity and his chief subjects.

Twentieth-century people have ceased to be more than momentarily shocked by explosions which kill a large number of people; but for three centuries the Gunpowder Plot continued to be regarded as a monstrously evil design, and a disgrace to the English Catholic community to which the plotters had belonged. The long survival of the Gunpowder Plot in the memory of the English people may have owed something to its dramatic simplicity as well as to the sense of outrage which it aroused. It had, indeed, a curiously two-dimensional quality, a lack of convincing depth, which would have been provided by evidence that the plotters had had a ramifying network of accomplices, or that they had formulated detailed plans for the future government of England.

Even before the end of the seventeenth century, these defects in the received story of the plot led to speculation that it might have been fabricated by the government, or more specifically by the Earl of Salisbury. For example, Bishop Godfrey Goodman wrote: '... some will not stick to report that the great statesman sending to apprehend these traitors gave special charge and direction for Percy and Catesby, "let me never see them alive," who, it may be, would have revealed some evil counsel given.'[14]

This idea has had an obvious appeal for some Catholic historians, attracted by the possibility of exonerating their long-dead co-religionists from the guilt of having plotted a treasonable massacre. The authenticity of the Gunpowder Plot was vigorously argued, especially at the end of the nineteenth century, when propounding ingenious solutions to historical mysteries enjoyed an academic vogue.[15] Modern scholars, for the most part, have turned contemptuously against this style of controversy. It is now generally doubted that the Gunpowder Plot can have been a government fabrication, for it seems unwarranted to attribute to a seventeenth-century secret service a degree of sophistication which similar departments in modern governments with their more elaborate resources seldom attain.

But if it is fantastic to suggest that the plotters were government agents destroyed by their own employers, it is more plausible to suppose that they were the dupes of at least one agent. This is the line of speculation followed by Archbishop Mathew: 'My own impression', he wrote, 'is that the Earl of Salisbury was familiar with the whole project from the beginning.... His methods were not very different from those traditionally associated with counter-espionage ... if Salisbury really had this knowledge, the next point is who was his agent?'[16] The Archbishop's question may remain forever unanswered. His own opinion was that Francis Tresham had joined the plot too late to have played the part, and that a more likely candidate was Thomas Percy, who was mortally wounded in the attack on Holbeach House.

An argument in favour of this hypothesis is provided by the story of Thomas Percy's relationship with the Earl of Northumberland, for whose disgrace Salisbury had patiently worked. In the secret correspondence with King James before his accession, Salisbury and Northampton had sought to discredit Northumberland, just as they had sought to discredit Raleigh. These small, unpleasant manœuvrings, which had failed in the one instance and succeeded in the other, had seemed important to the establishment of the alliance of Cecil and Howard as supreme in the King's counsels.

Either deliberately or fortuitously, the involvement of Thomas Percy in the Gunpowder Plot brought about Northumberland's disgrace. Thomas Percy was a member of the King's Band of Gentlemen Pensioners, an élite corps responsible for his personal safety. Northumberland was its Captain and, it was alleged, he had failed to administer to his cousin Percy the oath of supremacy, which was repugnant to the Catholic conscience, and which membership of the corps required. Northumberland, though not himself a Catholic, had Catholic sympathies which might well have led him to such an accommodation of his cousin. However, since Percy had played the traitor, it could be argued that Northumberland's indulgence to him had endangered the King's life. For this alleged guilt, Northumberland spent sixteen years as a prisoner in the Tower, where his favourite pastime of scientific experiments won him the popular reputation of being a magician, and the nickname of 'the Wizard Earl'.

If Thomas Percy was indeed Salisbury's agent, then the success of Salisbury in bringing about the downfall of Northumberland was complete. But the connection remains unproved.

Professor Joel Hurstfield seems to prefer Francis Tresham as his candidate for the role of government agent; but his final view is that the question of who was the agent is less important than the fact that the plot was not a fabrication: 'This hypothesis is riddled with far more contradictions and improbabilities than the traditional, and I think reasonable, view that the plot was the work of brave but incompetent idealists who wasted their lives in a noble cause....'

To Professor Hurstfield's adjectives describing the plotters, one may also add 'misguided', for in their zeal to serve the Catholic cause, the plotters inflicted almost as much damage upon their co-religionists as they had desired to inflict upon their enemies. They brought destruction upon fellow-Catholics far more worthy than themselves, and they brought renewed conflicts of loyalty and renewed persecution and suffering upon the whole Catholic community.

King James, of course, did not recognize his own role in the inception of the Gunpowder Plot, which was his disappointment of Catholic hopes which he had done so much to raise. He saw only the fact that his leniency had been repaid by treason, and this ingratitude quenched his sympathy towards his Catholic subjects for a long time to come.

CHAPTER SIX

The King and the Jesuits

... If the Pope doth not approve and like the practice of King-killing, wherefore hath not his Holiness imposed some severe censure upon the book of Mariana the Jesuit (by whom parricides are commended, nay highly extolled)? ...

James I, *A Remonstrance for the Rights of Kings*, 1615

THERE WAS ONE man in England to whom the Gunpowder Plot was as abhorrent as it was to the King: he was Father Henry Garnet, Superior of the English Jesuits.

Father Garnet bore no resemblance to the sinister Jesuit of Protestant imagination. He was not a subtle schemer who believed that the end justified the means; he was not a plotter of the destruction of Protestant princes. He was a devout and learned priest, an efficient organizer of the Jesuit mission, and a kindly spiritual adviser to the Catholic families for whom the practice of their religion was a dearly-bought privilege. According to a contemporary description, he was 'of a midelling stature, full-faced, fat of body, of complexion fair ... the hair of his head and beard grizzled ... his gait upright and comely for a fat man'. Obviously he had not lived the life of a man of action, expecting martyrdom like the Jesuit missionaries of the previous reign. He had been well protected as he lodged in the great Catholic households.

When the failure of the Gunpowder Plot was divulged, Father Garnet was at Coughton Court in Warwickshire, the house of a Catholic gentleman, John Throckmorton, whose stepsisters were the mothers of Robert Catesby and Francis Tresham. Staying in the house was the wife of Sir Everard Digby. The all-engulfing tragedy which the news of the arrest of the plotters brought to Coughton confronted Father Garnet with a situation which contained the probability of his own destruction.

Some months previously, Robert Catesby had made his confession to a Jesuit named Father Oswald Tesimond, at Hindlip House in Worcestershire, the home of Thomas Habington, Lord Monteagle's brother-in-law. Father Tesimond, horrified by the revelation of Catesby's plans, and immediately aware of their potentially disastrous effect upon the Catholic community as a whole, besides their inherent disobedience to the Pope, asked Catesby's permission to reveal the substance of his confession to the Superior, Father Garnet. Catesby agreed, but only on condition that Father Tesimond himself should do so in confession, thus ensuring that Father Garnet was subject to the seal of the confessional, and rendered incapable of divulging the plot, either to King or Pope.

Father Garnet was doubtless thankful that the plot had failed. The chaos which would have followed its success would have been unlikely to have resolved itself in accordance with Catesby's designs. In his ambiguous position, Father Garnet made an incorrect assessment of his wisest course of action: he wrote to the Earl of Salisbury to declare his ignorance of the plot. He then left Coughton and rode across country to Hindlip. Father Tesimond had gone abroad; he was received by Father Oldcorne, a Yorkshireman who wore a hair shirt.

As soon as Salisbury received Garnet's letter the hunt was up. Salisbury's paramount ambition in connection with the plot had been to establish convincing evidence that it owed its inspiration to the Jesuits; no better way could have been found of discrediting the order in England. So far, he had failed. Even in the course of interrogation under torture the plotters had denied that there was any connection between the Jesuits and the conspiracy. Salisbury interpreted the message of Father Garnet's letter as *qui s'excuse s'accuse*, which in a sense it was. He would have been wiser not to have written it.

Information on Father Garnet's whereabouts was provided by Humphrey Littleton of Holbeach, whose situation was no doubt extremely difficult after the use which the fugitive plotters had made of his house. Sir Henry Bromley, the local Justice of the Peace, occupied Hindlip, searched it, found several intricately constructed 'priests' holes', doubted that he had discovered all the secrets of the house, and settled down to wait until those secrets disclosed themselves.

In the meantime, the urbane Father Garnet, who enjoyed his 'sack' or sherry and his claret, and the ascetic Father Oldcorne were mewed up in a hiding-place which had evaded Bromley's scrutiny. Twelve days made the narrow confines of their self-imposed prison unendurable; arrest seemed preferable to asphyxiation in the foetid air. They came out and surrendered themselves.

Father Garnet was treated with courtesy, both on his journey to London and after his arrival at the Tower. Though he was interrogated on twenty-two occasions before his trial, he was lodged in comfort, provided with good food and wine, and permitted to buy a new pair of spectacles. At his trial he was forced to play the role of the influential Jesuit, not to be seen as a tortured martyr.

His trial opened on 28 March 1606. Lady Arbella Stuart attended to listen with intellectual interest to the revelation of a plot which happily had not sought to compromise her. No doubt her presence was a gesture of loyalty to the King. James himself was present, behind a screen.

Sir Edward Coke prosecuted in inimitable style, building up the credit of the accused in order to demolish it the more effectively: '... The principal person offending, here at the bar ... is by country an Englishman, by birth a gentleman, by education a scholar ... by art learned, a good linguist, and by profession a Jesuit and a superior.'[1]

Father Garnet attempted to explain how Catesby had confessed to Tesimond and Tesimond to himself, the information passing under the seal of the confessional: 'I was very much distempered and could never sleep quietly afterwards,' he concluded pathetically.

The Earl of Northampton took over from Sir Edward Coke, and delivered a supporting speech for the prosecution. 'The case stands now in this trial, Mr Garnet,' he said 'between my dear sovereign ... and you who were so well content to let the course of conspiracy run forward ... as though you, Mr Garnet, being then *Magister in Israel* and *Rector Chori*, could or would be ignorant of their prefixed end.'[2]

Father Garnet's end at least was not in doubt, from the moment of his arrest at Hindlip. He went to his execution on 3 May

1606. He was permitted to make the customary speech before his death.

> As for the treasons which are laid against me, [he said] I protest now at my death that I am not guilty of them, neither had any knowledge of the Powder Treason but in confession, and then I utterly disliked it and earnestly dissuaded it. Yea, I protest upon my soul I should have abhorred it ever, though it had succeeded. And I am sorry with all my heart that any Catholics had ever any such intention, knowing that such attempts are not allowable, and to my own knowledge contrary to the Pope's mind.[3]

The rabble which came to watch Father Garnet die probably heard his words without comprehension. The King, who had listened to the trial with attention, disliked the argument concerning the confessional. But he accepted that Father Garnet had not deserved death by plotting death. Father Garnet died in accordance with the penal laws, but James acknowledged the distinction between his foreknowledge and the plotters' guilt by commuting Father Garnet's sentence to death by hanging. Father Oldcorne did not come within the compass of his interest; he was executed outside Worcester without remission of the penalties.

It is a commonplace that James I had a neurotic fear of weapons and bloodshed. This condition had made it impossible for him to become expert in martial skills, as a king was still expected to be; but the fact that he had on occasion assumed military command during his reign in Scotland suggests that the extent of his neurosis may have become exaggerated.[4] Some of his biographers have too readily assumed that his fear of assassination was itself neurotic; but though neurosis may have heightened his fear, his reasons for experiencing it were genuine. James's father had been assassinated in 1567, and his Regent the Earl of Moray in 1570. There had been several unsuccessful attempts on the life of Elizabeth I. William of Orange, leader of the revolt of the Netherlands against Spain, had been murdered in 1584, King Henri III of France in 1589, and King Henri IV of France would die by an assassin's hand in 1610. Kingship, or headship of state, was a profession of high risk, as it has always been, and James had good reason to fear that he might share the fate of his fellow princes.

The doctrine of the justifiability of tyrannicide was held by both Protestant and Catholic political theorists. James's tutor George Buchanan had been a Calvinist exponent of it in the previous generation, and its most notorious contemporary exposition was in *De Rege et Regis Institutione* by the Spanish Jesuit Juan de Mariana. James blamed the danger of his situation partly upon the currency of this doctrine and partly upon the long-term effects of the excommunication of Elizabeth. Both, he believed, had tended to the derogation of the sacredness of kingship, and had contributed to forming the climate of opinion in which the Gunpowder plotters could believe that to have succeeded in their aims would have been spiritually meritorious.[5] But James recognized that this was the view of fanatics and extremists, and did not represent the state of mind of the majority of his Catholic subjects, which was exemplified by the reaction of the men who had refused the call to rebellion on Dunsmore Heath. He concluded that the way to differentiate between the potentially murderous fanatic and the man who wanted only to live in peace and worship in accordance with his conscience was to present an oath of allegiance to Catholics which would condemn in forceful terms the doctrines which could lead men to believe that the murder of a king could be an acceptable service to God.

The Oath of Allegiance, drafted by Archbishop Bancroft, required the man who took it to swear 'that our sovereign Lord King James is lawful King of this realm ... and that the Pope, neither of himself, nor by any authority of the Church or See of Rome ... hath any power or authority to depose the King ... or to authorize any foreign Prince to invade or annoy him ... or to discharge any of his subjects of their allegiance...'.

Mediaeval emperors and kings who had resisted the claims of the Papacy might have expressed themselves in similar terms; but unfortunately Bancroft, with James's approval, continued in more violent language, which made the oath a greater obstacle to the Catholic conscience that it need have been: 'And I do further swear, that I do from my heart abhor, detest and abjure as impious and heretical, this damnable doctrine and position, that Princes which be excommunicated or deprived by the Pope, may be deposed or murdered by their subjects....'*

An English Benedictine endeavoured to alleviate the Catholics' dilemma by writing in support of the oath: 'He claimed that the Pope's deposing power was not a matter of faith but a "probable" opinion on which the clergy could not legitimately give binding advice.'[6] Nonetheless, the violent language of the oath made it unacceptable to many Catholics, as did the application of the words 'impious', 'heretical', and 'damnable' to a doctrine or position which the Pope might hold.

Controversy concerning the Oath of Allegiance predictably divided the Catholic community. Among those who swore it was the Archpriest George Blackwell, who since 1598 had been head of the secular Catholic clergy in England. (He did not, of course, possess authority over the Jesuits, whose obedience was owed directly to their General, Father Claudius Aquaviva, and through him to the Pope.) Blackwell's action provoked an open letter from Cardinal Robert Bellarmine of the Society of Jesus, a man of personal sanctity, a great controversialist and a former pupil of Mariana, who, from the unassailable security of Rome, suggested that the taking of the oath was an unworthy compromise, and the acceptance of martyrdom the better course. Cardinal Bellarmine became a saint without undergoing martyrdom; we must presume that he would have embraced it had the need arisen. The Archpriest's example to the English laity was condemned in Rome, and Pope Paul v forbade English Catholics to take the oath.

These were the circumstances under which King James wrote his *Triplici Nodo, Triplex Cuneus, or an Apologie for the Oath of Allegiance* (1607), which, like some of his other works, was published anonymously and subsequently acknowledged to have been of royal authorship. This anonymity was purely conventional, for the text made no attempt to conceal the author's identity. Citing numerous precedents, the King defended the temporal rights of kings and recorded occasions on which the Popes had infringed them.

In 1608 Cardinal Bellarmine produced his *Responsio*, which, since James's *Apologie* had been anonymous, Bellarmine published as the work of his chaplain Matthew Tortus. James responded to the *Responsio* in 1609, by issuing a new edition of the *Apologie*, prefaced by *A Premonition to all most Mighty Monarchs, Kings, Free Princes and States of Christendom.* This 'premonition', or warning, was intended to caution all Christian princes against the pretensions of the Papacy. Inevitably it was unacceptable to Catholic rulers, because in writing it James had failed to understand that no Catholic ruler could digest discourteous references to the Pope. It was full of such incivilities, including a tedious attempt to prove that the Pope was Antichrist. This was a standard exercise of Protestant polemicists, which could not be omitted from an anti-papal work.

More worthy of attention, and of the greatest biographical interest, is James's account of his own religion, in refutation of the accusation that he was a heretic.

> I am such a Catholic Christian [he wrote] as believeth in the three creeds: that of the Apostles, that of the Council of Nice [Nicea], and that of Athanasius. And I believe them in that sense, as the ancient Fathers and Councils that made them did understand them; to which three creeds all the ministers of England do subscribe at their ordination....
>
> As for the Saints departed, I honour their memory, and in honour of them do we in our Church observe the days of so many of them as the Scripture doth canonize for Saints....
>
> And first for the Blessed Virgin Mary, I yield her that which the angel Gabriel pronounced of her ... that she is blessed amongst women.... I reverence her as the mother of Christ, whom of our Saviour took his flesh, and so the mother of God, since the Divinity and Humanity of Christ are inseparable....
>
> I may well be a schismatic from Rome, but I am sure I am no heretic....[7]

James was at pains to stress the ecumenical character of his own religion, which, had he lived at a period when ecumenicism was in fashion, might have done great service in reconciling separated brethren. As it was, his purpose in stressing his areas of agreement with Rome was to show that in areas of disagreement Rome was wrong.

Most of his objections to popular Catholic practices, however, though characteristically Protestant, were logically approached and not bigoted:

> As for prayer to Saints, [he began, regally]... what warrant we have to have recourse unto these ... Courtiers of God, I know not.... It sufficeth me to pray to God through Christ as I am commanded....

For relics of Saints, if I had any such that I were assured were members of their bodies, I would honourably bury them, and not give them the reward of condemned men's members, which are only ordained to be deprived of burial....

He turned to the subject of the veneration of the Cross:

But Christ's Cross must have a particular privilege, they say, and be worshipped *ratione contactus*.... [But] except they could first prove that Christ had resolved to bless that tree of the Cross whereon he was nailed, they can never prove that his touching it could give it any virtue.... Surely the prophets that in so many places curse those that worship images ... would much more have cursed them that worship a piece of stick....[8]

In these passages is found a quality of naturalness in which his writings suggest his conversational style. When he was not tempted into that area of Protestant mysticism which was concerned with the Antichrist, he was a very straightforward controversialist.

Though he was provoked by the *Responsio* of Cardinal Bellarmine and Matthew Tortus, James addressed his *Premonition* to his fellow princes. The task of crossing swords with the Cardinal's chaplain, which was beneath the dignity of a king, James delegated to an Anglican divine. As deputy controversialist he chose the holy and learned Lancelot Andrewes, whom he had appointed Bishop of Chichester in 1605. Andrewes swiftly produced a work in which he gave the punning title *Tortura Torti* ('The Torment of Tortus'). Cardinal Bellarmine himself answered, with *Apologia pro Responsio Sua*. Then James employed as collaborators Lancelot Andrewes and Isaac Casubon, who between them produced *Responsio ad Apologia Cardinalis Bellarmini*.

After these preliminary salvoes the battle of the books was joined in earnest. Professor Akrigg's summary of this literary action wittily sustains the metaphor of warfare:

In support of Bellarmine, Martin Becanus, another of the big guns of the Roman Church, thundered from Mainz his *Refutatio Torturae Torti*.... From Ingolstadt came a blast from the Jesuit Gretser. From Spain another Jesuit, Suarez, volleyed forth his *Defensio Fidei Catholicae*. Lessius and Scioppius added to the clamour against James. Eudaemon, Cofteteus, Peleterius joined them. Meanwhile Protestant theologians had rallied to the support of the embattled King. From Thorn in Germany Professor Conrad Graser led off with his *Plaga Regia*.... Battles developed within the battle. Barlow, Bishop of Lincoln, attacked the Jesuit Parsons in his *Answer to a Catholic Englishman*, only to have Parsons come back at him in *A Discussion of the Answer of Mr William Barlow*. William Tooker, Dean of Lichfield, ardent to distinguish himself before the gaze of his King, took on the mighty Martin Becanus in his *Duellum ... cum M.B.*, only to find himself confronted by M.B.'s *Duellum ... cum Gulielmo Tooker*....

...Today the old Latin books lie gathering dust in college libraries, the great fight forgotten which once was fought for the minds of men before blood arbitrated the issue in the Thirty Years' War.[9]

Meanwhile, what of the English Catholics, the civilians caught in the crossfire? They were unhappily trapped by the controversy engendered by the Oath of Allegiance, and they suffered from the renewed enforcement of the penal laws.

In the *Apologie for the Oath of Allegiance* James drew the attention of their co-religionists of Europe to the lenity which he had displayed before the Gunpowder Plot:

I may ... justly vindicate mine own fame, from those innumerable calumnies spread against me, in testifying the truth of my behaviour toward the Papists.... How many did I honour with knighthood, of known and open recusants? How indifferently [impartially] did I give audience, bestowing equally all favours and honours on both professions [religions]? How free and continual access had all ranks and degrees of Papists in my court and company? And above all how frankly and freely did I free recusants of their ordinary payments [fines]?[10]

He added that 'strait order was given out of my own mouth to the judges to spare the execution of all priests.'[11] For their renewed sufferings and disabilities the English Catholics, as James wished Catholic Europe to know, had the Gunpowder plotters to thank.

The English Catholics of the penal times revered the memory of the Elizabethan martyrs and of Father Garnet, Father Oldcorne, and Brother Nicholas Owen – who passed as Father Garnet's servant – a small man with a rupture, who worked unaided, dismantling and rebuilding stone walls, to construct 'priests' holes' in the great Catholic houses, and who died under torture in the Tower. It remained for a future generation, foolish enough to romanticize the violent revolutionary, to discern praiseworthiness in the actions of Robert Catesby and Guy Fawkes.

Unsurprisingly, after the discrediting effect of the Gunpowder Plot, and in the knowledge that following the peace with Spain of 1604, no diplomatic pressure from that quarter could be expected to alleviate their condition, English Catholics for a time practised a quietist religion, non-political, unostentatious, and characterized by a tendency to silent growth. Recent research has suggested that far from being a 'gradually receding community',[12] the English Catholic community grew from an estimated 35,000 in 1603 to an estimated 60,000 in 1640. This growth was due both to the quiet work of the secular clergy, who endeavoured to maintain a sense of continuity with pre-Reformation Catholicism, and to that of the Benedictine and Jesuit missionaries, who worked in England as they would have done in the conversion of a non-Christian country.

While news was made by the conversions of Court ladies, or of young noblemen who travelled abroad and were seduced by the glories of baroque Catholicism, the practice of the Catholic religion in England was truly maintained in missionary conditions, by many Jesuits working in conditions of extreme poverty. The comparison with countries in which the Catholic Church is persecuted at the present time is not far to seek.

Many years were to pass before men of different religions could co-exist on equal terms in Britain. But if the *trahison des clercs* of Mariana and other sedentary advocates of ultimate violence had not led a handful of fanatics to plot the overthrow of the state, the reign of James I would have brought toleration nearer.

CHAPTER SEVEN

The Poisoned Fountain

... a Prince's court
Is like a common Fountaine, whence should flow
Pure silver-droppes in generall; but if't chance
Some curst example poyson't neere the head
Death and diseases through the whole land spread.

(John Webster,
The Duchess of Malfi)

EARLY IN THE reign the Venetian representative in England, Giovanni Carlo Scaramelli, saw the King at Greenwich.

... Having arrived in the chamber where the King was, [he wrote] I found all the Council about his chair, and an infinity of other Lords almost in an attitude of adoration. His Majesty rose and took six steps towards the middle of the room, and then drew back one, after making me a sign of welcome with his hand. He then remained standing up while he listened to me attentively. He was dressed in silver-grey satin, quite plain with a cloak of black tabinet reaching to below the knees and lined with crimson; he had his arm in a white sling, the result of a fall from his horse when out hunting ... from his dress he would have been taken for the meanest among the courtiers, a modesty he affects, had it not been for a chain of diamonds round his neck and a great diamond in his hat....[1]

Most of the portraits of the King which show him dressed in jewel-encrusted clothes in the manner of Elizabeth I are probably misleading. James was notoriously impatient when he was obliged to sit for his portrait, and his lack of interest in portraiture probably led him to leave the artists free to complete the regal icons as they thought fit. He liked plain clothes and a few ostentatious jewels, a style which best expressed the type of kingship which he desired to personify. In later life, as he grew more careless of his personal appearance, his clothes became rather slovenly than plain, but in his prime the effect of his plainly clad figure surrounded by bejewelled courtiers was probably as impressive as he intended.

The first book which James wrote after his accession was an early example of propaganda against smoking, entitled *A Counterblaste to Tobacco*. The conclusion, which has long enjoyed the approval of non-smokers, condemns smoking as 'a custom loathsome to the eye, hateful to the nose, harmful to the brain, dangerous to the lungs, and in the black, stinking fume thereof nearest resembling the horrible Stygian smoke of the pit that is bottomless'.[2] Not so well known is the introduction, in which James described the sort of example which he thought that a king should set his subjects:

> ... It is the King's part (as the proper Physician of his Politic-body) to purge it of... diseases, by medicines meet for the same; as by a certain mild and yet just form of government, to maintain the public quietness ... by the example of his own person and court, to make us all ashamed of our sluggish delicacy ... likewise by his and his court's moderateness in apparel, to make us ashamed of our prodigality....[3]

It is evident from Scaramelli's description that at the beginning of the reign James was endeavouring to match his practice to his preaching, and to maintain the simple, dignified and relatively informal style which Sir Henry Wotton had described as characterizing the Scottish Court at the turn of the century.[4] However, the passage of a short time sufficed to reveal that this style of kingship was inappropriate to the English Court. The courtiers of Elizabeth had developed a glittering ostentation which they were reluctant to relinquish, and James was obliged to accept that despite his own preference for plainness, the brilliance of the Court had come to be regarded as the measure of the monarch's prestige. At the same time, Elizabeth had been a stern disciplinarian, who had striven, on the whole successfully, to impose upon her courtiers standards of morality befitting the votaries of a virgin goddess. By the end of her long reign there was a general weariness of this constraint.[5] The lowering of standards only required encouragement. Indeed, once that encouragement was given, constrained magnificence would turn to unbridled luxury, and imposed morality to extravagant sexual licence.

At first it did not appear that any encouragement to excess of either sort would be given by a king with a preference for plain living, or by a conjugally faithful and procreative royal couple, the model of conventional morality. The last children of James and Anne, born in England, were two daughters, the Princesses Mary and Sophia. Mary was born in 1605 and died in 1607; Sophia's life-span was one day of 1606.

A black-draped barge bore the corpse of the infant Princess by river to Westminster; a black marble tomb in the form of a baby's cradle received her remains in the Abbey. It is a remarkable monument, which expresses without sentimentality the pathos of a life extinguished almost as soon as it had begun. Next year the Princess Mary joined her sister in the small side chapel which they share with Queen Elizabeth I. She is commemorated by a conventional Jacobean effigy of a little girl in a stiffly carved black dress, propped upon her elbow in an attitude far more eloquent of intolerable discomfort than of eternal rest.

The tragedy of the successive deaths of these two children may well have influenced their parents to end their marital relations. Possibly the Queen may have been thought incapable of further childbearing, or may have thought herself so. But the succession was now secured, for Prince Charles was developing encouragingly, even though he continued to be overshadowed by his elder brother. Princess Elizabeth was healthy, and as proverbially lovely as a princess ought to be; she would be a worthy match for any prince in Europe. With the prospect of three royal marriages to be negotiated, all the requirements of diplomacy could be fulfilled. Queen Anne, who had experienced little conjugal or maternal ardour, could withdraw herself from her marriage bed with a justified consciousness of having done her dynastic duty. She turned to the innocent pleasures of her friendships and the roles which she delighted to play in the Court masques.

James had never been an uxorious husband. He had experienced a brief passion for his wife in the early days of their marriage. A few years later he had indulged in an extra-marital affair with Anne Murray of Tullibardine, who became Lady Glamis, and whose short tenancy of James's heart is commemorated by the love poems which he wrote her.[6] Another lady inspired one of the most accomplished of his sonnets. Her name, on the evidence of the theme of the poem, was Cicely:

> Fair famouse Isle, where Agathocles rang;*
> Where sometymes, statly Siracusa stood;
> Whos fertill feelds were bathed in bangsters'† blood
> When Rome and ryvall Carthage strave so lang;
> Great Ladie Mistress, all the Isles amang
> Which stands in Neptune's circle mouving flood,
> No, nather for thy frutfull ground nor good
> I chuse the[e] for the subject of my sang.
> Nor, for the ould report, of scarce trew fame
> Nor heertofor, for farelies‡ in the[e] found;
> But, for the sweet resemblance of that Name
> To whom thou seemest so sibb,§ at least in sound;
> If, then, for seeming so, thy prays bee such
> Sweet she her self doth merit more then much.[7]

The lady, who probably served to grace James's measure rather than to provide any genuine amorous inspiration, was identified by Dr Allan F. Westcott as Cicely Weymess, who married William Murray of Tullibardine, and thus became the sister-in-law of James's former mistress.[8] Cicely Weymess died before the end of 1603, and since the poem is not one of mourning, it was clearly written at an earlier date. The use of Scots language also suggests that it was written before James's accession to the English throne.

Though James had not shown himself wholly uninterested in women, he did not arrive in England with the reputation of a king who was likely to seduce the ladies of the Court. It was quickly recognized that he preferred to surround himself with male courtiers, some of whom were casually referred to as his 'favourites'. One of them was a Scot, James Hay, who was successively created Lord Hay, Viscount Doncaster and Earl of Carlisle; another was an Englishman, Philip Herbert, brother to the Earl of Pembroke, who was created Earl of Montgomery. Hay was a consummate courtier and a spendthrift charmer, whose motto – justified at least

* reigned.
† bullies, bravoes.
‡ marvels.
§ closely related – as in 'sibling'.

by the King's generosity to him – was 'Spend and God will send'. Herbert was endowed with exceptional beauty, which accorded oddly with his character. He was a boorish sportsman, drinker and womanizer, who was incapable of sharing the King's intellectual interests or of comprehending his emotions. These men dwelt in the suburbs of the King's affection; but that condition was sufficient to make their fortunes.

After some sixteen years of emotionally unrewarding marriage, James, at the vulnerable age of forty, was obviously likely to fall in love with someone, and a knowing courtier would have prophesied a male favourite. Although in *Basilikon Doron* James had condemned sodomy as an unforgiveable sin, probably he had convinced himself that other homosexual acts were not seriously blameworthy. His conscience would have freed him to follow the dictates of his inclinations. Under these circumstances the concluding of James's and Anne's conjugal relations can be seen as the severing of the bond of convention which had maintained the discipline of the English Court.

On King's Day, 24 March 1607, there was jousting in the tiltyard at Whitehall, in honour of the King's accession. It was an annual event characterized by elaborate pageantry. On another such occasion a letter of Dudley Carleton evoked the scene: 'The Duke of Lennox exceeded all in feathers; the Lord Walden in followers; and Sir Richard Preston in a pageant, which was an elephant with a castle on his back; and it proved a right *partus elephantis*, for it was a long time a-coming ... and was then as long a-creeping about the tiltyard....'[9]

Jacobean jousting was distinguished by such displays, which might be appreciated or unappreciated; but it was far less bloody than the mediaeval mock-warfare from which it was descended. According to the Jacobean custom the shields of the combatants were borne into the lists by mounted pages, each of whom in turn displayed the shield of his lord before the King.

At the King's Day celebrations in 1607 the shield of Lord Hay was carried by Robert Ker of Ferniherst, a cadet of a great Scottish Border family. His father, Sir Thomas Ker of Ferniherst, had served as Warden of the Middle March and had been a faithful friend of

Esmé, Duke of Lennox. Robert was the youngest of his sons, who had probably been born shortly, if at all, before his father's death; Sir Thomas had died in 1586, and Robert was reputedly about twenty when the years of his good fortune began. He was a handsome young man, 'straight-limbed, well-favoured, strong-shouldered and smooth-faced',[10] with fair hair and a pointed golden beard.

As he rode forward with Lord Hay's shield displayed, something upset his horse. Encumbered by the shield, he strove to control the increasingly maddened animal. It fell with him, and its convulsive struggle to regain its feet left him lying on the ground before the King with his leg broken.

James knew who he was. Where a member of a distinguished Scottish family was concerned enquiry would have been unnecessary. Indeed, according to the gossip-mongering Anthony Weldon, Robert Ker was already an object of interest to the King as

> a young gentleman ... who had his breeding in France; and was newly returned from foreign travel, a gentleman very handsome and well-bred, and one that was observed to spend his time ... with none but men of such eminences, as by whom he might be bettered. He did more than any associate himself with Sir Thomas Overbury, a man of excellent parts ... and drew the eyes of the court, as well as the affection of his master upon him; yet very few, but such as were the curious observers of those times, could discern the drawing of the King's affection.[11]

Whether this was the truth, or whether Weldon decorated his memory with hindsight, the King could have been expected to show concern for Robert Ker. The young man was carried to a nearby house to receive medical attention. Later the King visited him, 'and after, by his daily visiting ... taking all care for his speedy recovery, made the daybreak of his glory appear, every courtier now concluding him actually a favourite ...'.

'Lord!' Weldon continued, 'how the great men then flocked to see him, and to offer to his shrine in such abundance, that the King was forced to lay a restraint, lest it might retard his recovery, by spending his spirits; and to facilitate the cure, care was taken for a choice diet for himself, and chirurgeons with his attendants, and no sooner [was he] recovered, but a proclaimed favourite.'[12]

Before James's accession to the English throne Robert Ker had been a page at the Court of Scotland, where according to one account he had forfeited preferment by his barbarous rendering of a Latin grace. It sounds unlikely, for although James would have deplored bad Latin, he would have forgiven much in a charming young man of good family. Probably the truth was that when so many Scots followed James to England, some influential member of the Ker family thought that Robert would stand a better chance of making his fortune abroad. As a result he acquired from a sojourn in France a veneer of the European sophistication which James had found fatefully attractive ever since he had been allured by the graces of Esmé Stuart.

Robert Ker's ascent of the ladder of honours was not dazzlingly rapid: it had a steadiness which suggested a deep security in the King's regard. In 1607 Ker was knighted, and appointed a Gentleman of the Bedchamber; in 1609 he was given the manor of Sherborne, one of the last plumes plucked from Sir Walter Raleigh. In 1611 he was created Viscount Rochester, which made him the first Scot to take his seat in the English House of Lords. A few weeks later he was made a Knight of the Garter. In 1612 he became a member of the English Privy Council, and in 1613 he was appointed Lord Treasurer of Scotland. At the end of the same year he reached the summit of his glory, when James created him Earl of Somerset.

Ker identified himself with England. He anglicized his name to Carr. He showed no inclination to share his fortunes with his relatives; indeed, his isolation in this respect was curiously un-Scottish. Perhaps, as the last and late-born son of his father, he had little sense of identity with the older members of his family. The absence of nepotism which his career displays may be merely the consequence of lack of contact with hopeful relations, and not the creditable trait which it appears to be at first sight. However, in the context of his times it was certainly creditable that when a bribe was offered him he informed the King, and sought his approval before accepting a present, which thereby lost its power to buy his influence with the King, if not to enrich him. By Jacobean standards he showed in this respect an integrity unusual in a favourite, a minister of the Crown, or even a judge.

Apart from this unexpected quality, Robert Carr appears to have been a very ordinary young man. He was in no sense an intellectual, though he had sufficient intelligence to make use of men with better intellects than his own. His clever friend Sir Thomas Overbury, who was later to die a victim of murder and indirectly to bring about Carr's own ruin, was, at the beginning of Carr's career, not only 'his Pythias' but also a useful mentor to him. Later, when Carr became a power in the land, he would seek advice from the great antiquary Sir Robert Cotton. He was sensible enough not to attempt to usurp the influence of the Earl of Salisbury, and not to behave inimically towards Prince Henry, who took a jealous dislike to him. All in all, it seemed that James had lost his heart to a young man who showed sufficient intimations of good sense to hold out some hopes of future wisdom.

That Robert Carr did not become a wise man was not James's fault: at least he tried to make him a learned one by teaching him Latin. Whether Carr showed any aptitude at these lessons does not seem to have been remembered. James, as his books continue to remind posterity, had a strongly didactic streak in his nature; there was always a master and pupil aspect in his relationships with his later favourites. The other aspect, obvious to all who watched the King in company with them, was his emotional involvement, which he revealed without inhibition. In his youth, he had publicly kissed and embraced Esmé Stuart; he did the same with Robert Carr, and the favourite of his latter years, George Villiers. Indeed, according to a late contemporary, Sir John Oglander: '... he loved young men, his favourites, better than women, loving them beyond the love of men to women. I never yet saw any fond husband make so much or so great dalliance over his beautiful spouse as I have seen King James over his favourites....'[13]

The question naturally arises, what indeed was the nature of these relationships? They were self-evidently homoerotic in inspiration, and were obviously generally believed to be homosexual. King James's homosexual inclinations came to be accepted by his courtiers and contemporaries; as far as the details of his relationships were concerned, he kept the ultimate secret. But there does not seem any reason to suppose otherwise of him than of most people: that the loves which he displayed in public were consummated in private. A possible indication that this was so is that towards the end of Carr's years of favour James took occasion to write him a letter of reproach, in which he included among Carr's failings as a favourite 'your long creeping back and withdrawing yourself from lying in my chamber, notwithstanding my many hundred times earnestly soliciting you to the contrary ...'.[14]

In the meantime, the substitution of a favourite for his Queen as the person who enjoyed the closest intimacy with him could not fail to influence the moral climate of the Court. Once James had fallen in love, for the first time since his arrival in England, he seems to have lost his previous conviction that a king should set his subjects a somewhat austere example of personal conduct. When the King, who was the cynosure of the nation, forgot his role as the arbiter of morality, it was inevitable that his courtiers should feel that what was good enough for him was good enough for them.

The King probably never consciously relinquished his old belief that '... It is the King's part ... by his and his Court's moderateness in apparel, to make us ashamed of our prodigality ...'. Yet the increase in the prodigality of the Court, in every direction, may be laid at the King's door – though in this instance the cause was one of the pleasantest traits in his character: his extreme generosity.

James liked to give, and he liked to give pleasure by giving. He indulged his generosity throughout his life: quite possibly only in order to enjoy the delighted reactions of those to whom he gave; but he may also have deceived himself with the belief that not only the gratitude but also the love of the recipients was won by his princely gifts. There is a rather touching story told by Arthur Wilson, which shows that the King's generosity was at least charmingly spontaneous:

... being one day in the gallery at Whitehall, and none with him but Sir Henry Rich (who was second son to the Earl of Warwick) and afterwards Earl of Holland, a gentleman of excellent natural parts, but youthfully expensive, and James Maxwell, one of his Bedchamber, some porters passed them, with three thousand pounds, going to the Privy Purse. Sir Henry Rich, whispering [to] Maxwell, the King turned upon them and asked Maxwell 'What says he? What says he?' Maxwell told him, he wished he had so much money. 'Marry, shalt thou, Harry!' saith the King, and presently commands the porters to carry it to his lodging, with this expression, 'You think now you have a great purchase, but I am the more delighted to think how much I have pleasured you in giving this money, than you can be, in receiving it.'[15]

This was not an isolated example of generosity on such a grand scale. In the course of the year 1611, the Earl of Montgomery was given £8,000, Viscount Fenton £8,000, Lord Hay £5,000, Robert Carr, by that date Lord Rochester, £5,000, and the Earl of Essex £3,000. These sums of money must be multiplied many times to give an idea of what they represent in modern values. Present inflation makes the calculation all the more difficult: but reckoning on a twenty-four-fold increase in values, which was conservative even at the time of writing, the least of those gifts, the Earl of Essex's £3,000, becomes £72,000.[16]

Courtiers who were thus wonderfully and suddenly enriched expressed their good fortune in prodigality, and sometimes in merely vulgar ostentation. Lord Hay was credited with the invention of the 'ante-supper' or 'double supper', 'the manner of which was, to have the board covered at the first entrance of the guests with dishes as high as a tall man could well reach, filled with the choicest and dearest viands sea or land could afford. And all this, once seen, and having feasted the eyes of the invited, was in a manner thrown away, and fresh set on to the same height, having only this advantage of the other, that it was hot.'[17]

From one of the 'ante-suppers' an attendant of the King managed to secure a cold pie for himself and his family. It was 'reckoned to my lord [Hay] at ten pounds, being composed of ambergris, magisterial of pearl, musk, etc., yet was so far ... from being sweet ... that he almost poisoned his whole family, flying himself like the satyr from his own stink ...'.[18]

Gambling was a Court pastime which reached excessive proportions, and probably brought ruin to many courtiers who indulged in it beyond their means. There was a vogue for 'golden play', or gambling with gold coins only. John Chamberlain noted the sums which changed hands on the eve of Twelfth Night, 1608: '... there was great golden play at Court,' he informed Dudley Carleton, 'no gamester admitted that brought not £300 at least. Montgomery played the King's money and won him £750, which he had for his labour [i.e. the King gave him his winnings]; the Lord Monteagle lost the Queen £400, Sir Robert Carey for the Prince £300, the Earl of Salisbury £300 ... so that I heard of no winners but the King and Sir Francis Woolley who got above £800....'[19]

The increasing extravagance of the Court was probably most obviously expressed in the growing elaborateness of the clothes of both sexes. Both men and women curled and dyed their hair, drenched themselves in exotic and unpleasant perfumes, and covered themselves with the richest jewels that they could afford. Masks and wigs concealed the ravages of age; vivid cosmetics brightened the beauty of youth. The fashions themselves showed a natural development from those of the last years of the late Queen. The breeches of the men grew more grotesquely padded, the farthingales of the women yet more vast in circumference. On men's heads rested hats which spouted fountains of plumes; from women's headdresses blew veils which encompassed them like radiant clouds. The materials of Court dress grew richer, more brilliant in colour, more intricately embroidered in gold, silver and seed pearls. Ruffs and wired lace collars grew more fantastic and diverse in style, and an arbitress of fashion named Mistress Anne Turner invented a method of colouring starch with saffron, to dye the lace a rich golden yellow. The dresses of the court ladies, more exaggeratedly low-cut, exposed almost the whole of their breasts. Queen Anne, and other virtuous ladies, covered the fashionable décolletage with a film of gauze; but there were others who delighted to display themselves:

> Upon whose naked paps a lecher's thought
> Acts sin in fouler shapes than can be wrought....

It is notorious that the unfashionable equate fashion with immorality, but the fashions of the Jacobean Court provided some encouragement for this view. Consequently, it was not surprising that the country gentry and aristocracy, who encountered the morals, manners and fashions of the Court only through rumour, correspondence, or the occasional contacts provided by sessions of Parliament or royal progresses, imagined the prodigality and depravity of the Court to be greater than they were. The scandals which were to involve the King's most intimate associates in the middle years of the reign could only enhance this impression.

Old ideas die hard, and new ideas are swift to seed themselves. For those who adhered to the former, the Court remained the source of office, ennoblement, knighthood, and the fountainhead of honour. For those who accepted the latter it appeared to be a new Sodom or Gomorrah, a place where patrimony or virtue were lost as easily as a pocket was picked or a glove mislaid.[20]

CHAPTER EIGHT

'This Eating Canker of Want'

The only disease and consumption which I can ever apprehend as likeliest to endanger me is this eating canker of want, which being removed, I could think myself as happy in all other respects as any other King or monarch that ever was since the birth of Christ.

King James I to his Council, 1607

IT WAS NOT surprising that as early as 1607 the King began to experience the condition which he graphically described as 'this eating canker of want'. He arrived in England with the impression that he was the inheritor of great wealth, together with the English Crown, and he acted upon his first impression long after the facts of the situation ought to have disabused him. His actions appear in every respect to support the summing up of Professor F. C. Dietz:

Neither now [1603], nor at any subsequent time, is there the slightest indication that James had any sense of the value of money or of the meaning of the balance of debit and credit. He seems to have been incapable of understanding the fact that a considerable income and even the occasional presence of large amounts of coined money in the hands of the tellers of the exchequer were entirely compatible with a condition verging on bankruptcy.[1]

James's education by two strongly Calvinist classical scholars, George Buchanan and Peter Young, had been concentrated upon Latin, Greek, Calvinist Theology, political theory, history and modern languages. There had been some lessons in cosmography, and some rather half-hearted efforts to provide a grounding in arithmetic.[2] James thought that it was helpful for a king to know something of mathematics, because the subject had an application in warfare 'for the knowledge of the art military, in situation of camps, ordering of battles, making fortifications, placing of batteries, or suchlike'. He expressed this idea almost *en passant* in *Basilikon*

Doron.[3] Obviously it had occurred to neither of his tutors that the application of mathematics to the understanding of finance had a necessary place in the King's education. The royal finances would have been presumed to be the business of the Lord Treasurer of the kingdom, or, more particularly, of his underlings.

In addition to this large area of omission in James's education, which was not made good by natural aptitude or interest, there was the unfortunate fact that Scotland and England employed the same main unit of currency, the £; and at the end of the sixteenth century the £ Scots was worth approximately only one twelfth of the £ sterling, which made it obvious that an English income was worth a very great deal more than a Scots income of the same figure. Towards the end of James's reign in Scotland (taking the year 1599 as an example) the income of the Scottish Crown was £58,771; and at the time of his accession to the English throne, that of the English Crown was £110,000.[4] Besides the disparity in the figures themselves there was the disparity in the equivalent values of the two currencies, both of which would have contributed to James's impression that he had been prodigiously enriched.

Therefore, almost inevitably, James failed to grasp the seriousness of the fact that he had inherited from Elizabeth I a debt of approximately £430,000. It is most likely that he would have retained a tendency to think in Scottish values, and if he reminded himself that an English debt was really a more serious liability than a Scottish debt of the same sum, he had the ready comfort of reflecting that his English income was greater, to meet the greater debt. He may well have convinced himself that the inherited debt need not be a millstone for long, since he had such great resources with which to deal with it. Furthermore, Elizabeth had been obliged to make large outlays in directions in which James could justly economize. For example, there was the defence of the frontier, which was a frontier no more. There was the expense of the garrison which Elizabeth had maintained at Berwick; James required no garrison to defend one of his kingdoms against the other. There were the huge sums which Elizabeth had been obliged to expend on the subjugation of rebellious Ireland; Lord Mountjoy was completing this task, at which Essex had failed, at the time of James's accession. During the financial year ending at Michaelmas 1602 the war in

Ireland cost Elizabeth £342,074; but during the financial year 1607, English commitment in Ireland cost James £38,251.[5] That economy alone could have paid off a large proportion of the Crown's debt. If James could have economized in other directions his financial problems might have been short-lived.

Unfortunately economy proved impossible, for some reasons which were beyond the King's control. Queen Elizabeth I had had no family for the resources of the Crown to support, whereas James had a Queen and three children, for each of whom a separate household was required. For financial reasons alone it was perhaps fortunate that the royal family was not permanently increased in size after the King's accession to the English throne. On the 'childbeds' in which Queen Anne gave birth to her last two children, the short-lived Mary and Sophia, over £30,000 was spent. This expenditure seems quite disproportionate beside the £30,000 which was the whole cost of the upbringing of the Princess Elizabeth, who spent her childhood at Combe Abbey in Warwickshire, in the care of Lord and Lady Harington. On Elizabeth's marriage in 1613, James was unable to pay his debt to Lord Harington; he was obliged to discharge it by granting him the right to coin brass farthings.[6]

During the first decade of the reign James became increasingly encumbered by his debts. A number of reasons or excuses can be adduced – the expense of the royal family, the necessity of maintaining a certain regal splendour for reasons of prestige, the effect of inflation upon a fixed income – but when allowance has been made for all these mitigating circumstances, the fact remains that King James was incapable of understanding that he could not afford to spend his money as it pleased him most.

'Golden play' at the gaming tables, largesse to favoured courtiers and servants, lavish purchases of jewels – all combined to heap up a mountain of debt. The King might have understood the seriousness of the situation if he could have seen, in the form of an actual mountain of gold, the debts which he had incurred, but when he saw – if he saw – only the exchequer accounts, which were beyond his comprehension, his debts remained merely a matter of vague, though oppressive anxiety, to trouble his generous nature.

Inevitably, as the King sank deeper into debt, the wages of his servants fell into arrears. It was a natural progression that, when they did not receive what was due to them, they resorted to helping themselves. According to an undated report on peculation in the royal household, the royal bakers were making light-weight loaves and misappropriating what they saved. The officers of the buttery were selling the King's drink for their own profit. The cooks in the kitchen were selling the best of the meat delivered to them, so that only half of that supplied was served on the King's tables. The officers of the poultry were selling lamb, capon and fowl intended for the use of the household. The woodyard officers were charging for wood that never arrived, and half of what did come in was being stolen.[7] And unhappily, so it went on.

Bishop Goodman tells a story that when one of these delinquent officers lay dying he sent a contrite message to the King. James's response was a Christian assurance that he did 'freely and lovingly forgive him'. But he added with a touch of cynicism, 'I wonder much that all my officers do not go mad with the like thoughts; for certainly they have as great cause as this poor man hath.'[8]

At the apex of this pyramid of graft was Lord Treasurer Dorset, who had a reputation both for personal avarice and for lining his pockets with the unofficial profits of his office. An anonymous satirist mocked him when Death took him in an apt fashion in 1608. Old Dorset was about to confront a man accused before the Privy Council with the evidence of his guilt. 'Here is this which shall strike you dead,' he said; and as he rose up to exhibit the document, he fell dead at the table. The witty epitaph was passed around:

> Discourteous Death that wouldst not once confer,
> Or deign to parley with our Treasurer:
> Had he been Thee, or of thy fatal tribe
> He would have spared a life to gain a bribe.[9]

King James was at least sufficiently aware of the seriousness of the financial situation to recognize that the next Lord Treasurer must be a man of the highest ability and, if possible, of integrity. One man appeared to combine both qualities, and to have proved his trustworthiness to the King since the beginning of the reign: Robert Cecil, Earl of Salisbury, accepted the great office which had been the summit of his father's career and was the crown of his own ambition. In so doing he took on a killing burden of overwork.

For all his greatness, Salisbury's position was unenviable, for inevitably, with the passage of time, the King's gratitude for his part in securing the succession gradually faded. Furthermore, Salisbury's appointment as Lord Treasurer coincided with the early years of the rise of Robert Carr. Under the new circumstances created by the presence of a young favourite at the King's side, Mathew's observation that it was not easy for Salisbury's role as the 'little beagle' to maintain its initial charm is probably sadly true. Salisbury had taught himself to assume the informal style which pleased the King, as, in a letter to Lord Dirleton in 1606, intended for the King's eyes, he described himself as 'being newly come home from a long and late session in Parliament, and being close by my chimney's end, a proper place for beagles ...'.[10] He was the master also of the incense-laden style which was appropriate in official communications, such as a letter from the Privy Council to the King which proclaimed that '... if your Majesty may repute it for the least part of happiness to be served by us, how much more may we appoint ourselves thrice happy to be guided and governed by such a King, from whom not only we receive a kind of influence to the enabling of our advice and councils, but ... all the Kings of the earth might be glad as from the oracle to take instructions from the King of Great Britanye.'[11]

Probably Salisbury well understood the necessity of stretching himself continually to retain the King's regard. His appointment as Lord Treasurer was the heavier burden in that it came when the King had grown accustomed to his capacity to work himself to the utmost, and when he had already given the King his great house of Theobalds, which had so much delighted James at first sight. Salisbury had nothing more to give the King, except his service in the essentially thankless task of attempting to make him solvent. It was thankless principally because the only means by which it might be achieved were the unpopular means of rigid economies and intricate forms of extortion.

Salisbury appears to have made one attempt to bring home to James, in visual terms, the reality of his extravagance. According to an anecdote of Francis Osborn, James wrote a warrant for £20,000 to be paid out of the Exchequer as a gift. Salisbury had the money piled up for the King to see: 'Thereupon the King fell into a passion, protesting he was abused, never intending any such gift: and casting himself upon the heap, scrabbled out the quantity of two or three hundred pounds, and swore he [the intended recipient] should have no more.'[12]

Momentary shocks such as this might have a salutary effect, but obviously the lesson would be as speedily forgotten. Salisbury attempted the resource of urging the King himself to resist the temptation of giving; he persuaded James to go so far as to command his courtiers not to tempt him. In 1610 a 'Declaration of his Majesty's Royal Pleasure in the Matter of Bounty' contained the words 'we do expressly . . . forbid all persons whatsoever, to presume to press us, for anything that may . . . turn to the diminution of our revenues and settled receipts. . . .'[13]

But in the long run Salisbury recognized that the solvency of the Crown demanded more radical measures. He turned his lucid and practical mind to the question of devising them.

He thought of the desperate expedient of selling Crown lands to pay off substantial portions of the debt. Such sales would reduce the annual income of the Crown in the future, so the measure may be regarded as one of doubtful wisdom. However, Salisbury selected for sale those properties of the Crown which were themselves the least profitable. Among them were hundreds of mills, manors and rectories. The loss in rents was some £14,500 per annum, but the sales assisted in bringing the King's debts down from £597,337 at the outset of Salisbury's treasurership to £300,000 at the beginning of 1610.[14]

Salisbury endeavoured to counteract the loss of annual income by seeking new areas of gain. A means was provided by a test case of 1606, when a merchant named Thomas Bate appealed against the import duty on currants imposed during the previous reign. The Court of Exchequer dismissed Bate's appeal and ruled that the King possessed the power to regulate trade by other such 'impositions' if he saw reason to do so. Accordingly, in 1608 Salisbury issued a new 'Book of Rates', in which the range of impositions was extended. Conversely, he worked at unearthing old debts to the Crown, and possible causes of fines, such as the enclosure of common land or the creation of 'assarts' or clearings in the royal forests. He was able to boast that these researches had led him to impose

£730 in fines for illegal enclosures in a single day, and £300 on the day following.[15]

He brought the Crown's debt down as best he might by such means as fines for long-forgotten misdemeanours, and by pressing the King's feudal rights, like the 'aid' which was payable on the knighting of his eldest son. This feudal aid was collected when Prince Henry was knighted in 1609. Another aid was sought for the marriage of the Princess Elizabeth, but on this occasion the response was poor.

For all Salisbury's resourcefulness none of his expedients was likely to be of lasting effect while the King's expenditure exceeded his income by £80,000 per annum. His gifts to courtiers amounted to nearly £100,000 in the year following his accession, while one courtier alone, the spendthrift James Hay, was reputed to have received a total of £400,000 from the King in the course of the reign, though 'on his death he left not a house or acre of land to be remembered by'.

Salisbury's largest and most hopeful scheme was to provide the King with an adequate annual income guaranteed by Parliament, through the sacrifice of the Crown's surviving feudal rights. To enhance the bargaining power of the Crown to the utmost, Salisbury made the fullest use of the opportunities to exact those rights in the period preceding his presentation of his plan to Parliament. Fines, impositions, and the rights of the Court of Wards, by which the Crown administered the estates of minors of gentle and noble blood, were all made to yield the greatest possible profit, as a result of which the King's debt was reduced to £280,000 during 1610. At the same time, the previous taxation granted to the King by Parliament after the revelation of the Gunpowder Plot was being collected; the Crown had benefited from the yield of three subsidies and three fifteenths by the end of 1609.

The King's position therefore appeared relatively strong when Salisbury was ready to present his proposal of a 'Great Contract' by which Parliament would provide the King with a permanent income of £200,000 per annum in return for his abandonment of his remaining feudal rights, which had long been causes of grievance. Besides the rights which Salisbury had made to yield the highest profit, there was also that of Purveyance, by which the provisions for the royal household could be purchased by the officials called Purveyors, at prices fixed by themselves, well below the current market prices. There was no need for Salisbury to enhance the profitability of Purveyance, for it was one of the aspects of household administration which was most subject to malversation; it was a burden on the ordinary subject, and Parliament would have been delighted to see an end to it. James himself had no wish to permit the right of Purveyance to be applied extortionately, and he made many good resolutions to end an evil situation; but for so long as he remained in financial difficulties he was powerless to enforce honesty upon the officers of his household.

To negotiate a scheme as revolutionary as the Great Contract in the end proved beyond the powers of Salisbury, not only because both the King and Parliament were somewhat distrustful of it, but because the means of implementing it were scarcely developed. James had always doubted the basic wisdom of bargaining with his Parliament. It appeared to him that the increasingly critical spirit which the Commons displayed must be the direct consequence of Salisbury's use of certain areas of the royal prerogative for the purposes of such bargaining. The devaluation of the monarchy itself he could envisage as the final result. At the same time, Parliament was accustomed to the idea that taxation was 'extraordinary', to be requested and granted in times of emergency, such as wartime, but not to be required every year. During the last years of Elizabeth there had been an almost continual state of emergency provided by the war in Ireland, and the long-continued hostilities with Spain, which gave frequent demands for taxation an official justification. Yet the theory survived that the sovereign should 'live of his own', by which was meant not only that he should maintain himself and his family and household out of his own resources, but that he should bear the costs of government out of them as well. If this had once been feasible, it was so no longer. Elizabeth's practice of what is politely called rigid parsimony, but which was in fact the acute miserliness which had characterized her grandfather Henry VII, had enabled her to do so for so long as her government had no crisis to meet. But her commitments in the Netherlands and in Ireland had put an end to the possibility of holding her balance of payments during her later years. As a result she had left her successor with the large debt which lay at the root of his problems so long as the same financial theories pertained.

Salisbury's efforts to reduce the King's improvidence as much as he could, and to increase the effectiveness of the means by which money could be raised through the exercise of the King's feudal rights, preceded his attempt to change the inherited attitude of the English Parliament towards taxation. Bravely, Salisbury tried to introduce the new concept that Parliament had a duty to support the Crown financially in the burden of government, in return for the surrender of those aspects of the royal prerogative which had become anachronistic or were themselves burdensome.

Parliament was deeply suspicious of this new view, and also doubtful of the desirability of paying large sums into the hands of a King who was well known for his proclivity for giving generously to his courtiers, men who were as extravagant as himself and, so far as anyone could see, were undeserving, and some of whom, moreover, were unpopular Scots.

Possibly Salisbury committed a decisive tactical error on attempting to drive a delicate bargain with an experienced Parliament, which contained members who knew one another well, and who had had ample opportunity in the successive sessions of Parliament to form their personal impressions of the King and the Court. None of the last six Parliaments of Elizabeth I had sat for more than six months and none for more than two sessions[16]; whereas the first Parliament of James I had already sat for long enough to gain a new sense of corporate identity, and a new confidence in negotiating with ministers of the Crown.

Parliament drove a long and hard bargain with Salisbury, and at the end of July 1610 a recess was granted so that the Commons could consult with their constituents on the best means of raising £200,000 annually.

After the recess the mood of both King and Commons had changed. Parliament now strongly doubted the wisdom of providing the King with means to become independent of the need to make requests for 'extraordinary' taxation. In theory the Commons possessed considerable powers conferred by the privilege of granting or withholding taxation; these powers they had not yet learnt to use to the best advantage, but they were aware of a potential source of strength which they might be foolish to bargain away.

The King on his side had second thoughts about yielding any areas of his prerogative, and thus suffering, however slightly, a diminution of his personal power in return for an income which might not hold its value in real terms in the years to come. In view of continuing inflation, Salisbury's plan, which has been much praised for its statesmanship and lamented for its failure, might in the end have presented a serious problem of re-negotiation to King James in the later years of his reign, or to his successors. In the event, these conjectural problems were replaced by others.

After the consultative recess, when Parliament reassembled in October 1610, James had decided that he wanted more money in return for the rights which he was to forgo, and the Commons refused to agree. They especially disliked his essentially reasonable demand that the officers of the Court of Wards, which was to cease to function, should be compensated for their loss of employment. On this note of disagreement, James prorogued Parliament in December, and dissolved it early in 1611.

The 'eating canker of want' continued to be treated by desperate expedients such as the creation of the Order of Baronetage, which took its place in the scale of honours as the lowest hereditary titled order, and was in effect an hereditary knighthood. Baronetcies were originally based on the fiction that each baronet should maintain thirty foot soldiers for service in Ireland. The soldiers were supposed to be paid eightpence a day for three years – thus £36.10s. This sum made up the price for which the first baronetcies were sold – £1,095. The original creation brought in £120,000.[17] So successful an expedient was tried again in later years. 1619 saw the creation of a new order of baronets, those of the Kingdom of Ireland. In the last year of the reign followed the baronets of Nova Scotia.

Other honours were sold irrespective of the merits of the purchaser. As early as 1603 the King commanded all subjects who had an income of £40 per annum or upwards derived from land to claim the right of knighthood – for a fee of £30 – or to make payment in lieu of taking the title. While knighthood thus fell into some disrepute, there were many men ambitious to acquire peerages, and willing to pay many thousands of pounds for them. For example, in 1616 Sir John Roper paid £10,000 to become Lord Teynham – and received the mocking nickname of 'Lord 10m'.[18]

Whether the Great Contract would have yielded enough to make such ingenious methods of fund-raising unnecessary may be doubted; but whether or not it would have done so, Salisbury, who may have devised the scheme for the first order of baronets, had little time left to think of further plans to make his sovereign solvent. At the beginning of 1612 it was recognized that he was dying.

Since he had given Theobalds to the King, Salisbury had made time between his labours as Lord Treasurer to build the greatest of Jacobean palaces, Hatfield House, beside the old royal manor house of Hatfield, which James had given him in return. Salisbury's Hatfield still stands, the perfect monument to his taste and to the taste of his age, a fit setting in which a powerful minister could receive his King, and the whole Court. It is also a monument to the fact that Salisbury was himself extravagant, and that he had not scorned to take profits from the great appointments which he had held. Neither had he scorned to accept a pension from the King of Spain.

After his death no-one had a good word to say for him. His sexual immorality and his deformity provided material for many cruel epitaphs, such as

> Here lies Robert Cicil
> Compos'd of back and pisle.

None found compassion in the realization that, while wealth and power had enabled him to command pleasure, his disability had made his chances of receiving love very slight. At least it was said that his youthful marriage to the sister of Lord Cobham had been happy.

It was the King's misfortune that there was no immediately obvious successor to him as Lord Treasurer. Salisbury's greatest oversight or failing had been that he had taken no thought to train a successor. His loyalties were closely familial, and his son Lord Cranbourne was not a sufficiently intelligent man to be considered. Unfortunately his enmity to his brilliant cousin Francis Bacon had remained constant. It appeared that he had cared only to retain power in his own hands.

Salisbury's old ally the Earl of Northampton at first hoped to succeed him at the Treasury, but Northampton's greatest gift was to inspire mistrust. His sycophancy was too profound to convince anyone that it had even the slenderest basis of sincerity. James was accustomed to Northampton. He would keep him always where he had been since the beginning of the reign: near, but not at, the centre of affairs.

James appointed a Treasury commission, which was composed of the Earls of Northampton, Suffolk and Worcester, Lord Wotton, who was the Treasurer of the King's Household, Lord Zouche, and the Chancellor of the Exchequer, Sir Julius Caesar. They found that the debt which Salisbury had once spectacularly reduced had risen to £500,000.

CHAPTER NINE

'The Expectancy and Rose of the Fair State'

> ... it may be doubted, whether it ever lay in the power of any Prince merely human, to bring so much felicity into a nation, as they did all his life propose to themselves at the death of King James.
>
> Francis Osborn, of Prince Henry

THERE ARE MANY portraits of King James's eldest son. When Prince Henry reached maturity he was, according to the description written by Sir Charles Cornwallis, the Treasurer of his household, '... of a comely, tall, middle stature, about five foot and eight inches high, of a strong, straight, well-made body ... with somewhat broad shoulders, and a small waist; of an amiable, majestic countenance, his hair of an auburn colour, long-faced and broad forehead, a piercing grave eye, a most gracious smile, with a terrible frown; courteous, loving and affable....'[1]

A fine equestrian portrait, attributed to Isaac Oliver, shows the Prince clad in richly decorated armour. His hat is adorned with the Prince of Wales's Feathers; in his hand is an upraised whip, perhaps symbolic of discipline. His face is portrayed in an expression of stern benignity.

Prince Henry was the idol of the English nation, and the memoirist Francis Osborn was probably correct in his opinion that it was beyond the power of any prince 'merely human' to fulfil the hopes which were centred upon him. Cornwallis, whose view of him verged upon idolatry, wrote that '... he had a certain kind of extraordinary unspeakable excellence ... gathered (out of question) by him long ago from the plentiful garden of his father's all-admired *Basilikon Doron*, long since in his youth dedicated unto him'.[2]

Prince Henry, it may be remembered, had been born and brought up in Scotland by the second Earl of Mar and the Dowager Countess, his mother, who had been the foster mother of James himself. Prince Henry, as Cornwallis discerned, was formed in the image of the kingship which James had personified in Scotland, and which he had defined in *Basilikon Doron* as an appropriate model of kingship for his son. If Henry had reached the years of discretion while his father was still ruling in Scotland he would have seen the model which had been presented for his instruction still running in perfect order. As it was, he became conscious of his father's style of kingship only when James had modified it as a result of his contact with the more elaborate Court style of England. To Henry, it could only seem that what his father had preached he did not – or did no longer – practise.

Prince Henry was a very dutiful son; had he not been so, his relations with his father would have been far more strained than ever they became. James loved and was proud of his son. Henry reverenced his father's abilities and qualities, yet many of his own practices and actions contained implicit criticisms of King James. For instance, it was notorious that the King swore habitually and thoughtlessly, and when he was checked by some divine who had the temerity to do so, laughed and said that he hoped God would not hold it against him since it was done in the heat of anger and without premeditation; whereas Prince Henry gave instructions 'to have boxes kept at his three standing [permanent] houses, Saint James's, Richmond and Nonsuch, causing all those who did swear in his hearing to pay moneys to the same, which were after duly given to the poor ...'.[3]

James's ecclesiastical policy, which had not commended itself to the more fanatical among the Puritans, they imagined Prince Henry would alter:

> Henry the 8 pull'd down abbeys and cells
> But Henry the 9 shall pull down Bishops and bells

chanted his Puritan admirers.

In particular, Henry came nearest to open criticism of his father over the matter of his favourites: 'He oftimes protested, that neither fantasy nor flattery should move him to confer upon any a superlative place in his favour, but would to the uttermost of his understanding measure unto all according to the merit of their services, as holding it not just to yield unto affections....'[4]

Perhaps in consequence of his idealistic reaction against the low morality of his father's Court, Prince Henry has sometimes been portrayed as a cold and priggish young man. But he had the susceptibilities common to most young men. He admired, and according to some Court gossips was thought to have been seduced by, the lovely young Frances Devereux, Countess of Essex. However, when some courtier picked up a glove which she had dropped and presented it to the Prince, Henry, who had discovered that she was at the same time indulging in an intrigue with Robert Carr, spurned the token, saying that he scorned her glove which had been stretched by another. Whether contempt for the lady, for the reputed lover, or for his father's affections was the strongest motive, the amateur psychologist may judge.

The most obvious contrast between James and his son was in Prince Henry's enthusiasm for everything that pertained to war. He practised martial sports, he went on long marches to strengthen himself in readiness for real warfare: '... also delighting to confer ... of all manner of wars, battles, furniture, arms by sea and land, disciplines, orders, marches, alarms, watches, stratagems, ambuscadoes, approaches, scalings, fortifications, encampings....'[5]

While James's personal motto was '*Beati Pacific*' (Blessed are the Peacemakers), the motto which Prince Henry chose for himself was '*Fax Mentis Honestae Gloria*': the economy of the Latin is difficult to render, but the message is 'Glory is the guiding light of a mind filled with thoughts of honour.' Henry IX would have been a warlike King.

Prince Henry was sixteen years old in 1610. On 4 June, with splendid ceremonies, James created him Prince of Wales. Henry as a result received a degree of independence of action which he enjoyed to the full, and in which he gave promise of the efficiency and authority that he would bring to the ruling of his kingdoms when his turn came.

As Prince of Wales Henry was given a larger and more formal household, which in its organization resembled the households of his parents. Besides his devoted Treasurer, Sir Charles Cornwallis, he had his Chamberlain, Sir Thomas Chaloner; his Groom of the Stole was his closest and best-loved attendant, Sir David Murray, who had slept in his Bedchamber ever since he was a child at Stirling. His tutor, Adam Newton, became his secretary. He had numerous other officers of the household, and his establishment contained a total of almost five hundred persons. This large household, or 'family' as the pleasant custom of the seventeenth century called it, the young Prince of Wales managed with an efficiency which the hard-pressed officers of the King's household must have wished that James himself possessed.

In yearly income Prince Henry received from the Principality of Wales £11,713. Rents from his Duchy of Cornwall brought him approximately £1,713. The Cornish coinage and customs brought him another £2,000, and the pre-emption of Cornish tin £8,000. He received £282 from the earldom of Chester. Altogether, Prince Henry's rents, from these and other sources, brought him an income of about £25,000 per annum.[16] The Prince did not live above his means. According to Cornwallis he created an impression that he lived in a style of appropriately princely magnificence, and yet he was provident without appearing to be stingy. As a result he was able to save 'a yearly spare of some thousands of pounds, which he reserved for a store of treasure to be ready for all events and occasions accidental'.[7]

However, the Prince of Wales, for all his exemplary providence – which must have annoyed King James as much as did Henry's ostentatious avoidance of his own particular pleasures and failings – delighted in the Court ceremonial, of which the masque was both the most lavish and the most exquisite. In the hands of Ben Jonson and Inigo Jones the Jacobean and Carolean court masques became perhaps the most elaborate theatrical spectacles ever to be performed by amateurs. Certainly they were the most elegant celebrations of the cult of monarchy which the Court of Great Britain ever witnessed. It would be interesting to know whether the participants in general were aware of the remarkable quality of the short-lived art form in which they played their parts. Probably they were not, for if Jonson could hold the contribution of Jones in contempt, as he did, it is likely that the less artistically-conscious courtiers were interested only in the importance of what they themselves were doing. Jones imported from Italy new concepts of stage design, which remained basically unchallenged until the twentieth century. But when Jonson the poet and Jones the designer, both of them difficult and self-important men, eventually fell out, Jonson wrote a bitter *Expostulation with Inigo Jones*, which condemned his preoccupation with spectacle in the lines

> O shows! shows! Mighty shows!
> The eloquence of masques! What need of prose
> Or verse or sense t' express immortal you?
> You are the spectacles of state! ...
> Oh, to make boards speak! There is a task –
> Painting and carpentry are the soul of masque...[8]

At this level the masque was a courtly entertainment, apparently frivolous in that it lost a great deal more money than the King, or any courtier, could in reality afford; in that it was an apparently purposeless excuse for courtiers and their ladies to dress up in extravagantly rich costumes and dance till dawn; in that each masque seemed superficially to be a confection of nonsense, in which nymphs and satyrs, or obscure characters from classical mythology, excavated by Ben Jonson's learning and clothed in poetry, provided an excuse for all these revels. But Prince Henry at least would have known that he was taking part in an almost liturgical celebration of the cult of monarchy; and that, in paying the ritual homage to his father, which every masque offered in some form, he was investing in the ever-growing veneration upon which it was intended that the monarchy of Great Britain would be able to draw in the future. The purpose of the masque as Jonson conceived it, the King approved it and Prince Henry understood it, was to celebrate the blessings of order which a good monarchy existed to bestow. The 'argument' of each of the symbolic stories which the elaborately costumed masquers enacted was dedicated to the same end – to present this message in visual terms.

The masque, as it was developed at the Jacobean court, consisted of the 'Entry', or arrival of the masquers; the 'Main', or dance of the masquers; the 'Revels', or dancing of the masquers with the spectators, and the 'Going Out', or concluding dance. Jonson developed the importance of the 'Antimasque', which was a grotesque or comic 'curtain-raiser', which gradually extended in length and developed in scope as it grew in popularity.

The royal or noble masquers did not speak; they danced their parts in silence, while the speaking parts were often taken by professional actors. James himself was not a participant in the masque. He provided the centrepiece, and was the object of worship to which the performance was directed. He sat on the 'State', a raised and canopied chair in the centre and forefront of the audience. Queen Anne was the most enthusiastic masquer of all, and Inigo Jones's most valued patron. To her the costumes and sets were certainly of greater interest than the verse. Prince Henry, on the other hand, though he enjoyed the splendour which was dedicated to glorifying the regality and power of his family, and though he conscientiously patronized all aspects of the arts, was probably far more interested in the poetry and its content.

On 1 January 1611 Jonson's *Oberon, the Fairy Prince* was performed before the King, the Queen, and the Princess Elizabeth, with Prince Henry dancing the title role. The simple story was that Oberon brought his subjects, the Fays, to pay homage at the throne of King Arthur (or James). Who the Fays were was explained in a speech by one of their attendant Sylvans. Oberon's intention, the speaker proclaimed, was to offer

> A night of homage to the British court,
> And ceremony, due to Arthur's chair,
> From our bright master, Oberon the fair;
> Who with these knights Attendants, here preserved
> In Fairy Land for good they have deserved
> Of yond high throne, are come of right to pay
> Their annual vows, and all their glories lay
> At's feet...[9]

As Oberon and his entourage approached, the Prince drawn in a chariot by two white bears, an exquisite song in honour of the enthroned James was sung:

> Melt earth to sea, sea flow to air,
>   And air fly into fire,
> Whilst we, in tunes, to Arthur's chair
>   Bear Oberon's desire;
>   Than which there nothing can be higher
> Save James, to whom it flies:
> But he the wonder is of tongues, of ears, of eyes.

Who hath not heard, who hath not seen,
Who hath not sung his name?
The soul that hath not, hath not been
But is the very same
With buried sloth and knows not fame,
Which doth him best comprise:
For he the wonder is of tongues, of ears, of eyes.[10]

If the flattery, however exquisitely expressed, seems rank, it must be remembered that Jonson was not only praising his own sovereign, but the ideal of monarchical authority as the source of all those blessings, of justice, order, peace and prosperity, which he saw as the sum of civic good. Prince Henry was not only saluting his father, whose shortcomings he privately disapproved, he was also saluting the ideal of the type of monarchy which he aspired, at some future time, to personify to the utmost of his power.

Jonson, the poet, scholar and satirist, the man whose bluff exterior seemed to suggest that he was the very antithesis of the court sycophant, could, however, produce flattery which would not have disgraced the talents of Northampton. A choice example is his epigram addressed to the ghost of the Roman poet Martial:

Martial, thou gav'st far nobler epigrams
To thy Domitian than I can my James:
But in my royal subject I pass thee,
Thou flatterd'st thine, mine cannot flatter'd be.[11]

Prince Henry had not his father's complacency in accepting flattery as his due. Sir Charles Cornwallis tells a story that when a courtier – who is surmised to have been Robert Carr – wrote a letter to the Prince which concluded with the words 'Yours before all the world', the Prince refused to agree to the courtesies with which Cornwallis concluded the reply which he wrote on Henry's behalf, and made him write out the letter again, omitting those words, because, he said, 'his hand should never affirm what his heart thought not.'

James's boredom with flattery, which has been remarked before, showed itself in different ways. Probably he never troubled to question its sincerity, which perhaps he did not doubt in any case. He became wearied by the repetitiousness of the sentiments which were addressed to him by Councillors, courtiers, poets, characters in the masques, year in, year out. He has been criticized by admirers of the masque as an art form for his failure to appreciate the peculiar magic of that form of dramatic art which owed its inspiration to the cult of his kingship. But it is not surprising that he was numbed by the soothing liturgy of such lines as

> He is a god, o'er kings; yet stoops he then
> Nearest a man when he doth govern men,
> To teach them by the sweetness of his sway,
> And not by force. He's such a king, as they
> Who're tyrants' subjects or ne'er tasted peace
> Would, in their wishes, form for their release...[12]

He came to prefer the comic relief of the Antimasque. He was particularly delighted by the Antimasque to the anonymous *Masque of Flowers*, which was performed by the Gentlemen of Gray's Inn at the marriage of Robert Carr, in 1613. An exotic character named Kawasha (a corruption of the name of the supposed Virginian Deity Kiwasa) disputed with Silenus the relative merits of tobacco and alcohol. According to Kawasha

> Silenus taps the barrel, but
> Tobacco taps the brain,
> And makes the vapours fine and soot
> That man revives again.
> Nothing but fumigation
> Doth chase away ill sprites,
> Kawasha and his nation
> Found out these holy rites.[13]

In spite of, or even because of, his strong disapproval of smoking, James was so amused by this that he insisted on having the Antimasque played again. By contrast, Prince Henry, with his uncompromising idealism, was apparently devoid of humour. To everything he did he brought the same quality of passionate concentration; there were no equivalents of the Antimasque in any department of his life.

Prince Henry was scarcely out of childhood before negotiations for his marriage were initiated. Apparently Henry was prepared to accommodate himself to whatever alliance his father should conclude on his behalf. In 1612 there was preliminary diplomacy in connection with a marriage between the Prince and a daughter of the Duke of Savoy, or alternatively with a sister of the boy King Louis XIII of France. James requested his son's views on the matter, and Henry made the response that he would conform himself with his father's decision. He added, 'Your Majesty may think that my part, which is to be in love with any of them, is not yet at hand.'[14] Diplomacy was slow, the daughters of France and Savoy were children, and the Prince was probably already experienced enough to know that numerous ambassadors would spend their masters' substance before any agreement was reached. At the same time, Henry had privately expressed his aversion for marriage with a 'Papist' bride. He may have been hoping that if he made a show of dutiful obedience, time would give him the opportunity to make his own choice among the available Protestant princesses.

Time, however, would show little generosity to Prince Henry. In the very year in which his marriage was first seriously considered his health began to be a matter of anxiety. In the early months of 1612 he began to grow pale and listless. He reacted by forcing himself to the limits of his physical endurance, as though he could drive away his illness by violent exertions. He hunted, riding hard. He played tennis 'for the space of three or four hours', in his shirt, which Cornwallis considered more suitable for an artisan than for a prince. During the summer of 1612, while he was staying at Richmond, he would go swimming in the Thames 'to the dislike of many, who did see him swim after supper, his stomach being full, affirming it to be full of danger, and that it was heedless for him to adventure himself in the water; but no remedy ...'.[15]

During those warm summer nights, while he struggled to throw off his weakness, he would 'also delight many times to walk late at night by the river's side in moon light to hear the trumpets sound an echo, which many suspected, because the dew then falling did him small good.'[16]

As the autumn came on the Prince grew weaker, yet in spite of his weakness he endeavoured to maintain the same exacting regime of hard exercise. But he began to suffer from a 'continual headache, laziness and indisposition increasing (which notwithstanding ... he strove mightily to conceal), whereas oft before, he used to rise early in the morning to walk the fields, he did lie abed almost every morning until nine of the clock, complaining of his laziness, and many mornings before his rising, ask the grooms of his bedchamber, "How do I look this morning?" ... which they, fearing no danger, would put off with one jest or another ...'.[17] They began to notice, however, that he had 'dead, sunk eyes'.

On 25 October 1612, the Prince listened to a sermon preached on the text 'Man that is born of woman is of few days and full of trouble. He cometh forth like a flower, and is cut down: he fleeth also as a shadow and continueth not.' (*Job* 14: 1–2). The text was appropriate, for that day was afterwards taken as having marked the onset of the Prince's fatal illness.

'Oh Death!' wrote Cornwallis, 'was there no remedy? Do sweet-smelling flowers so much delight thy grisly, ghastly senses' appetite that thou wouldst gather none but our fairest, well-beloved, scarce blown rose?'[18]

Cornwallis went on to describe in unremitting detail the agony of the Prince's last days, and the double agony of the medical treatment which he received. 'Clysters' [enemas] were administered although he had suffered on 13 October from 'a great looseness, his belly opening twenty-five times'.[19] He endured numerous 'bleedings' and was given 'a gentle medicine of boiled senna and rhubarb' which resulted in 'incredible pain'. Even more desperate remedies, such as powdered unicorn's horn [probably narwhal's horn], pearl, and the bone of a stag's heart, were offered to him as his life ebbed away. He became delirious, and his head was shaved and the cloven bodies of warm dead birds were pressed against it.

In his last suffering Henry turned to Sir David Murray, calling over and over again 'David! David! David!' to the faithful attendant who was beside him, but whose face he could no longer see. He complained that he could not endure the light of the candles which were placed by his bedside. He asked for his sister Elizabeth, whose marriage was being deferred by his fatal sickness.

He died on 6 November 1612. Neither of his parents was present, and while it is true that both of them had a horror of deathbeds, it was not to be expected that either the king or the Queen would attend a deathbed at which contagion might be encountered. Their absence was probably occasioned by reasons of state and not by callousness; the grief which both James and Anne experienced was not in doubt.

'Wherefore now since his soul resteth in heaven,' wrote his devoted Cornwallis, 'let us also leave him ... where the fears, jars, jealousies, discontentments, mutinies, uproars and dissentions of state shall never vex him; where he shall hunger no more, thirst no more, desire no more, having all tears wiped from his eyes, in place of those frail ones, which could not here endure the sight of the candle, now beholding Him Whose eyes are ten thousand times brighter than the sun, following the Lamb whithersoever He goeth, and in the heaven of heavens enjoying the blessed fruition of his God, in the company of millions of His saints and angels....'[20]

The effect of the death of Prince Henry upon the future of the Stuart dynasty, and upon the kingdom which had centred so many hopes upon him, is imponderable. Whether he would have been a good king or a bad king it is impossible to estimate. Certainly he was idealistic in his conception of kingship, but his early dedication to the arts of war suggests that he might have been an expensively 'glorious' king. His ambitions, had he pursued them unchanged in adult life, must undoubtedly have cost the lives and borne heavily upon the livelihoods of many of his subjects. Perhaps the '*Beati Pacifici*' of his father was a better motto for a king who desired to serve his subjects well than the '*Fax Mentis Honestae Gloria*' of Prince Henry would have proved to be in the long run.

After the death of Prince Henry the succession was still secure, for his place was taken by his brother Charles, who was created Prince of Wales in 1616. Prince Charles was readily acknowledged to be a better scholar than his elder brother. He was conscientious and dutiful. Like Prince Henry, Charles had digested the lessons of *Basilikon Doron*; he too wanted to be an ideal king. The great difference between them was that Prince Charles was unknown to his future subjects, and he lacked his brother's instinctive ability to endear himself to a crowd which did no more than glimpse him. This instinct was not inborn in Prince Charles, and he did not acquire it by experience.

James may have felt resentment of the easy popularity of his elder son; yet the loss which the English people believed themselves to have sustained was also James's loss. Much is forgiven a king who has a popular heir. But henceforward James would be dependent on his own merits to command his subjects' regard; and those merits, though many and varied, were seldom appreciated and even more seldom comprehended.

CHAPTER TEN

The King's Daughter

> ... By vertue first, then choice a Queen
> Tell me, if she were not design'd
> Th' eclipse and glory of her kind?
>
> Sir Henry Wotton, on Elizabeth,
> daughter of James I

THE ONLY SURVIVING daughter of King James I was praised for her beauty with a universality of agreement and a sincerity of expression which preclude the possibility that she received merely the conventional homage which the plainest of royal ladies might expect. In later life, when misfortune had stripped her of all the advantages of royalty except that of birth itself, she still found devoted supporters and admirers. But her portraits for the most part do not suggest the kind of beauty which would make her instantly recognizable as 'Th' eclipse and glory of her kind'.

The Princess Elizabeth bore a strong resemblance to her father, who in the prime of life was considered a sufficiently regal and impressive figure of a king, but was never regarded as a man pre-eminent for his good looks. Yet in Elizabeth a similar facial structure was mysteriously metamorphosed into beauty. Her bright auburn hair and luminous dark eyes combined with charm, vivacity and appropriate regality to make her seem the quintessence of a beautiful princess.

Even had she been distressingly ugly, the daughter of the King of Great Britain could have expected to make a great marriage; as it was, she was sought by kings and princes for both personal and political motives. One of her earliest suitors was the young King Gustavus Adolphus of Sweden, but his suit was rejected through the opposition of Anne of Denmark. While the possibility of a marriage with a daughter of the Duke of Savoy was under discussion for Prince Henry, there was talk of a double marriage, with the Princess at the same time marrying the Duke's son. The heir to the throne of France, who succeeded as Louis XIII in 1610, was another possible candidate. Though all these projects came to nothing, an even more exalted suitor appeared in the person of the widowed King Philip III of Spain. Queen Anne thought this a sufficiently glorious match to be worthy of her daughter, but the Earl of Salisbury opposed it, despite his acceptance of Spanish subventions, which, after all, were intended to secure his influence on behalf of Spain. No doubt he felt that his integrity survived if he maintained the independence of his judgement. He judged against the Spanish marriage for the English Princess, and his influence, even at the very end of his life, was strong enough to counteract successfully that of Queen Anne.

King James, who had made haste to conclude peace with Spain at the outset of the reign, was increasingly attracted to the possibility of a closer alliance, cemented by the marriage of one of his children with the Spanish royal house. But the time was not yet at hand, nor were the diplomatic contacts formed through which the later negotiations would take place.

It is fascinating, if fruitless, to speculate what would have been the result had Elizabeth made any of the three royal marriages which were suggested for her. Possibly England might have been forced to play a more than peripheral role in the Thirty Years' War, but at least Elizabeth would not have been united with one of its most unfortunate political victims. As it was, the hand of Elizabeth was sought and won by a prince who would, in time, make it appear that any of the other proposed marriages would have been preferable.

Frederick V, Elector Palatine, was the official leader of the Evangelical Union, an alliance of German Calvinist Princes which had been formed through the influence of a specious and sanguine politician, Prince Christian of Anhalt, who acted as Frederick's chancellor. As a result of Anhalt's manœuvrings, and more profoundly as a result of the strategic importance of his principality, Frederick acquired a significance in the affairs of Europe which his personal character did not equip him to sustain. He was 'gentle, trustful, equally incapable of anger, hatred, or resolution .... Ironic fate had given him no vices, and all the virtues most useless to a ruling prince.'[1]

Frederick's mother was Louisa Juliana, daughter of William 'the Silent', Prince of Orange. She sent her son to be brought up at the court of her sister and brother-in-law, the Duke and Duchess of Bouillon, at Sedan. The Duke was a sovereign prince, and the leader of the French Calvinists. His court was French-speaking, as was that of the Palatinate, at Heidelberg. Thus both branches of the young Elector's family had a background of French Calvinist culture, 'tied by their religion to the French language, through Calvin and his works and through French-speaking Geneva'.[2]

This was the background of King James's own religious persuasion, and in part, of his education; for his second tutor, Peter Young, had been educated at Geneva under Calvin's successor, Theodore Beza. The world of French Calvinism had remained familiar to him as the area of cultural contact with Europe maintained by the kirk of Scotland. 'At this time,' said a contemporary writer on religious affairs, 'most of the professors in the academies at Samure, Montalban, Sedan and Lescar were Scotsmen.'[3] Indeed, the Duke of Bouillon had courteously consulted James before offering Andrew Melvill a chair at the University of Sedan.

These contacts would have led James to suppose that he was acquainted with, and could adequately assess, the conditions which would provide the future setting of his daughter's life. But this would have been a false impression, for he could scarcely have been aware of the long-term ambitions of the Evangelical Union, or even of the problems which Frederick would have had to face in due course, even if Christian of Anhalt had sown no dragon's teeth at all.

Frederick was one of the Electoral Princes of the Holy Roman Empire, whose privilege it was to elect the new Emperor when the imperial throne fell vacant. There were three clerical Electors, the Archbishops of Mainz, Treves and Cologne, and four secular Electors, the Princes of Saxony, Brandenburg and the Palatinate, and the King of Bohemia. To complicate the matter, the throne of Bohemia was itself electoral, and had been for some time firmly under the control of the imperial dynasty of Hapsburg. But the whole electoral system, which the Hapsburgs had successfully managed throughout their tenure of the Empire, was about to be jeopardized, from their viewpoint, by the Evangelical Union.

At the time when Frederick's marriage was being negotiated there were three Catholic Electors, the three Archbishops, who could be expected to remain faithful to a Hapsburg Imperial candidate; and there were three Protestant Electors, the three Princes of the Empire. The aims of the Evangelical Union required that the throne of Bohemia should be wrested from Hapsburg control before the next Imperial election, when a Protestant majority on the electoral college might secure the election of an Emperor of its own choice.

King James added his signature to the Evangelical Union when he agreed to the marriage of Frederick and his daughter, but, 'while the Elector's advisers assumed that James I would help them put . . . [the project] into action, the king had equally assumed that these remote German follies would never enter into the actual policies of Europe. . . .'[4] At the same time it is unlikely that James had given much thought to the geography of the Palatinate, though it would inevitably play a part in a situation which was already to some extent foreseen. In 1621 men who paid attention to the affairs of Europe supposed that there would be war. In that year the Twelve Years' Truce between Spain and the Protestant United Provinces of the Netherlands was due to expire. Not only was Frederick bound by the closest ties of blood and religion to the United Provinces, whose survival from attempted Spanish reconquest his grandfather William of Orange had played the chief part in securing, but his hereditary lands straddled the route which the commander of the Spanish armies would need to traverse when he marched from his recruiting grounds in Northern Italy to the attack on the United Provinces.

Ambrogio Spinola, the Genoese general who held this command, and whose appearance is familiar as a courteous and elegant victor in Velasquez' picture 'The Surrender of Breda', was already planning his attack. From Milan to Brabant his way would be through the Valtelline, along the northern shore of Lake Constance, through Alsace, and northwards following the Rhine through the lands of the Catholic Bishop of Strasbourg. So far he would be traversing the territory of co-religionists, but between Catholic Strasbourg and Treves lay approximately fifty miles held by the Calvinist Elector Palatine: the conquest of this inimical principality was essential to Spinola's plans.

The Evangelical Union also had a function as an organization formed in readiness to meet this aspect of the Hapsburg threat. It was Elizabeth's tragedy that her father's view of the European situation was utterly at odds with that of the politicians with whom he negotiated her marriage.

The Elector Frederick arrived in England on 16 October 1612, before the death of Prince Henry, who was an enthusiastic supporter of the alliance which was about to be sealed by his sister's marriage. On the 18th Frederick was received by the King and Queen in the Banqueting House at Whitehall. He kissed the hand of a future mother-in-law to whom his status was a bitter disappointment. It is perhaps significant of the fact that Anne was not alone in her attitude that in England Frederick was never called 'the Elector', but always 'the Palsgrave', which was an anglicization of his German title of 'PfalzGraf'. Possibly it may have seemed that the title of Elector 'implied in England some inferiority in the sense that he was an elector of some other sovereign'.[5] Queen Anne, who could scarcely bring herself to be courteous to Frederick, also vented her disappointment on her daughter by mockingly calling her 'Goodwife Palsgrave', a sneer which would play a part in the history of Europe to

> Mock mothers from their sons, mock castles down...

At the time Elizabeth was said to have retorted that she 'would rather be the Palsgrave's wife than the greatest Papist Queen in Christendom'.[6] But perhaps the gibe wounded her nonetheless, for some years later, when there was a throne in prospect for her husband, her view had changed; then, it was said, she declared that she would rather eat sauerkraut with a king than roast meat with an Elector.[7]

Frederick himself was immediately popular in England. He was good-looking, affable and charming. All his attractions were instantly obvious; his weaknesses would be revealed only under the stresses of adversity.

The moment of his meeting with his bride could not fail to charm both her and the onlookers, as '... stooping low to take up the lowest

1 King James VI of Scotland and I of England in the year of his accession to the English throne.

2 A medal of King James struck to commemorate the peace with Spain of 1604; beneath is an example of the King's signature.

3 The Lyte Jewel c. 1610: a gold locket enamelled and surrounded by diamonds, containing a miniature of the King attributed to Nicholas Hilliard. It was given by James to Thomas Lyte of Lyte's Carey, Somerset, as a reward for drawing up a genealogy of the Kings of Britain.

4 A portrait of King James c. 1610, by an unknown artist.

5 A portrait of Queen Anne of Denmark attributed to William Larkin. The Queen is believed to be portrayed in mourning for her son Prince Henry, who died in 1612.

6 Henry Prince of Wales c. 1610, attributed to Isaac Oliver.

7 Portrait of Prince Charles in adolescence attributed to A. van Blijenberch; a painting which clearly reveals that Charles lacked the glamour and self-confidence of his elder brother.

8 Miniature of Robert Carr, later Earl of Somerset, by an unknown artist.

9 Portrait of Robert Carr, Earl of Somerset, in later life by an unknown artist. He is shown wearing the Order of the Garter, of which the King generously did not deprive him after his disgrace.

10 *and* 11 Illumination of King James in the initial letter J of a patent of nobility of 1617, and, below, an engraving of King James, which probably portrays him at the same period of his life.

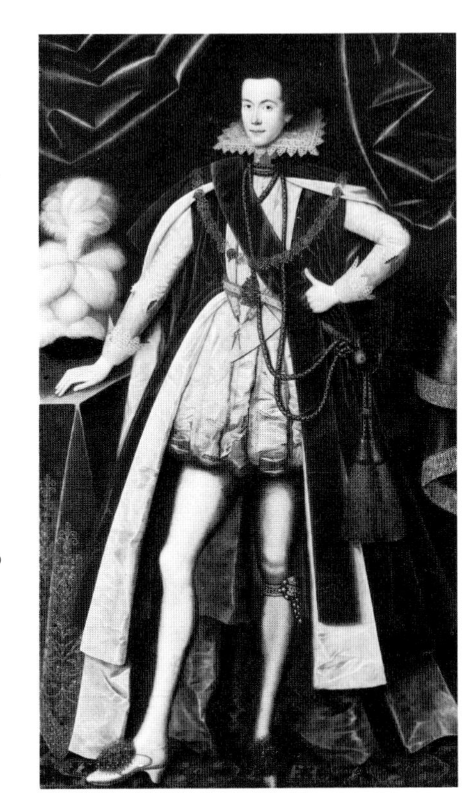

2 Sir George Villiers, later Duke of Buckingham, attributed to William Larkin. This portrait was probably painted in 1616 to ommemorate Villiers's creation as a Knight of the Garter.

3 A family group of George Villiers, Duke of Buckingham, with his wife and children, after Gerard Honthorst, 1628. The little girl on the left of the picture is Mary or 'Mall', of whom King James was fond.

14 King James enthroned, surrounded by his family, living and dead. Prince Henry, Queen Anne and the Princesses Mary and Sophia are shown leaning on skulls, to show that they have died; the palms and rose-crowns of the little princesses symbolize that their souls are in heaven. On the right are Elizabeth of Bohemia and her husband Frederick, whose children's names are inscribed on the banner held by the cherub. On the left stands Prince Charles, his hand on the Bible, to symbolize his constancy in the Protestant faith. Engraving by William van de Passe.

15 A portrait of Prince Charles, towards the end of his father's reign, by David Mytens. Charles's regal dignity, portrayed by Van Dyke, is already prefigured in this picture.

16 A crude engraving of the betrothal of Prince Charles and the Infanta Maria receiving the blessing of Christ.

17 The last official portrait of King James, by Daniel Mytens, 1621: this sombre portrayal of the ageing King is appropriately adorned with his motto 'Beati Pacifici', on the tapestry behind him.

part of her garment to kiss it, she most gracefully courtesying [sic] lower than accustomed, and with her hand staying him from that humblest reverence, gave him at his rising a fair advantage (which he took) of kissing her'.[8]

She fell in love with him, and he with her. Their idyllic relationship survived the terrible hardships which resulted from the follies into which they led each other. At least, it is unlikely that she would have found as much personal happiness with the dedicated warrior Gustavus Adolphus, the lethargic Catholic bigot Philip III, or the bisexual Louis XIII. Future troubles were happily concealed from both the lovers at the beginning of 1613, when the English court put aside its mourning for Prince Henry, and prepared to celebrate the marriage which was the most popular alliance that King James's foreign diplomacy ever achieved.

Appropriately the marriage took place on St Valentine's Day, 14 February, in the Chapel Royal of Whitehall. The bridegroom, dressed in cloth of silver, was escorted to the Chapel by sixteen noble bachelors, to symbolize the sixteen years of his age. The bride, likewise dressed in silver, her long, loose hair – symbolic of her virginity – entwined with ropes of pearls, was escorted by sixteen bridesmaids.

King James doubtless outshone the bridal pair, for he wore jewels which were estimated to be worth £600,000. He was adorned with the greatest of the English Crown Jewels, 'the faire great pearle pendante called the Bretherin, the Portugall Dyamond and the great table diamond sett in gould called the Mirror of France'.[9] The English Court gave the appearance of dazzling riches, but the financial situation was in reality extremely disturbing, for with Salisbury gone, and the Great Contract repudiated, the King's debts were steadily mounting, and with his daughter he had been obliged to give a dowry of £40,000 paid in cash. Fortunately for King James's capacity to enjoy himself, his awareness of his financial problems was at best intermittent.

'Contented and insolvent',[10] he watched the masque which were performed as part of the wedding celebrations, and the production of *The Tempest*, for which Shakespeare is believed to have written the interpolated Masque of Goddesses as an addition in honour of the occasion. At least some of the benedictions which the goddesses pronounced upon Ferdinand and Miranda were granted to Frederick and Elizabeth:

> Honour, riches, marriage blessing,
> Long continuance, and increasing,
> Hourly joys be still upon you!
> Juno sings her blessings on you.

If in nothing else, the marriage of the Elector and his wife was blessed with hourly joys, and the increase of thirteen children.

While the marriage was being celebrated, the last act of an obscure tragedy was being played out. The Lady Arbella Stuart was imprisoned in the Tower of London, soon to die.

After James's accession Arbella had enjoyed the favour and affection of the royal family. Gifts and pensions from the King had helped her to maintain a style which befitted the first lady of the Court, after the Queen herself. The sudden alteration in her fortunes, after the exile in the country to which the late Queen had condemned her, had brought her exalted suitors. Among them were Queen Anne's brother, Ulric, Duke of Holstein, and the egregious Prince Christian of Anhalt.

James was loath to allow her to marry a foreign prince, whose issue might at some future time contest the title to the English throne, as he had once feared that Arbella herself might contest that title with him. Time passed, and it seemed that Arbella would be condemned to live out her life as a scholarly spinster, decreasingly ornamental to the Court.

Arbella wanted a husband. She promised the King, however, that she would not attempt to make a marriage abroad without his agreement; he in turn assured her that he would be content if she chose a husband who was a loyal subject to the English Crown. Like Herod, trapped by his rash promise into taking the life of John the Baptist, James had forgotten that he had one subject who should have been made an exception to his assurance. The one subject who might beget children which could endanger the succession of James's own issue was William Seymour, grandson of the Earl of Hertford.

Hertford had married Lady Catherine Grey, the sister of Lady

Jane Grey, the nine days' Queen of England, both of whom were grand-daughters of Mary Tudor, sister of Henry VIII. If there was any marriage in England which James could reasonably forbid to Arbella, it was a marriage with a descendant of Henry VII in the female line. His refusal to sanction such a marriage would be the more reasonable in that Henry VIII had by his will excluded the Scottish descendants of his sister Margaret and her husband James IV of Scotland from the English succession. This will had been overriden, but there was no reason to suppose that at some future time it might not be remembered and invoked. In the interests of his own posterity, King James might be expected to limit the number of possible competitors for the English throne, when it lay in his power to do so (see Genealogical Table).

As though the Fates had selected Arbella Stuart to be their victim, by a singular misfortune she fell in love with William Seymour. In February 1610, James, learning of a budding affair between the young man, who was twenty-three years old, and Arbella, who was thirty-five, ordered the imprisonment of them both. They were released again, when Seymour had explained that he did not mean any harm. Undoubtedly he did not, and neither did Arbella. Seymour declared that '... myself being but a younger brother ... of mean estate ... and therefore my fortune to be raised by mine own endeavour, and she a lady of great honour and virtue, and as I thought of great means: I did plainly and honestly endeavour lawfully to gain her in marriage....'[11]

Arbella can never have known of this confession of his motives in proposing marriage to her, which Seymour made to the Privy Council; but when, after their release from imprisonment, Seymour asked her to free him from his promise to marry her, she refused. So, in accordance with her wishes, they were married in secret on 21 June 1610.

As soon as their secret was known, which was in scarcely more than a fortnight, they were arrested again. The *dénouement* of their story was foreseeable. They contrived to escape, planned to cross the Channel in disguise, and intended to live in exile until such time as the King should feel disposed to forgive them.

Their misadventures would have resembled the plot of a Shakespearian comedy, if they had not led directly to Arbella's tragic end.

Disguised in 'a pair of great French-fashioned hose over her petticoats ... a man's doublet, a man-like perruque with long locks over her hair, a black hat, black cloak, russet boots with red tops, and a rapier by her side', Arbella made her way, after endless difficulties, to Leigh at the mouth of the Thames. There she and her two servants persuaded the master of a brig to take them out to a French ship which friends had arranged should be waiting to take them to France. Seymour, who had failed to meet Arbella at the original rendezvous at Blackwall, also failed to catch up with her anywhere along the route. The captain of the French ship insisted that they should sail without him. When he arrived at Leigh he was lucky enough to hire a collier to take him across to Calais. Seymour reached France in safety, but Arbella was arrested in mid-channel by Captain Griffin Cockett, of the *Adventure*, an aptly named ship, which had been sent in pursuit when her escape was discovered. Arbella was lodged in the Tower, whence she wrote piteous letters, entreating aid from all who might have influence in pleading her cause to the King.

James was not moved, which is not surprising if it be considered how much anxiety the counter-claim of Arbella to the English throne had cost him during his reign in Scotland. He must have remembered the favour, the kindness and the generosity which he had shown her after his accession, and wondered over and over again if her choice of William Seymour as a husband had not shown her, after all her apparent submissiveness, to have been a wolf in sheep's clothing. He did not risk forgiveness, though later he forgave Seymour, after the marriage had proved childless.

In the meantime, poor Arbella remained a prisoner in the Tower, hoping for pardon, and even planning her reappearance, in the finery which so delighted her, at some great occasion at Court. She had high hopes of the opportunity offered by the marriage of the Princess Elizabeth. She ordered four dresses to wear at the festivities, the grandest at a cost of £1,500; but the marriage took place without her, although the young Elector heard her sad story and himself petitioned the King for her release.

On 25 April 1613 the Elector and his bride left England, and almost two and a half years later, on 25 September 1615, Arbella Stuart died in the Tower, wandering in mind and emaciated in body. Her life was nothing more than a tragic illustration of the hazard of being born too close to a throne at a time of dynastic change; there was nothing remarkable in her career, or dangerous in her actions.

CHAPTER ELEVEN

'The Hearts of Kings are Deep'

Then, since fortune's favours fade,
You, that in her arms do sleep,
Learn to swim, and not to wade,
For the hearts of Kings are deep.

Sir Henry Wotton, *Upon the sudden restraint of the Earl of Somerset, then falling from favour*

SOVEREIGN PRINCES DO not care to be fooled. For this reason alone, if he had had no stronger objective causes, King James would have been expected to show high displeasure at the secret marriage of his cousin Arbella. The older members of his Court would have compared his anger with that of Queen Elizabeth I at the secret marriage of her favourite Robert Dudley, Earl of Leicester, to Lettice Devereux, widow of the first Earl of Essex. Elizabeth's wrath, they would have remembered, had not been easily assuaged, and in her eyes it had been fully justified by Leicester's betrayal of both her favour and her trust. Yet even when secrecy had not been employed to pre-empt royal disapproval, Elizabeth had taken a somewhat crabbed view of marriage; whereas James, with his taste for influencing events through personal intervention, delighted in matchmaking. He was especially pleased if he could promote such good ends as the making or linking of fortunes, the intermarrying of Scots and English, or the reconciling of old enemies.

Such a reconciliation was James's purpose in arranging in 1606 the marriage of Robert Devereux, third Earl of Essex, and Frances Howard, daughter of the Earl of Suffolk. There had been enmity between the Devereux and the Howards ever since the Howards had been instrumental in bringing Elizabeth's last favourite, the second Earl of Essex, who was Lettice's son and Leicester's stepson, to the block in 1601.

On the eve of Twelfth Night 1606, the pretty, precocious bride, who was thirteen years old, and the quiet, gauche bridegroom, who was one year older, were married in the Chapel Royal of Whitehall, in the presence of the whole Court.

The culmination of the wedding celebrations was the performance of Ben Jonson's masque *Hymenaei*. It was an admirable exposition of some of Jonson's most exalted ideas, but it was also an unhappy example of historical irony. Jonson celebrated the blessings of union, '... not simply the union of Robert Devereux and Frances Howard, of two great English families, but the new union of England and Scotland, the union of King James and his kingdom, the cosmic union wrought by the power of love'.[1] Unfortunately the union of the bride and groom was destined to be unhappy, the union of the noble families to be undone, the union of Scotland and England finally to be repudiated by Parliament the following year, and the 'cosmic union wrought by the power of love' to be made a hideous travesty by the power of hatred.

These unhappy events were hidden in the future as the Court watched the elegant dances of the masque. After the wedding the young couple separated; they were considered as yet too young to co-habit. Essex travelled to the Netherlands, where he laid the foundations of his future career as a soldier. His wife remained at court, where her status as a married lady gave her a certain freedom of action which would have been denied to an unmarried girl. During the four years which passed before her husband's return, the Countess of Essex may at first have hoped to become Prince Henry's mistress. Prince Henry had spurned her, according to court gossip, when he learned of Rochester's interest in and possible success with her. It is probable that the entrapping of Rochester in what Arthur Wilson called her 'gulf of beauty' was at first the suggestion of the Earl of Northampton, the Countess's great-uncle.

After the death of Salisbury, the pre-eminence of the Howards was threatened by an opposing group of influential courtiers, ministers and churchmen, including the Lord Chancellor Ellesmere, Archbishop Abbott of Canterbury, the Earl of Pembroke, the Earl of Southampton, who was the self-appointed patron of young Essex, because he had been the closest friend of Essex's unfortunate father, and Sir Ralph Winwood, who was appointed to the secretaryship of state made vacant by Salisbury's death. The alliance of the King's favourite with the Howards, in the face of this grouping of enemies, would be undeniably advantageous. If the eyes of Rochester strayed in the direction of the Countess of Essex, then Northampton would have been swift and subtle in his suggestion to her of the advantages of such a conquest. She made it easily.

A portrait which is traditionally identified as Frances, Countess of Essex, on the evidence of its resemblance to the only certain representation of her, a rather crude wood-engraving, shows a girl who has bright and calculating eyes, lively eyes, though scarcely the 'wombs of stars' which John Donne praised. She has a faint, sly smile playing about the lips of her generously sensual mouth. Her large breasts are ostentatiously displayed in accordance with court fashion. Her jewels are few, perhaps because she had little need to gild her own lilies.

Robert Carr fell in love with her, and felt his own inadequacy by comparison with her brilliant attraction. He turned to his friend Sir Thomas Overbury, who had considerable literary ability, for help in composing love letters eloquent enough to express his passion. Overbury complied, though he hated the Howards, and his own ambition had led him to follow the faction of Ellesmere, Abbott and Winwood. Perhaps he may have thought Frances Devereux a mere whore, and amused himself with the idea that his friend's affair with her would sully the reputation of her family. If so, he miscalculated, for the love which both Northampton and Overbury may have regarded as an intrigue to be manipulated became an all-consuming passion which both Frances Devereux and Robert Carr determined must be sanctified by their marriage.

Overbury was outraged. One night one of his servants overheard an angry exchange between him and Rochester in a gallery of White-hall Palace.

'What do you here at this time of night?' demanded Overbury. 'Will you never leave the company of that base woman? And seeing you do so neglect my advice ... I will leave you free to yourself, to stand on your own legs.'[2]

Rochester inevitably replied that he was perfectly capable of standing on his own legs – or feet, as we should now say – and he and Overbury parted in anger.

Dr Beatrice White, in her study of the death of Sir Thomas Overbury, has suggested the basis of this quarrel between him and Robert Carr:

> It should not ... be forgotten that in those days a friendship between two men often – and openly – involved emotional and sexual attachment ... and there can be little doubt that the friendship between Carr and Overbury was of this nature. Both of them were strikingly handsome; of Carr especially it can be said that his face was his fortune – though Overbury, who never married, may have been more naturally homosexual.[3]

Under such circumstances the homosexual lover of a bisexual or heterosexual friend is almost inevitably the loser, though he is seldom required to pay so high a price as Overbury paid.

Overbury had no friends. He was only the client of powerful allies, who had no more use for him when he forfeited his influence with the King's favourite. He was hated by James, who naturally detested the influence of any other man upon one of his favourites, and was jealous of any close friendship with other men which his favourites attempted to maintain. Overbury was doomed when Rochester became resolved to marry the Countess of Essex, and Northampton took it upon himself to suggest to the King that the marriage was possible.

Northampton told the King that while Essex and his wife had lived together for the three years which had passed since his return to England, they claimed that they had frequently attempted to have intercourse with each other, but the marriage still remained unconsummated. There was therefore a case for declaring the marriage to be no marriage.

King James was willing to admit that his reconciliation of the Devereux and the Howards had been a failure, and he was ready to allow the marriage to be declared null in the full knowledge that a successful nullity suit would be followed by the marriage of Frances Devereux and Robert Carr. It was a curious aspect of the King's character that, while he was bitterly jealous of his favourites' male friends, he always showed himself willing, and indeed eager, to arrange advantageous marriages for them. He had intended a match between Robert Carr and Lady Anne Clifford, daughter and sole heiress of the Earl of Cumberland. It was unfortunate for Carr that this marriage did not take place, for the diminutive and formidably virtuous Lady Anne would have saved him from any form of trouble, and had he forfeited the King's favour in the natural course of events her great possessions would have ensured his continuing prosperity. However, James abandoned his projected match-making in deference to his favourite's desires, and appointed a commission to hear the nullity suit.

In the meantime, it was necessary to both the anxious lovers that Sir Thomas Overbury should not be present while the case was heard. He had angered Carr and mortally offended Frances by gross attacks on her moral character. The success of her nullity petition depended on her claim that after three years of living with her husband she was still a virgin. Overbury presumably knew, after his activities as a surrogate wooer, that she had been Carr's mistress. She had little doubt that he would not scruple to say so, and she determined that he should never have the chance. Carr himself was equally determined, though as events were to show, he was less unscrupulous as to the means which might be employed to silence him.

The pair had an invaluable ally in the Earl of Northampton. He was naturally eager that the nullity case should succeed and the marriage take place, and he appreciated the necessity of ensuring Overbury's silence. James, though he was unaware, so far as can be discerned, of any plotting, accepted a suggestion that Overbury should be offered a diplomatic post abroad. He disliked the man sufficiently to be delighted at Carr's sudden willingness to be separated from him; furthermore, he had received many bitter complaints of his insolence from Queen Anne. He offered him the post of ambassador to Russia.

Overbury knew that the embassy to the ends of the earth represented exile, not advancement. He procrastinated, hoping that Carr would intercede for him, despite their recent quarrel. Thinking of the past, he may have believed that Carr lacked the confidence to do without him; obviously he miscalculated the stronger influence of Frances, which had been at work upon his friend. His hesitancy led the Privy Council, on the King's behalf, to send Sir Dudley Digges to him, to demand that he should attend and give his answer. He unwisely decided to rely on Carr's assistance to support him in refusing, and he gave Sir Dudley Digges proud words, which may have masked a deep disquiet: 'I know my precious chief [Carr] better than you do, and my precious chief knoweth the King's pleasure better than any other doth. And therefore I rely upon my precious chief and will not go.'[4]

It had been a Court quip that Overbury ruled Carr and Carr ruled the King, a jest which was not calculated to amuse James. Overbury's words to Digges sounded a suspiciously similar note. Overbury was committed to the Tower for contempt of the King's pleasure in refusing the Embassy.

He had been eliminated from the public scene very neatly, and it has been suggested that Northampton's was the mastermind which worked out the scheme that ensured that heads or tails Overbury would go – to Russia or to the Tower. Though the Tower was not so far, it might be the safer form of banishment. Northampton revealed his presiding presence when he secured the appointment of a new Lieutenant of the Tower, Sir Gervase Elwys, who was ordered to keep Overbury from any contact with the outside world. Thus he was successfully silenced before the nullity case was heard.

The Commissioners appointed to hear it were the Archbishop of Canterbury, Bishop King of London, Bishop Lancelot Andrewes of Coventry and Lichfield, the two Chancellors of the Exchequer, Sir Thomas Parry and Sir Julius Caesar, Sir Daniel Dunn, the Dean of the Court of Arches, Sir John Bennet, and two Doctors of Law named James and Edwards. They sat in June 1613, to hear the Countess of Essex claim that after three years of married life she was still a virgin, because of the impotency of her husband, although she had done all that she could to facilitate the consummation of the marriage. The Earl of Essex was ready to admit that so far as his wife was concerned he had proved impotent, but he was not prepared to admit the disgrace of total impotence, and he declared that he was perfectly capable of intercourse with other women. This raised the question of whether he might have been bewitched.

This whole topic was profoundly repugnant to Archbishop Abbott. He wrote a letter to the King, setting forth his misgivings, and stating that in his reading of the Early Fathers he could find nothing to support the belief that *maleficium* [witchcraft] could cause impotence in marriage. James was extremely displeased by this letter. He wanted the Essex marriage to be nullified, and he wanted Carr and Frances to be united. As always, he wanted his wishes to be supported by the forms of legality, and he was not prepared to allow Abbott's scruples to stand in his way. Furthermore, he may have believed in the power of *maleficium* to bring about the described condition, although as he grew older he grew less and less credulous concerning the power of witches. He wrote a long reply to Abbott, with scholarly refutations of the authorities which the Archbishop had cited, and he suggested that a glance at his own book *Daemonologie* might be instructive.

Abbott was not convinced, and James realized that if the Commission were to reach a satisfactory decision, it would be necessary to nominate two more members, who would vote predictably to ensure a majority. He added Bishop Buckeridge of Rochester and Bishop Bilson of Winchester.

On 25 September the Commission voted that Essex and his Countess were not man and wife. Frances was free to remarry, but to secure her freedom she had been obliged to declare herself willing to submit to an examination by twelve noble ladies to testify to her virginity. For reasons of modesty, it had been agreed that she should present herself for examination in a veil, and there were many courtiers who said that the veiled virgin had not been the Countess of Essex. Some even claimed to know who she was: according to some she was Sir Thomas Monson's daughter, according to others she was Frances's cousin, Katherine Fiennes. A substitution appears to have been a likelihood, for if Frances had been a virgin, the silencing of Overbury would not have been necessary.

Only a few weeks after the nullity case Sir Thomas Overbury died, still a prisoner in the Tower of London. In the excitement of a sensational case, and in the ensuing preparations for the marriage of Carr and Frances, nobody spared a thought for the unfortunate prisoner. He had been generally hated for his arrogance while he lived. He was unpitied when he died.

In preparation for his marriage, Robert Carr was created Earl of Somerset. It was the apogee of his career as the King's favourite, and it was also a mark of the King's favour to the Howards, for it ensured that Frances should suffer no loss of precedence on her second marriage.

John Donne wrote an *Eclogue ... at the marriage of the Earl of Somerset*, which contained the lines:

> May these love-lamps we here enshrine,
> In warmth, light, lasting, equal the divine.
> Fire ever doth aspire,
> And makes all like itself, turns all to fire,
> But ends in ashes; which these cannot do,
> For none of these is fuel, but fire too....[5]

One can imagine that he might have paused after he had written the words 'ends in ashes', for with his wide experience of the transitoriness of passion, and with his poetic vision and his worldly wisdom, he might have seen that the relationship which the court was celebrating could indeed end in ashes. But he was writing a courtly poem, and with a resolution which defied his knowledge of reality he might well have written those words 'which these cannot do'....

The marriage took place on St Stephen's Day, 26 December 1613. The officiating cleric was the Bishop of Bath and Wells, who was also Dean of the Chapel Royal of Whitehall, and who had also officiated at Frances's marriage to the Earl of Essex. But there was no other suggestion that the occasion was a matter of repetition: to emphasize for all to witness that she had never been a married wife, Frances wore her hair loose in the manner of a virgin bride. The unbound hair which symbolized maiden purity was not only loose, but in riotous overstatement it was 'pendant almost to her feet'.

The year 1614 was a difficult year for Somerset. In June the Earl of Northampton died, which left the Howards without an effective head. The Earl of Suffolk became Lord Treasurer, and Somerset replaced him in his previous office of Lord Chamberlain. The King on appointing him said that 'no man should marvel that he bestowed a place so near himself upon his friend, who he loved above all men living.' Nonetheless, Somerset did not feel secure. He had neither Overbury nor Northampton to advise him, and in all probability his conscience troubled him concerning Overbury. He had connived in having him removed from the Court, and when he was in the Tower he had deceived him with assurances that he was labouring to secure his release. It was a sufficient sin against friendship and honour to trouble a man's conscience. But he may also have feared that Overbury had not died a natural death; or in time he may have come to know that he had not. Any or all of these thoughts would have been enough to make the Earl of Somerset a less easy companion to the King than he had once been.

James had genuine reasons to be dissatisfied with the conduct of his favourite. As a married man Somerset had naturally less time to spend wholly at the King's beck and call. He was in love with his wife, and she with him. Perhaps they were unwise in giving too much of themselves to each other, and allowing too little to the very source of Somerset's fortunes. Undeniably Somerset took James's love too much for granted. It had endured for a long time, and he forgot, as all lovers, husbands and wives are apt to forget, that love requires constant attention, like a plant, not only to make it grow, but to keep it alive.

Somerset had a multitude of things on his mind. The Court factions provided not the least of his problems. The Howards, to whom he was irrevocably committed by his marriage, had their enemies, who had become his own. The Archbishop of Canterbury had become hostile to him in consequence of the friction with the King which had resulted from the nullity case. The Secretary of State, Sir Ralph Winwood, was inflexibly inimical to the Howards. He opposed the close relationship with Spain which the Howards advocated and which Somerset had also come to support. Somerset was probably quite profoundly ignorant of foreign politics, but he had to have a view. With Northampton dead he cannot have known where to turn.

In 1614 James began to show interest in the young George Villiers, who was presented to him at Apethorpe in Northamptonshire during his summer progress. Somerset was soon aware that in consequence of this interest his own enemies had begun to cultivate the young man. His temper grew short, and scenes between him and the King increased in number and bitterness. He wrote the King a long and angry letter about the Court factions. James took the trouble to reply in detail. He was obviously saddened by the deterioration of his relationship with his favourite. The letter which he wrote is a chronicle of that deterioration, and it is also remarkably self-revealing. For this reason it is worth quoting at some length.

First, [James wrote] I take God, the searcher of all hearts, to record that, in all the time past of idle talk, I never knew, nor could, out of any observation of mine, find any appearance of any such Court faction as you have apprehended; and so far was I ever free from overseeing or indirectly feeling of it (if I had ever apprehended it), as I protest to God, I would have run upon it with my feet, as upon fire, to have extinguished it, if I could have seen any sparkle of it.

Next, I take the same God to record, that never man, of any degree, did directly or indirectly let fall to me anything that might be interpreted for the lessening of your credit with me....

... I am far from thinking of any possibility of any man ever to come within many degrees of your trust with me, as I must ingenuously confess you have deserved more trust and confidence of me than ever man did – in secrecy above all flesh, in feeling and impartial respect, as well to my honour in every degree as to my profit. And all this without respect either to kin or ally, or your nearest and dearest friend whatsoever.... And in those points I confess I never saw any come towards your merit: I mean, in the points of inwardly trusty friend and servant. But as a piece of ground cannot be so fertile, but if either by the own natural rankness or evil manuring thereof it become also fertile of strong and noisome weeds, it then proves useless and altogether unprofitable; even so, these before rehearsed rich and rare parts and merits of yours have been of long time, but especially of late, since the strange frenzy took you, so powdered and mixed with strange streams of unquietness, passion, fury and insolent pride, and (which is worst of all) with a settled kind of induced obstinacy, as it chokes and obscures all these excellent and good parts that God hath bestowed upon you. For although I confess the greatness of that trust and privacy betwixt us very well allow unto you an infinitely great liberty and freedom of speech unto me, yea, even to rebuke me more sharply and bitterly than ever my master [i.e. Buchanan] durst do, yet to invent a new act of railing at me ... cannot come within the compass of any liberty of friendship....

... You have, in many of your mad fits, done what you can to persuade me that you mean not so much to hold me by love as by awe, and that you have me so far in your reverence, as that I dare not offend you, or resist your appetities. I leave out of this reckoning your long creeping back and withdrawing yourself from lying in my chamber, notwithstanding my many hundred times earnestly soliciting you to the contrary....

To conclude, then, this discourse proceeding from the infinite grief of a deeply wounded heart – I protest in the presence of Almighty God, that I have borne this grief within me to the uttermost of my ability, and as never grief since my birth seated so heavily upon me, so have I borne it as long as possibly I can....

What shall be the best remedy for this, I will tell you, be kind. But for the easing of my inward and consuming grief all I crave is, that in all the words and actions of your life you may ever make it appear to me that you never think to hold grip of me but out of my mere love, and not one hair by force.... I told you twice or thrice, you might lead me by the heart and not by the nose.

God is my judge, my love hath been infinite towards you.... Let me be met, then, with your entire heart, but softened by humility.... Hold me thus by the heart; you may build upon my favour as upon a rock that shall never fail you, that shall never weary to give new demonstrations of my affection towards you; nay, that shall never suffer any to rise in any degree of my favour, except they may acknowledge and thank you as a furtherer of it....

Thus have I now set down unto you what I would say, if I were to make my testament; it lies in your hands to make of me what you please – either the best master and truest friend, or, if you force me once to call you ingrate, which the God in heaven forbid, no so great earthly plague can light upon you! In a word you may procure me to delight to give daily more and more demonstrations of my favour towards you, if the fault be not in yourself.[6]

For all that he had to say of love and grief, the King's letter was far more one of warning than of reassurance. The penultimate paragraph contained the most important passage relating to Somerset's hypothetical future as a favourite: rightly interpreted, it required him to follow the example of Lord Hay and be content to dwell in the suburbs of favour, letting his place, with his blessing, be taken by some other, who 'may acknowledge and thank you as a furtherer of it'.

Somerset showed how little he was prepared to heed this lesson when, in the summer of 1615, James sent Sir Humphrey May to inform him that the recently knighted Sir George Villiers would call upon him to offer his services, which Somerset was expected to accept. Villiers duly arrived, and said, 'My Lord, I desire to be your servant and your creature, and shall desire to take my Court preferment under your favour and your lordship, and your Lordship shall find me as faithful a servant unto you, as ever did serve you.'

Somerset answered ill-advisedly, but with spirit, 'I will none of your service, and you shall none of my favour. I will, if I can, break your neck, and of that be confident.'[7]

Bishop Goodman had some shrewd comments to make concerning the decline of Somerset:

> The true fall of Somerset was this, [he wrote] that love and affection, though they are the strongest passions for the instant, yet they are not of longest continuance, for they are not grounded in judgement, but are rather fancies which follow the eye.... A man may be glutted with one favourite, as he is feeding upon one food, though it be manna; therefore to have choice of dishes best pleaseth the palate: so truly I think the King was weary of an old favourite.[8]

Somerset had in effect already fallen before revelations concerning the death of Sir Thomas Overbury led to his being placed under house arrest, in October 1615.

CHAPTER TWELVE

Poison in the Tower

Sir Thomas never ate white salt, but there was white arsenic put in it.

James Franklin, apothecary, on trial
for the murder of Sir Thomas Overbury,
1615

MANY YEARS LATER, Archbishop Abbott recalled the time when Somerset was declining in the King's favour and Villiers was rising: he wrote an illuminating account of how Villiers was first given official recognition as a favourite, when he was knighted on St George's Day, 23 April 1615, some six months before Somerset's final ruin.

It was now observed [the Archbishop wrote] that the King began to cast his eye upon George Villiers, who was then cup-bearer, and seemed a modest and courteous youth. But King James had a fashion, that he would never admit any to nearness about himself but such an one as the Queen should commend unto him, and make some suit on his behalf; that if the Queen afterwards, being ill-treated, should complain of this dear one, he might make his answer, 'It is long of yourself, for you were the party that commended him unto me.' Our old master took delight in things of this nature.

That noble Queen ... knew her husband well; and, having been bitten with favourites both in England and Scotland, was very shy to adventure on this request.... The Queen would not come to it, albeit divers Lords ... did earnestly solicit her Majesty thereunto. When it would not do, I was very much moved to put my helping hand, they knowing that Queen Anne was graciously pleased to give me more credit than ordinary.... I laboured much but could not prevail; the Queen oft saying to me 'My Lord, you and the rest of your friends know not what you do. I know your master better than you all; for if this young man be once brought in, the first that he will plague must be you that labour for him; yea, I shall have my part also. The King will teach him to despise and hardly intreat us all, that he may seem to be beholden to none but himself.' Noble Queen! How like a prophetess or an oracle did you speak!

Notwithstanding this we were still instant, telling her Majesty that the change would be for the better. For George was of a good nature.... In the end, upon importunity, Queen Anne condescended, and so pressed it with the King that he assented, which was so stricken while the iron was hot, that in the Queen's Bedchamber, the King knighted him with the rapier which the Prince [Charles] did wear.[1]

Obviously King James had suffered considerably from the Queen's complaints of Somerset – for whom she had never felt anything but a sharp dislike – that he should have developed this adroit method of circumventing any complaints which she might make against Villiers, of anyone else, in the future. In fact, the King's precautions proved unnecessary, for Villiers went out of his way to woo the Queen, and although Abbott and his allies may have felt that the Queen had spoken like an oracle when she promised them that they would regret having abetted his advancement, Anne herself never had cause to complain of him. Indeed, he won her over so successfully that she wrote to him addressing him by the friendly nickname of 'My Kind Dog'.

Villiers habitually used the imagery of dog-like devotion in his letters to the King, which he signed with the unchanging formula 'Your Majesty's humble slave and dog'. It was probably many years after he had first begun to employ that formula that he wrote to James and told him that he had been asking himself 'whether you loved me now ... better than at that time which I shall never forget at Farnham, where the bed's head could not be found between the master and his dog'.[2] James and Villiers had visited Farnham during the summer progress of 1615, and the implication of the letter is obviously that there they had become lovers. The much argued question of the nature of James's relations with the last of his favourites appears to be answered in one sentence of Villiers' letter.[3]

Villiers was offered a great deal of advice during his early days as the King's favourite, but in reality he had little need of it. He was highly intelligent, and he had ample opportunity of observing Somerset's mistakes: he profited by them through learning not to repeat them. Possibly Villiers was assisted by the knowledge that James had not fallen in love with him at first sight: he did not start out with the overweening confidence which results from being the recipient of such love. He had gained the King's attention in the first place as the candidate of the Howards' enemies, who had bought him the post of Cup-bearer in the hope of investing in the foreseeable fall of Somerset. Villiers was cast in the role of a courtesan for a long time before he aspired to play that of a statesman.

In the autumn of 1615 the insinuating charm of the young Villiers was winning him the golden opinions of all who had grown tired of Somerset's pride and ill-temper. Somerset's impending fall was greeted with mocking verses:

> I.C.U.R. [I see you are]
> Good Monsieur Carr
> About to fall.
>
> U.R.A.K. [You are a Kae*]
> As most men say,
> But that's not all.
>
> U.O.Q.P. [You occupy]
> With your annullity
> That naughty pack
>
> S.X.Y.F. [Essex's wife]
> Whose wicked life
> Hath broke your back.[4]

The last days of Somerset's greatness were troubled not only by the rise of Villiers and the turning away of courtiers who had previously fawned upon him, but by the increasingly confident repetition of rumours concerning the death of Overbury.

Sir Ralph Winwood had ever since Overbury's death been quietly investigating all the rumours which were whispered in the Tower of London itself. A fellow prisoner of Overbury's had been the Countess of Shrewsbury, incarcerated for conniving at the secret marriage of Arbella Stuart. She had willingly relayed to Winwood all that she heard. Then, from an unexpected quarter, new and dramatic evidence came.

* Kae=Jackdaw i.e. a jackdaw in peacock's feathers

During the summer a young Englishman named William Reeve lay dying in Brussels. He wished to unburden his conscience of a state secret, and he asked to be visited by servants of the English Ambassador. William Reeve told them that he had been apprenticed in London to a French apothecary, Paul de Lobell, who had sent him to the Tower to administer an enema to Sir Thomas Overbury. He said that he had been bribed by the Countess of Essex, as Lady Somerset had then been, to poison the enema with mercury sublimate, and as a result of it Overbury had died the following day.

The English Ambassador at Brussels, Sir William Turnbull, returned to London with this tale, which he immediately told to Sir Ralph Winwood. With some knowledge of Overbury's end, based on the hearsay which he had collected, Winwood approached Sir Gervase Elwys, the Lieutenant of the Tower, who had been put in that position at the instance of Northampton, and told him that he would be well advised to clear himself of the gathering suspicions concerning the unnaturalness of Overbury's death. This approach was a gamble, for if Elwys had held his peace there was little that Winwood could have done about it. However, Elwys was only too eager to unbosom himself, ultimately to his own destruction.

The unfortunate Elwys knew too much to exonerate himself from some share of blame, but he attempted to give an account of Overbury's death which placed him in as good a light as possible. Soon after his appointment, Elwys had discovered that poisons of various kinds were being sent to Overbury, in tarts and jellies, which were supposedly being sent to the prisoner as kindly offerings to alleviate the drabness of his diet. These pleasant delicacies had turned black before they could be brought to the prisoner's table; and Elwys said that he had substituted other, wholesome things, and had served them to Overbury on his own initiative. Furthermore he had prevented Richard Weston, the under-keeper who was specially deputed to look after Overbury, from mixing with his food a phial of poison, which had been sent to Weston by the Countess of Essex, and delivered to him by her confidante, Mistress Anne Turner, the same lady who had originated the fashion for yellow-starched ruffs. Frances, it appeared, had been impatient to hasten Overbury out of the world, and had made numerous successive attempts to poison him, only to have her efforts frustrated by the vigilance of

Sir Gervase Elwys, until William Reeve had been successful in administering the poisoned enema.

Winwood decided that he now had a strong enough story to reveal the matter to the King. He did so, and James immediately ordered Elwys to set down the whole of it in writing. Faced with Elwys' appalling story, James realized that the entire business could have been fabricated with the destruction of Somerset as its ultimate purpose. He appointed a commission consisting of Lord Zouche, Sir Thomas Parry, Sir Fulke Greville, and Winwood himself, to examine the circumstances of Overbury's death, and he instructed them to remember: 'There be two things in this cause to be tried, and the verity can be but in one of them: first, whether my Lord of Somerset and my Lady were the procurers of Overbury's death; or, that this imputation hath been by some practised to cast an aspersion upon them....'[5]

Though James was weary of his old favourite, he would have been thankful to have found him wholly free from the imputation of murder. However, the under-keeper Weston confessed his attempt to poison Overbury, and implicated the Countess of Somerset. James had no choice but to command a full investigation, and the trial of all concerned. He placed the matter in the hands of the implacable Lord Chief Justice, Sir Edward Coke. Coke's investigations led to the examination of over two hundred people, and provided him with a huge and saddening dossier of human weakness and wickedness on which to base the prosecution.

Weston's confession implicated the most significant figure in the case after the Countess herself. This was Anne Turner, who may have been Frances's evil genius from the beginning. Anne had been a waiting gentlewoman in the service of the Howards, and had spent her early life as in part a servant and in part a companion to Frances. She had married a Doctor Turner, a respectable physician, who had soon left her a widow. The doctor's widow had proved herself to be a resourceful woman, who had learned how to prosper by exploiting the weaknesses of other people. She used her house as a place of assignation, where courtiers could meet to consummate their illicit love affairs; she provided them with the aphrodisiacs which they sometimes required; she introduced them to practitioners of magical arts which were mostly employed for sexual purposes. From this, it was not a long step to providing drugs and potions to secure the opposite effect to that which her clients usually sought. Anne Turner, it transpired, had long ago supplied Frances with drugs which were intended to prevent the unfortunate Earl of Essex from consummating his marriage.[6]

This was not relevant to the death of Overbury, but it led up to it, for when Frances turned from wanting preparations to make her husband impotent, and sought poisons to render her enemy silent, Anne Turner was not the woman to refuse her help. Aphrodisiacs and magic philtres she was accustomed to obtain from a learned charlatan who still has a certain fame of his own, Dr Simon Forman, to whom Frances had once written letters addressing him as her 'Sweet Father', and appealing for help against her husband's natural desires. Forman, whatever hopes Frances may have had of him, was not a poisoner; but the knowledgeable Anne Turner discovered one, an unscrupulous apothecary named James Franklin, who provided seven varieties of poison which might be mixed with Overbury's food.

'Sir Thomas', Franklin declared, in a discernible tone of professional pride, 'never ate white salt, but there was white arsenic put in it. Once he desired pig, and Mrs Turner put into it *lapis costitus*. At another time he had two partridges sent him from the Court, and water and onions being in the sauce, Mrs Turner put in cantharides instead of pepper.... For these poisons the Countess sent me rewards.... She was able to bewitch any man.'[7]

In view of this statement, and others to the effect that poison after poison had been sent to Overbury in one form or another, it is remarkable that he survived as long as he did. Possibly this was to some extent the work of Sir Gervase Elwys, possibly Frances paid for many more poisons than were ever delivered to the Tower. She was rich, extravagant with money, inexact in her knowledge of how the poisons were supposed to work, and so eager to be rid of her enemy that she was prepared to go on and on investing in the means to procure his death. It must have been an irresistible temptation to Turner and Franklin to take from her as much as she was prepared to give. But the time came when Overbury had to die: when Frances's patience wore thin, and before her suspicions were aroused.

Overbury was known to be ill in the Tower, and as a state prisoner of some importance – who, though he had incurred the King's displeasure, was considered as being under his protection – he was visited by the King's physician, the French doctor Sir Theodore Turquet de Mayerne. When Mayerne left London with the Court, he deputed the care of Overbury to his countryman, the apothecary Paul de Lobell, whose corruptible servant William Reeve was finally responsible for Overbury's death.

Though Reeve was dead, Weston was still available to stand trial for his attempted murder of Overbury; and once his attempt was established, the prosecution could be extended to the accessories, Turner, Franklin, and the unfortunate Sir Gervase Elwys. The trials of the Earl and Countess of Somerset would come later.

Weston was convicted and went to his execution on 10 November 1615. If ever callous purveyors of death, who had no personal motive but acted only for gain, deserved to die for their crimes, Turner and Franklin were among their number. Sir Gervase Elwys was not another such. However, he was technically guilty as an accessory before the fact, because he had known of the attempts to poison Overbury, and he had neither denounced the poisoners nor saved his prisoners from their attentions. In fact, Elwys had been in an impossible position. He had been an unknown, though worthy, knight without friends at Court; and as such his appointment as Lieutenant of the Tower had been, on the face of it, surprising. He had owed the occasion of his appointment to a fellow Lincolnshireman, Sir Thomas Monson, who had recommended him to the Earl of Northampton, who in turn had secured his nomination as Lieutenant, in succession to Sir William Wade. He was so much a nonentity, so dependent upon patronage, that when he discovered that Overbury was the victim of attempted poisoning, he could not denounce the attempt for fear that no-one would have believed him, and indeed that he would have been in trouble for slandering great persons, without the means of substantiating his accusation. This was probably why he was so eager to tell all to Sir Ralph Winwood; but telling the truth proved to be no means of saving his life.

He was executed on 20 November, and he summed up the story of his own tragedy aptly enough when he confessed that 'when it was in his power to have hindered the proceedings of the poisoners he suffered them to go on to the murthering of an honest gentleman'. But how much it was indeed in his power to have hindered the proceedings more than he did may be doubted.

The prosecution of those connected in the Overbury case had a curious effect upon Sir Edward Coke. He seems to have imagined that he had not merely discovered the truth concerning the murder of Overbury, but that he had discovered the tip of a huge iceberg of conspiracy. Sir Thomas Monson was arraigned for his part in acting as broker in the appointment of Sir Gervase Elwys. Coke failed to establish any connection between Monson's part in this affair and the poisoning of Overbury; thereupon he hinted darkly that the whole story was not known, and that if Prince Henry's death were fully investigated, a link between it and the poisoning of Overbury would be revealed, and 'if this had not been found out, neither the Court, City, nor any particular family had escaped the malice of this wicked cruelty'.[8]

The proceedings against Monson were immediately dropped, and James, who had been angered by the unwarranted reference to the death of his son, placed the prosecution of the Somersets in the hands of Sir Francis Bacon. Coke had felt a strong draught of royal displeasure.

The small fry among the purveyors of Overbury's death left this world before the end of December 1615. The Somersets did not stand their trial until the spring of the following year.

The pregnancy of the Countess was the occasion of the first delay: on 9 December she gave birth to a daughter. But the trial continued to be delayed by the steadfast refusal of Somerset to plead guilty. Frances had confessed her guilt in the face of the statements of Weston, Turner, Franklin and Elwys, but she had firmly declared the innocence of her husband.

The tragedy of Frances Howard is that in all her evil doings she was inspired by her basically blameless desire to be the wife, not the mistress, of Robert Carr. Had she been content to conduct an adulterous affair with him, she could have done as many Court ladies did, and taken her pleasure while incurring little censure. But to secure the status of a wife she had been prepared to resort to administering dubious drugs to a husband who had hoped to love her, and for long had not understood her aversion to him; then she had procured the death of the man whose testimony could have prevented her from gaining the annulment of her marriage, which was the only means through which she could attain to a legal union with Robert Carr. In fact, Frances deserves far more pity than is usually accorded her, for had she lived in the twentieth instead of in the seventeenth century, she could have had all that she desired without any disgrace at all, and her indomitable will, which enabled her to triumph so briefly over the accepted morality of her time, might have been brought to bear upon a more worthy cause. As it was, she lost the love of the man whom she had fought so hard to win, for her criminality brought about his ruin.

Frances stood her trial on 24 May 1616. Dressed all in black, except for a ruff and cuffs of white lawn, she faced an assize of her peers and listened to the prosecuting speech of Sir Francis Bacon, which was laced with reassuring references to the merciful nature of King James, who had not, since the beginning of his reign, caused noble blood to be shed, not even that of traitors. She pleaded Guilty, and heard the sombre voice of Lord Ellesmere condemn her to death. There was a general supposition that the King's mercy would spare her.

The following day Somerset stood trial in his turn. He entered a plea of Not Guilty, no doubt for the simple reason that he was not guilty. He admitted that he had connived at Overbury's imprisonment: 'I design'd it for his reformation,' he said, 'not his ruin.' He placed himself in a dubious light by his conduct after Overbury's death. Then he had endeavoured to regain the letters which he had written to Overbury in the Tower, and he had tampered with the dating of the letters which Overbury had written to him. Evidently, after Overbury's death he had suddenly realized that his own conduct might not bear close scrutiny, or else he had learned of what his wife had done, and had hoped that he might be able to do something to conceal it.

The best evidence that he had known nothing of Overbury's murder was provided by the letters which the late Earl of Northampton had written to Elwys at the time of Overbury's death. Somerset, once his friend was dead, and in the first flush of guilt-stricken regret, had urged that Overbury be given an honourable burial, but Northampton had gone out of his way to urge upon Elwys the necessity of getting him buried 'instantly'.[9] It was fortunate for Northampton that he had died before the storm broke, for even he might have found that he had too much inconvenient knowledge to explain away.

Somerset had at first refused to believe that the King would have him brought to trial, and when he had realized that he would indeed have to face trial, and the concomitant possibility of condemnation to death, he had attempted to force the King to change his mind by threatening to make certain disclosures which would have been damaging to James's reputation. James supposed that Somerset had the intention of 'laying an aspersion upon me of being in some sort accessory to his crime'.[10] What indeed Somerset was threatening to reveal has been much discussed, but it appears obvious that the meaning of the King's words was that he supposed Somerset would seek to blame the death of Overbury ultimately upon him by referring to the fact that Dr Mayerne had been sent to attend Overbury in the Tower at his instance; that Mayerne had sent Lobell, and that Lobell had sent Reeve, who had committed the murder. The chain of connection, though imaginary in terms of intention, would have been damaging indeed if it had been uttered in the form of a slanderous suggestion.

Somerset should have known James better after all his years of intimacy with him. Though James might fear the consequences of Somerset's threat, he was not vulnerable to intimidation. During his early years in Scotland he had learned in a hard school how to outface it. Somerset went to his trial, though Anthony Weldon observed that '... who had seen the King's restless motion all that day, sending to every boat he sees landing at the bridge, cursing all that came without tidings, would have easily judged that all was not right, and there had been some grounds for his fears of Somerset's boldness ...'[11].

However, if Somerset had planned to say anything detrimental to the King, he thought better of it. He defended himself with dignity, though not with great effect. In accordance with the custom of the times he was not permitted legal representation, and it was pointed out to him that he was being accorded a singular grace in that he was allowed to make notes on which to base his defence. Nevertheless he began courageously: 'I am confident ... in mine own cause, and am come hither to defend it.'[12]

His explanations of his conduct were simple, but, unfortunately for him, impossible to prove. Regarding the poisoned tarts he said, 'Whereas it is pretended that I should cause poisoned tarts to be sent him to the Tower, my wife in her confession saith, that there were none sent but either by me or her, and some were wholesome, and some not. Then it must needs follow, that the good ones were those which I sent, and the bad hers.'[13]

Again he reiterated his intentions concerning Overbury's imprisonment: 'My furthest intent in his imprisonment was that he should be no impediment to my marriage, and this I communicated to my Lord of Northampton and Elwys.'[14]

At the end of his defence Somerset addressed a dignified speech to the assize of his peers which was about to sit in judgement on him:

> My Lords, [he said] before you go together, I beseech you give me leave to recommend myself and cause unto you: as the King hath raised me to your degree, so he hath now disposed me to your censure. This may be any of your own cases, and therefore I assure myself you will not take circumstances for evidence: for if you should, the condition of a man's life were nothing. In the meantime, you may see the excellence of the King's justice, which makes no distinction, putting me into your hands for a just and equal censure. For my part, I protest before God, I was neither guilty of, nor privy to, any wrong that Overbury suffered in this kind.[15]

Nonetheless, the lords were neither convinced by Somerset's defence, nor perhaps unmindful of the King's previous desire that he should plead guilty. After consultation with the Lord Chief Justice of the King's Bench, Sir Edward Coke, and the Lord Chief Justice of the Common Pleas, Sir Henry Hobart, they reached a unanimous verdict of guilty. Somerset, like his wife, was condemned to death, with a similar expectation in the minds of everyone present that he would receive the King's mercy.

James, as always, desired to show himself as a just and a merciful ruler. It was unfortunate that the meting out of justice upon the small fry, and the exercise of the prerogative of mercy upon the fallen favourite and his wife, did not perfectly create this impression.

The Earl and Countess of Somerset in their turn became prisoners in the Tower, where predictably a 'great falling out' occurred between them. Somerset's eyes were cleared of the illusions of his love, and he saw Frances as Overbury had seen her: as a wicked woman who would be – and now had been – his ruin. The revulsion of her husband against her was the cruellest punishment that Frances could have endured, for all her crimes had been committed solely to win him for her husband. Perhaps King James's mercy was a crueller punishment to both of them than would have been that of sending them to the block.

In 1616 Frances received her pardon, a dusty reward for her plea of Guilty; Somerset, for his recalcitrance, had to wait for his pardon until 1624. However, in January 1622 both were released from the Tower and sent to live at Rotherfield Grays, in Oxfordshire, under an extended house arrest, which permitted them to enjoy a three-mile radius of freedom. 'They lived,' according to Arthur Wilson, 'though in one house as strangers one to another.'[16]

Frances died in 1632, and Wilson recounted the manner of her death with an unpleasant satisfaction which suggests that his sympathy for her first husband Essex may have led him to regard it as a judgement on her: 'Her death was infamous ... for that part of her body which had been the receptacle of most of her sin, grown rotten (though she never had but one child), the ligaments failing, it fell down and was cut away in flakes, with a most nauseous and putrid savour, which to augment, she would roll herself in her own ordure in her bed [and] took delight in it ...'[17]. It is only fair to say that Bishop Goodman denied the truth of this story.

Somerset survived her, and died in 1645. A portrait which was painted of him during his later years shows his handsome face grown haggard, his eyes sombre. Round his neck is the George of the Order of the Garter, which James, to the surprise of many, refused to take from him after his conviction. This generous gesture suggests that, although Somerset had utterly lost his place in the King's favour, James had not forgotten the last vestiges of that once deep love which he had recorded in the anger and disillusionment of the letter which he had written to Somerset before the Overbury scandal.

King James was not closely in touch with public opinion, and therefore possibly he did not realize the damage which his reputation suffered through the trial of the Somersets for Overbury's murder. The impression which the rise of Somerset had created in the minds of the country gentry and the nobility who did not frequent the Court was as nothing compared with that created by the fall of Somerset and the manner in which it occurred. Yet Archbishop Abbott, who was neither naïve nor time-serving, could say that the King's life was 'so immaculate and unspotted from the world ... that even malice itself could never find true blemish in it'. James, who himself took this view, may have shown naïvety in supposing that malice would not.

CHAPTER THIRTEEN

Golden Mirages

... there was never a mine of gold in the world promising so great abundance.

Sir Walter Raleigh, on his
proposed voyage to Guiana

IF KING JAMES I had been a private individual, during the years between 1613 and 1616 he might have been obsessed by little else but the failure of his relationship with Robert Carr, and the scandal which resulted from the criminality of Carr's wife. But, since he was King of Great Britain, James had many preoccupations outside the scope of his private life.

The financial necessities which had grown increasingly pressing since the death of Salisbury were decisive in leading the King to summon a new Parliament in 1614. The occasion had been delayed by the various temporary expedients which had been tried after the failure of the Great Contract. The first creation of baronets has been mentioned previously. A 'Forced Loan', raised during the winter of 1611–12, had yielded £116,000; but this was, of course, an addition to the existing debt, although it may have afforded an impression of immediate relief.

The King faced the necessity of summoning a new Parliament chiefly as a result of the representations of the advantages of such a course which were set out for him by Sir Francis Bacon, to whom at this time he was turning increasingly for advice. Bacon urged the wisdom of ensuring that the new House of Commons should consist of 'what persons in particular in respect of their gravity, discretion, temper and ability to persuade are fit to be brought in to be of the house *bonis artibus*, without labouring or packing ...', and should exclude 'what persons in particular, as violent and turbulent, are fit to be kept back from being of this house, *bonis artibus*, without labouring or packing ...'[1]. This advice sounded very reasonable, but by what arts Bacon proposed that the ends should be achieved was not obvious. However, as a result of listening to Bacon's arguments, James decided that the summoning of Parliament might provide the solution to his financial problems.

James was not unastute in thinking that it might be possible to revive in principle the idea of the Great Contract, and to negotiate with some influential members a similar bargain, though inevitably on a smaller scale.[2] The idea was feasible, though the King may have been unwise in attempting to make his bargain with men who had not yet been elected to their seats. His hope was probably that, if the members in question were already primed with an idea which was part of the royal policy, they might be able to present it to their fellows much as the Lords of the Articles presented the legislation which the King desired to the Scottish Parliament.

The man who was responsible for the preliminary stages of this negotiation was Sir Henry Neville, who, before the appointment of Sir Ralph Winwood to the Secretaryship of State, was ambitious for that office himself. Neville told the King that he 'dared undertake' to secure the success of the scheme in the Lower House. This assurance may have been merely sanguine, but Neville's words, no doubt after exaggerated repetition, led to a widespread belief among the new members of the Commons that they were about to be subjected to the machinations of 'undertakers'. When Neville and his supporters took their seats, they found that this pejorative name had made them already 'dis-credited and vilified men'.[3]

Despite the presence in the House of a number of representatives of the official world and the Court, royal control proved insufficient to contain the explosion of anger against the 'undertakers', whose villainy was imaginary and whose capacity to act was pre-empted by the reaction to the belief that the King was trying to control Parliament through private bargaining.

Sir Ralph Winwood, who had been appointed Secretary of State only a few days before Parliament met, had not sat before, and he lacked both the experience and the tact to present the King's policy in a favourable light. But the King evidently did not appreciate the extent to which ability to do so would be needed. He was probably satisfied by the number of assured supporters who were sitting in the Commons. Besides Winwood, there was Sir Thomas Lake, who was appointed his Co-Secretary of State; Sir Francis Bacon, who was now Attorney-General, Sir Henry Yelverton, the Solicitor-General, Sir Robert Hitcham, Attorney-General to the Queen, and other, lesser men, to the total of eighteen Court and Government officials.[4]

The King opened Parliament on 5 April 1614, and dissolved it on 7 June. In his opening speech James admitted his great need for money, and expressed his hope that the second Parliament of his reign might prove to be a 'Parliament of Love'. As is well known, it was called by posterity not the 'Parliament of Love' but the 'Addled Parliament', because during the few weeks that it remained in session no single bill received the royal assent. The whole session was characterized by a mood of wilful refusal to co-operate, and every aspect of the King's policy was the subject of attack.

If the King was misunderstood, it was scarcely his fault, for in the many speeches he made to his Parliaments he was always at pains to define and to elucidate his views, and he never shrank from addressing the Lower House himself, although he became increasingly aware that his words were not given a fair hearing. As he put it to the Parliament of 1621:

> I have made many long discourses, especially to the gentlemen of the House of Commons, and to them I have delivered as I myself have said, a true mirror of my mind and free thoughts of my heart. But as no man's actions, be he never so good, are free from sin, [he] being a mortal, sinful creature, so some, through a spice of envy have made all my speeches heretofore turn like spittle against the wind upon mine own face, and contrary to my expectations, so that I may truly say with our Saviour, I have often piped unto [you] and you have not danced, I have warned and you have not lamented.[5]

On 4 May 1614, James made a speech in defence of his right to levy impositions, which had again come under attack.[6] In his response to the attacks on his policy and ideas to which he was consistently subjected, James showed a moderation and a regard for legality which might be thought more characteristic of constitutional monarchy than of such would-be absolutism as James is usually represented as having practised.[7] 'Kings', he told the Parliament of 1614, 'that are not tyrants or perjured, will be glad to bind themselves within the limits of ... law.... For it is a great difference between a King's government in a settled state and what Kings in their original powers might do....'[8] It was not therefore surprising that when this studied moderation was met with immoderate contentiousness, James dissolved Parliament without the desired grant of taxation, which was obviously not forthcoming except at a price which he considered too high to be worth paying. That price would have been the abandonment of his right to levy impositions. But after the dissolution of the Addled Parliament impositions continued to be levied without the consent of Parliament until the outbreak of the Civil War. According to the opinion of Dr Conrad Russell, 'In this, the only profound constitutional conflict of the reign of James I, the result had been such an overwhelming victory for the King that there can hardly be said to have been a contest.'[9]

One of the members, Sir Thomas Roe, thought that he had witnessed 'a dissolution not of this, but of all Parliaments'.[10] He might have been right, to judge by the parallel case of the *Etats-Généraux* of France, which was dissolved in 1614 and did not meet again until 1789. James certainly had no wish to summon Parliament again if he could avoid it. 'The House of Commons is a body without a head,' he complained to the Spanish Ambassador, Count Gondomar, 'the members give their opinions in a disorderly manner; at their meetings nothing is heard but cries, shouts and confusion. I am surprised that my ancestors should ever have permitted such an institution to come into existence.'[11]

James's strictures on his Parliament may have been justified, but after the dissolution, his financial problem remained, as intractable as before.

Don Diego Sarmiento de Acuna was created Count of Gondomar in the course of his embassy in England, but for the sake of clarity he will be called from the outset by the title which is his most familiar designation.

Gondomar arrived in England in 1613. At this time a marriage between Prince Charles and Christine of France, sister of Louis XIII, was under negotiation. Gondomar at first supposed that it would be impossible to prevent this marriage from taking place;

but his ambition was to revive the project of a Spanish marriage for the heir to the throne of Great Britain. Philip III of Spain had an eligible daughter, the Infanta Maria. James's need for money – and not for a moderate sum, but for a vast fortune, such as an Infanta's dowry might be expected to provide – would give Gondomar's proposal a decidedly appealing aspect. On his first arrival in England, however, he could not broach the matter, for he had no official instructions from his sovereign, and without them 'the French would see it not as a serious offer ... but simply as malicious wrecking of their diplomacy'.[12] While Gondomar sought the instructions which he needed, he took advantage of James's immediate liking for him, and sedulously cultivated the King's friendship.

Gondomar has had a bad reputation with English historians because he was so much hated by contemporary Englishmen that the lampoons, satires and dramatic misrepresentations of his character which were written at the time have created an almost indelible impression of him. Only in recent years has its veracity begun to be questioned.[13]

The Count of Gondomar was a Castilian aristocrat. Like James himself he was both non-military and learned. He could converse in Latin, which the King enjoyed, and his approach was a blend of deference and informality, which James found agreeable. It would have been easy for a hispanophobe who possessed only a very slight impression of him – which meant almost any Protestant Englishman outside the King's closest circle – to imagine him as a combination of Mephistopheles and Machiavelli, each of whom contributed a proverbial adjective to the English language.

Thomas Middleton, in a popular play, *A Game at Chess*, satirized him in the character of the Black Knight, and described him as

> ... The mightiest Matchiavel-politician
> That e'er the devil hatch'd of a nun's egg.[14]

The reason for this caricature's appeal to the audience was that the old Elizabethan view that Spain was the national enemy had healthily survived the peace treaty which had been signed at the beginning of the reign. Old enmities are always slow to die. When the talk of a Spanish marriage for Prince Charles became common property, the majority of Englishmen were of the opinion that it would be better for the King to get Spanish gold not by negotiating for an Infanta's dowry but by authorizing English sea captains to plunder the Plate Fleets, which brought the gold of the New World to Spain. This manner of dealing with the Spaniards was nostalgically associated in their minds with the heroic days of the last reign, in which the winds and the waves had shown the direction of God's favour in assisting England to defeat the Spanish Armada. James himself had been inspired to write a sonnet on the subject.

With such ideas and memories occupying the popular mind, the friendship of the King with the Spanish Ambassador would have seemed like the most incomprehensible folly, if not like the work of the devil through the Spaniard's influence. The two lines quoted from Middleton's play make the existence of this view strongly apparent. But King James, as a result of his diplomatic contacts with Catholic Europe, thought very differently from the mass of his subjects, and, indeed, differently from his younger self. However, the crude Jacobean view that the Spanish Ambassador was an evil genius who played upon the King's simpler nature survived its first currency and became an historical cliché.

Recently the traditional view of Gondomar as a villainous arch-intriguer has undergone a change. For instance, he was not a great spy-master, 'partly because he did not trust anyone who would betray secrets for money, partly because few spies ... had access to information of the order of importance in which he was most interested.'

Gondomar had the simplest method of seeking the information which he desired: he asked the King, whose custom it was to receive ambassadors in private. This habit illustrated the strength of James's conviction that the conduct of foreign policy was an inviolable area of the royal prerogative. James talked freely to Gondomar, and frequently appeared to talk indiscreetly; but he would not have regarded himself as obliged to talk to the Ambassador truthfully. Gondomar was sufficiently well aware of the problems which James's conception of 'kingcraft' raised in diplomatic terms to remain upon his guard. His successes were achieved to the accompaniment of nagging anxiety that he was the King's dupe, and not of conviction that the reverse was true. The Spanish marriage was discussed in the context of an unusual friendship which lacked the basic element of trust.

Once Gondomar had received his instructions which permitted discussion of a marriage between the Spanish Princess and the English Prince, he was able to encourage the King to appoint an ambassador to represent him in Spain. For this intricate diplomacy, King James chose a man of intelligence and exceptional honesty, Sir John Digby. The Spanish conditions for the marriage, which Digby reported from Madrid in May 1615, sounded almost preposterous in England, yet they were the inevitable requirements of a Catholic monarchy: the children of the marriage were to be baptized as Catholics; their religious education was to be at the discretion of their mother, and if they elected to become Catholics they were not to forfeit their rights of succession; the Infanta was to have Catholic servants, and a chapel which was to be a public place of worship for the English Catholics, against whom the penal laws were to be rescinded.

While these conditions sounded exorbitant to King James, and would have sounded totally untenable to almost anyone else (as they did to Digby), if the Infanta had been on offer to a Catholic bridegroom it would have been unnecessary to state any of them. The serious aspects of the contract would have lain elsewhere. But there had never been a marriage between an Infanta and a non-Catholic; the immutable Catholicism of Spain, once considered, makes the conditions perfectly understandable.

Repulsive as any form of Protestantism appeared at the Spanish Court, the fact remained that Spain needed peace, if only as a period of recovery between wars, and the supply of bullion from the New World needed securing from the interference of English privateers. From the Spanish viewpoint, it was worth negotiating the marriage of the Infanta to the English Prince – if necessary, of selling the Infanta in the economic interests of Spain – but the conditions under which the marriage could be permitted to take place had to be acceptable to Catholic sentiment.

So far as James was concerned, much the same was true, from the opposing viewpoint. He badly needed the Infanta's dowry – and the really astonishing sum of an equivalent in Spanish currency of £600,000 was mentioned – but at the same time the conditions had to be within certain limits of acceptability. James had told the Parliament of 1614 that no religion had gained by persecuting its enemies, yet he knew that he could not go so far as to rescind the penal laws, for even his suspension of them at the beginning of the reign had proved unworkable.

The Spanish conditions shocked him by their unacceptability to what he knew was the prevailing condition of religio-political opinion in England; but the size of the sum of money which he knew might be gained by successful negotiation continued to attract him. While negotiations remained open nothing was lost and much might be won. When Gondomar returned to Spain in 1618, after his first period of residence in England, James made a spectacular gesture of goodwill in releasing a hundred Catholic priests from prison and allowing them to accompany the Ambassador out of the country.

Financial necessity led James, as it has led many other people, to follow paths which he would not have followed had he been free of its influence. It led him in 1616 to release Sir Walter Raleigh from his long imprisonment in the Tower of London.

Raleigh had his supporters in the Government, among them Sir Ralph Winwood, who reached the apogee of his influence after he had twice gambled successfully, once in assisting at the fall of Somerset, and once in backing the rise of Villiers. Archbishop Abbott, the Earl of Southampton and Pembroke, and the rest of the anti-Howard and anti-Spain faction were natural enthusiasts for Raleigh's project to bring gold from Guiana.

Raleigh's description of the source of the gold was tantalizing; it lay only a few inches under the ground 'in a broad slate, and not in small veines, there was never a mine of gold in the world promising so great abundance'. This incredible invitation to human greed, according to local hearsay, was close to the Orinoco delta. The area had been visited by Captain Lawrence Keymis, sent by Raleigh in 1596, who had been told by natives of the gold. It lay theoretically within the territories of the King of Spain, but at the time of Keymis's visit the relations between England and Spain had been simplified by a state of war. Peace, however, did not necessarily make the acquisition of the gold impossible.

Between the delta of the Orinoco and the mouth of the Amazon there were settlements which had been founded in the names of the Kings of Spain and Portugal. Since the union of the Spanish and Portuguese crowns in 1580 there was, in theory, an unbroken chain of allegiance owed by the whole length of that vast coast. But there was even less sense of unity between the Spaniards and the Portuguese than between the English and the Scots; there was no liaison between their settlements, and in these immense tracts of land this meant that there was no unity at all. It might be arguable that there were large areas of coastline that no-one had claimed, or had occupied insufficiently for such a claim to be realistic.

James had left the British Isles only once, to make the relatively short voyage across the North Sea when he sailed to claim his bride. His geographical imagination was therefore necessarily limited; he was reliant upon descriptions of the coast of the New World, which he could not visualize. Raleigh did not suffer from this disadvantage, but his view of Anglo-Spanish relations had been formed while he was still a free man. A voyage to seek gold in Guiana would invoke very disparate responses in the minds of King James and Sir Walter Raleigh.

However, neither Raleigh's plan nor James's acceptance of it was irresponsible or unrealistic. In the course of the reign there had been three attempts by Englishmen to colonize the empty areas of the South American coast. In 1604 Charles Leigh, with a ship pacifically named the *Olive Plant*, had established an English settlement for two years on the banks of the river Wiapoco. A longer-lived venture, encouraged by Prince Henry, had sailed under Robert Harcourt, and had maintained an existence in Guiana until 1613. In 1610 the third expedition to Guiana was led by Sir Thomas Roe, and Raleigh invested £600 in it. When Raleigh proposed his own venture he was not suggesting a plan which would have appeared an inevitable violation of international relations, and he was not pressing the King to countenance a project of a kind which he had not countenanced before.

Raleigh's ship, the *Destiny*, was launched in 1616, and James assured Gondomar, who naturally raised objections to the proposed expedition, that Raleigh's purposes were entirely peaceful. Raleigh, however, from the moment of his release, imagined himself as winning great prizes from the Spaniards by acts of piracy, and thereby regaining James's favour with treasure too vast to be resisted for considerations of policy.

The story of Raleigh's last voyage is almost too well known to need re-telling. In brief, the *Destiny* reached the Orinoco without incident, and Raleigh, whose health had not stood up well to the rigours of the voyage, sent the faithful Captain Keymis, who had accompanied him, to locate the gold mine. Keymis, with Raleigh's elder son, Walter, took an expeditionary force inland. They found their route barred by a Spanish settlement, San Thomé, the existence of which was probably not known to them. Keymis made a disastrous decision to attack it, and in the ensuing fight Raleigh's son was killed. Keymis returned to the *Destiny* with nothing but tragedy to recount and, realizing that the trail of ruin which his action would cause was not yet ended, he committed suicide. He had acted like a fool, but perhaps he was in truth the victim of Raleigh's wild talk on the outward voyage.

Raleigh sailed home in the knowledge that he must be sailing to his death; he was still under the death sentence which had been passed on him at the beginning of the reign. He thought to save his life by sailing the *Destiny* to Brest, but a mutinous crew forced him to take her in to Plymouth. Soon after he landed he was arrested by his kinsman Sir Lewis Stukeley, the Vice-Admiral of Devon. He was brought to London and lodged under house arrest; a late attempt to escape to France was carefully overseen and foiled. He was permitted to make his way to Woolwich on a boat which was to take him out to a French vessel. After he had compromised himself by secret dealings with the French, he was recaptured and taken to the Tower.

On 18 August 1618 he appeared before the commissioners who had been appointed to examine him. There was an appearance of equity in the fact that they were not men who would have been predisposed against him. Archbishop Abbott had been his supporter, the Earl of Worcester was old and detached from faction. The others were Sir Francis Bacon, who had risen a step further in official life to become Lord Keeper, and Sir Edward Coke, who had been dismissed from his position as Lord Chief Justice of the King's Bench after endless clashes with the King over the demarcation of the jurisdictions of the Prerogative Courts and the Courts of Common Law; Sir Julius Caesar, who had become Master of the Rolls, and Sir Robert Naunton, who had been appointed Secretary of State in the place of Winwood, who had died during Raleigh's absence. The death of Winwood may have appeared a disaster to Raleigh, but the Secretary, even at the height of his power, would not have had the influence to save him. In turn, the commission has been aptly described as representing 'the Protestant royalism of the English law'. The temper of such an assembly was not intrinsically inimical to Raleigh, but no gathering of Jacobean officialdom would have been unmindful of the King's will, which was entirely inimical to him. Raleigh had transgressed the King's policy of international peace, and therefore he had to die.

It is difficult to divorce the rest of Raleigh's story from the accretion of heroic myth which clings to it. He was not, until the time of his death, a hero; he was a man whose imprisonment had gained him a degree of sympathy which he had not enjoyed at the outset of the reign. At that time he had been one of the most detested men in England. He was still not well regarded at Court. Though Prince Henry had admired him, that was no help to him in 1618. Anne of Denmark interceded for him, but her influence was strictly circumscribed. He was a proud, unpopular man, whose successes belonged to the previous reign, and whose chance to reinstate himself had failed. However, he died like a hero, and left his own immortal epitaph:

> Even such is Time, which takes in trust
> Our youth, our joys, and all we have,
> And pays us but with age and dust;
> Who in the dark and silent grave,
> When we have wandered all our ways,
> Shuts up the story of our days:
> And from which earth, and grave, and dust,
> The Lord shall raise me up, I trust.

King James's mind had been poisoned against Raleigh long ago, through the correspondence which Sir Robert Cecil and Lord Henry Howard had conducted with him before he became the King of England and they the Earls of Salisbury and Northampton. The root of Raleigh's tragedy was that he had never been able to reverse the King's first opinion of him. But the end of Raleigh's story was not the conclusion hallowed by tradition, that a weak Scottish King executed an English hero to cancel out an offence against Spain. Had it been so, it would have been an act of appeasement, as it is generally supposed to have been. In fact, it was an act of *realpolitik*. James, as an international politician, executed a man who was usable but expendable in his schemes; and James's guilt is not that he executed Raleigh but that he made cynical use of him. For surely the King's reasoning was that, if Raleigh brought gold from Guiana without making trouble with Spain, he could be forgiven for the sake of his usefulness; if he brought gold at the cost of trouble, at least it would illustrate to Spain the danger of not being on good terms with England; if he made trouble with Spain and did not bring gold, then he would have to die.

Raleigh died, but one golden mirage succeeded another. James's eyes turned again to the mirage of the Infanta's dowry, which derived ultimately from those distant Spanish possessions the fruits of which Raleigh had thought to plunder.

CHAPTER FOURTEEN

The Last Favourite

You are now the King's Favourite, remember well the great trust you have undertaken...

Sir Francis Bacon to Sir
George Villiers, 1616

THE TRAGIC CONCLUSION of Sir Walter Raleigh's career coincided with the glittering beginning of that of the King's last favourite.

In April 1616 Sir George Villiers was created a Knight of the Garter. There is a well-known full-length portrait of him in Garter robes, which was probably painted in honour of this occasion. The picture shows him as a tall young man with slender limbs and graceful proportions. Although he had been born in 1592 he still looks like an adolescent youth. He is clean-shaven and apparently perfectly smooth-faced. His dark hair is combed back from his forehead, and curls forward around his temples and ears. His grey eyes are intelligent and attentive beneath his finely-arched brows; his well-shaped mouth is composed in an amiable smile. His head is framed by a semi-circular standing collar of wired lace, and he is posed in the dark space between looped-back folds of heavy green velvet curtains. His unusual beauty is probably enhanced by the conventional background, and the formal grandeur of the robes, which are usually seen in portraits of much older men. The red velvet and white satin panels of the mantle separate to display his legs clad in white stockings. They are extraordinarily long and slender, like the legs of a thoroughbred colt. It is not surprising that he excelled at running, leaping and dancing.

Villiers's prowess as a dancer was exhibited on Twelfth Night, 1618, by which time he had become Marquis of Buckingham. The Court masque of that year bored the King, and the dancers, who were tired, according to the Venetian Horatio Busino, who described the scene, began to lag:

> ... whereupon the King, who is naturally choleric, shouted aloud 'Why don't they dance? What did they make me come here for? Devil take you all, dance!' Upon which the Marquis of Buckingham, his Majesty's favourite, immediately sprang forward, cutting a score of lofty and very minute capers, with so much grace and agility that he not only appeased the ire of his angry lord, but rendered himself the delight and admiration of everybody.[1]

The rise of Buckingham was remarkably rapid, 'so quick', as Clarendon aptly observed, 'that it seemed rather a flight than a growth'. In 1616, shortly after his admission to the Order of the Garter, he was created Viscount Villiers, and in 1617 Earl of Buckingham; in 1618 he was not only created a Marquis but also appointed Lord High Admiral. There he paused until, in 1623, the King created him the only Duke who was not of the royal blood.

'The Duke', wrote Clarendon, many years later, 'was indeed a very extraordinary person; and never any man, in any age, nor, I believe, in any country or nation rose, in so short a time, to so much greatness of honour, fame and fortune, upon no other advantage or recommendation than of the beauty and gracefulness of his person.'[2] The Puritan memoirist Lucy Hutchinson expressed a harsher opinion when she wrote that the Duke of Buckingham had been 'raised from a knight's fourth son to that pitch of glory, and enjoying great possessions, acquired by the favour of the King, upon no merit but that of his beauty and his prostitution'.[3] That this belief was widely held and expressed outside Court circles[4] raises again the question of the nature of the relations between Buckingham and James. Though that question appears to be settled by Buckingham's letter referring to 'that time ... at Farnham', the reference is so brief that some further discussion of a matter which had been a cause of considerable controversy may be required.

Some historians and biographers have doubted that James and Buckingham were indeed lovers, chiefly on the grounds that this relationship would have rendered impossible the later friendship between Buckingham and Prince Charles. But perhaps this is to give too much weight to what Charles would have thought had he *known* what was the nature of their relationship. Throughout his life, until the very last months, Charles showed a rare capacity for blinding himself to the truth of a situation which he did not wish to face. In this case his well-known purity would have assisted him to do so, and no enemy of Buckingham would have had the temerity to speak of the matter to him; for during the last years of the reign Charles was 'the rising sun', and nobody would have risked losing his favour even to have the satisfaction of bringing down Buckingham.

The opinion of Dr Roger Lockyer, in his new biography of Buckingham, is that 'By giving himself to James, Buckingham confirmed his supremacy, for what he had to offer was a combination of qualities which the King could find nowhere else – youth, beauty, high spirits, sensuality, sweetness of character, and devotion.'[5] This is a very much more charitable representation of Lucy Hutchinson's view.

It seems almost self-evident, from outward appearances, from the single reference made by Buckingham himself, and from the intense feeling expressed in the many letters which James and Buckingham exchanged – some of which will be quoted in their context – that the relationship of the King and his favourite was homosexual. But perhaps this was a relatively short-lived phase in a changing relationship, for Buckingham, unlike almost all other royal favourites, showed that he was able to detach himself gradually from the King without loss of favour. This was possible because the relationship proved itself to be grounded in genuine attachment on both sides, and it seems probable that by 1620, when Buckingham and Prince Charles became close friends, the passionate phase of James's relations with Buckingham had ended. While this suggestion is hypothetical it is inherently likely, because, whereas James was in vigorous middle life at the age of forty-eight when the young Villiers was first presented to him, after he was fifty his health steadily deteriorated. During his later years, affection, not passion, was probably what he required from his favourite.

At the end of 1616 James resolved to make his long-deferred return visit to Scotland. Before he had left his native kingdom in 1603, he had promised that he would return every three years; not only had he failed to keep his promise, but even a single return had been delayed year after year. No doubt the distance and the expense had exerted more influence than he had ever imagined that they would, but without such considerations the momentum of events had left him scarcely an opportunity of undertaking a journey which would necessarily take him away from England for many weeks.

He was obeying a strong impulse, and taking advantage of a chance which he believed to be the first, and sensed would be the last, when he decided to make the journey. He wrote to the Scottish Privy Council, on 15 December 1616:

> We are not ashamed to confess that we have had these many years a great and natural longing to see our native soil and place of our birth and breeding, and this salmon-like instinct of ours has restlessly, both when we were awake, and many times in our sleep, so stirred up our thoughts and bended our desires to make a journey thither that we can never rest satisfied till it shall please God that we may accomplish it.[6]

The King's resolution was unpopular with his English courtiers, none of whom wished to go with him on a progress of unprecedented length to the northern kingdom where, they imagined, cold, discomfort and barbarism awaited them. Even the Queen had no desire to accompany her husband. Some people imagined that she hoped that if she remained behind she would be made regent in his absence. But since she must have known that such an eventuality was far from likely, it is more probable that lethargy and a complete lack of nostalgia for Scotland explained her remaining at home.

Apparently there was no implication of ill-feeling between Anne and James. A certain warmth of affection between them was attested by John Chamberlain, who wrote in the summer of 1613:

> ... about a fortnight since, the Queen, shooting at a deer, mistook her mark and killed Jewel, the King's most principal and special hound, at which he stormed exceedingly a while, but after [he] knew who did it, he was soon pacified, and with much kindness wished her not to be troubled with it, for he should love her never the worse, and the next day sent her a diamond worth £2,000, as a legacy from his dead dog....[7]

However, with the passage of a few years their relationship grew increasingly attenuated; and with Viscount Villiers to accompany him, James was not disposed to insist upon Anne's coming. At the beginning of the journey, as though it were a reward for his compliance with the King's wishes in accompanying him readily when others were reluctant, Villiers received his earldom. His response to the King's wishes was always calculated with skill.

Certain English and Scottish lords received invitations, which were necessarily to be interpreted as commands, to attend the King on his northern progress. Among them were his Scottish kinsmen, the Duke of Lennox and the Marquis of Hamilton, and the English brothers, the Earls of Pembroke and Montgomery. There were three English bishops in the King's entourage: Andrewes of Ely, Neile of Durham, and Montague of Winchester, who in 1616 had edited the King's *Collected Works.* James rode north from Theobalds on 15 March, and retraced his stately journey of thirteen years before. On 13 May he reached Berwick and crossed the Tweed, to re-enter his native country.

He had not come purely on a visit. Still possessed by the chimera of unification, he sought to enforce on the Kirk the notorious 'Five Articles of Perth', which would have had the effect of bringing the practice of the Kirk into line with that of the Church of England. The Five Articles required that in Scotland Holy Communion should be received kneeling; that the Kirk should celebrate the festivals of the Christian Year; that Confirmation should be administered only by bishops and not by ministers; and that private baptism and communion should be permitted in cases of grave sickness. (The controversy which had taken place over private baptism at the Hampton Court Conference in 1604 may be remembered.) These apparently moderate requirements seemed to the ministers of the Kirk to be redolent of 'popery', and they were met with vehement opposition. Though the Articles were formally adopted, in deference to the King's desires, by the General Assembly of the Kirk which met at Perth in 1618, the King subsequently recognized the resentment which they had occasioned, and did not enquire too closely into the extent to which they were imposed in practice. Though James had been for many years a non-resident monarch, he was well-attuned to the opinions and prejudices of his countrymen, and he never lost his fine sense of touch in dealing with them. Unfortunately his son Charles I, who in later years sought with more zeal than wisdom to anglicanize the Kirk, lacked the experience to know when he had crossed the limits of implacable prejudice.

James had gone as far as he could in bringing Scotland candles and choristers, and a chamber organ from the Chapel Royal of Whitehall for use in that of Holyroodhouse. 'The organs are come before, and after comes the Mass,' said a Calvinist divine who ought to have known the King better.

But for the most part James was received with a rejoicing which could almost be described as idolatrous. Indeed the flattery of the English Court could yield nothing to that of the orator who welcomed the King when he visited Glasgow: 'Honourable and worthy auditors,' declaimed one William Hay, 'stay your minds and eyes with me, and contemplate here the only Phoenix of the World. Here is that great peacemaker and composer of our mortal – no, immortal – wars. Behold the man who, what neither by wit, nor force, nor blood, could be performed, hath accomplished – made a yoke of lions, united two [of] the most warlike nations of the world....[8]

James was happy to renew his acquaintance with the scenes of his youth, and to receive the adulation of his original subjects, which was offered him with more humility and enthusiasm than it had been during the years when he was struggling to assert his authority over a kingdom grown almost ungovernable during the chaos of the Reformation and its aftermath, and the long turbulence of his own minority. He savoured the fruits of his success in receiving the thankfulness of his subjects for the stability of 'King James's Peace'.

He rode southward again in the late summer, leaving Carlisle at the beginning of August. 'He set off through that wild northern country, which no other English sovereign had passed for centuries.... He was far from the line of Queen Elizabeth's progresses. He went to houses where he would be the only royal visitor, to Wharton Hall and Hornby Castle, which belonged to Monteagle's father old Lord Morley, and Hoghton Tower. He passed through the country of the Pendle witches....'[9]

The King's entourage, ill-attuned to the northern ethos, was thankful to regain the Midlands. One Englishman set down his impressions of Scotland in a disagreeably satirical manner. Sir Anthony Weldon, recently knighted, was one of the Clerks of the

Green Cloth, a member of the department which was responsible for keeping the accounts of the Royal Household.

For the country [wrote Weldon], I must confess it is too good for those that possess it, and too bad for others.... There is great store of fowl – as foul houses and shirts, foul linen, foul dishes and pots, foul trenchers and napkins, with which sort we have been forced to fare....

The country, although it be mountainous, affords no monsters but women.... To be chained in marriage with one of them were as to be tied to a dead carcase and cast into the stinking ditch; formosity or a dainty face are things they dream not of....

And therefore to conclude, the men of old did no more wonder that the great Messias should be born in so poor a town as Bethlem in Judea, as I do wonder that so brave a Prince as King James should be born in so stinking a town as Edinburgh in lousy Scotland....[10]

Weldon wrote a good deal more in the same vein, and unfortunately for him he took it to work with him when he returned to Whitehall, no doubt for the pleasure of sharing his humour with his colleagues, and it was discovered among the records of the Board of Green Cloth. Not surprisingly, Weldon was dismissed, as 'unworthy to eat his bread whose birthright he had so vilely defamed'. But, although the King granted him a compensatory pension, Weldon exacted a revenge which far outweighed his punishment, for he went away to write his famous 'Character' of King James, which was published as anti-royalist propaganda after the Civil Wars, in 1650:

He was [wrote Weldon] of a middle-stature, more corpulent through his clothes than in his body ... his clothes ever being made large and easy, the doublets quilted for stiletto-proof.... He was naturally of a timorous disposition ... his eyes large, ever rolling after any stranger that came in his presence.... His beard was very thin; his tongue too large for his mouth, which ever made him speak full in the mouth, and made him drink very uncomely, as if eating his drink, which came out of the cup at each side of his mouth. His skin was as soft as taffeta sarsnet, which felt so because he never washed his hands, only rubbed his finger-ends slightly with the wet end of a napkin; his legs were very weak, having had, (as was thought), some foul play in his youth ... that weakness made him ever leaning on other men's shoulders; his walk was ever circular, his fingers ever in that walk fiddling about his codpiece....[11]

This description of King James, though it is obviously a caricature, has been accepted (partly through the evil offices of Sir Walter Scott, who based on it his portrayal of the King in *The Fortunes of Nigel*) as an accurate pen-portrait. It has been quoted at the expense of other contemporary descriptions of the King because it is vivid, and it has been quoted regardless of when it was written as though it were a description of the King as he appeared throughout his adult life. However, if a caricature is to have any relevance, it is necessary for it to have a basis of truth, and the truth which Weldon's 'Character' reveals about King James is that when it was written – i.e. after 1617 – he was an ageing, ailing man, who had deteriorated in appearance and in physical capabilities.

A detailed picture of the deterioration of James's health is provided by the case history written by his doctor, Sir Theodore Turquet de Mayerne. Towards the end of the King's life Mayerne wrote a description of his condition, and a summary of the illnesses from which he had suffered. It is worth quoting at some length:

The liver ... is liable to obstructions and generates much bile.... He often swells up with wind.... Sometimes he is melancholy from the spleen in the left hypochondrium exciting disorders ... he becomes very irascible ... often his eyes become yellow but it soon passes off; he glows with heat and his appetite falls off; he sleeps badly; he readily vomits and at times so violently that his face is covered with red spots for two or three days; he sometimes has difficulty in swallowing.... Vapours from his stomach precede illness. The alvine discharge is uncertain.... He sweats easily owing to his delicate skin. He often suffers bruises from knocking against timber, from frequent falls, rubbing of greaves and stirrups and other external causes which he carefully scrutinizes and notes in a book to show to his physicians that it was not from an internal disorder and so avoids having to take medicines which he detests. He is of exquisite sensitiveness and most impatient of pain.

Colic: Very often he laboured under painful colic from flatus (an affliction from which his mother also suffered) ... with vomiting and diarrhoea, preceded by melancholy and nocturnal rigors.

Diarrhoea: He has been liable to diarrhoea all his life, attacks are usually ushered in by lowness of spirits, heavy breathing, dread of everything and other symptoms ... pain in the chest, palpitation, sometimes hiccough. In 1610 his life was in acute danger with persistent vomiting. In

1612 another fit of melancholy with the same symptoms and again in 1615 and subsequent years.

In 1619 the attack was accompanied by arthritic and nephritic pains, he lost consciousness, breathing was laboured, great fearfulness and dejection, pulse intermittent and his life was in danger for eight days. A similar attack in 1623 was followed by lameness and debility.

Nephritis: He often passed urine red like Alicante wine (which are His Majesty's own words) but without attendant pain. In July 1613 blood-red urine with frequent severe vomiting, pain in the left kidney, and other nephritic symptoms. They recurred later in the year and again in 1615 even worse....

Arthritis: Many years ago he had such pain and weakness in the foot that it was left with an odd twist when walking. In 1616 pain and weakness spread to knees, shoulders and hands, and for four months he had to stay in bed or in a chair. Three times in his life he was seized with excruciating pain in his thighs ... which, as if by spasms of the muscles and tendons, most pertinaciously twitched at night. His legs became lean and atrophied due to lack of exercise not calling forth the spirits and nourishment to the lower limbs.[12]

In the joint opinion of Dr Ida Macalpine and Dr Richard Hunter in their monograph entitled *Porphyria, a Royal Malady*, Mayerne's 'observations on James I are so complete that porphyria can be diagnosed'.[13] They advanced the theory that certain members of the Stuart family suffered from the rare hereditary disease of porphyria, which they passed on to their descendant George III, whose sufferings from it were so intolerable that they drove him to apparent insanity. Whether or not the contention that James I suffered from porphyria can be established beyond reasonable doubt, at least Mayerne's graphic descriptions of his sufferings serve to explain some of the details of Weldon's 'Character'. For example, the sensitiveness of James's skin, not a personal preference for uncleanliness, explains his wiping his fingers on a napkin instead of washing his hands, and the onset of arthritis explains his need to walk leaning on other men's shoulders. Some insight into what James suffered at times makes Weldon's caricature of him seem particularly tasteless.

The King's declining health no doubt played a part in forming Buckingham's determination to make his own position unassailably secure. He would have observed that Somerset's neglect to advance any of his relatives had left him isolated at the crisis of his fortunes. Indeed, the only strong alliance which Somerset had formed had been his marriage into the Howard family, and that connection had proved valueless to him since the cause of his disgrace had been the criminal conduct of his wife. At the time of Buckingham's ascent to favour the power of the Howards was like an old and rotten tree – vast in appearance, but frail in reality, and ready to be cut down. Buckingham, who owed his first backing at court to enemies of the Howards, would be instrumental in bringing about their fall when his own power was fully secured.

Buckingham made use of his family to help establish his position. The most influential member of it, himself excluded, was his mother, to whom he was devoted. She had been born Mary Beaumont, and was descended from an impoverished branch of a great mediaeval family. As a young woman she had been a waiting-gentlewoman to her cousin, Lady Beaumont of Coleorton, a situation which contained no great prospect of advancement. But her youthful beauty attracted the attention of a widowed Leicestershire knight, Sir George Villiers, who already had children. He married her, and begot several more. Sir George's eldest son, William, inherited his lands, leaving nothing much for the sons of his second wife, John, Christopher and George. However, George in the days of his good fortune was able to secure for his brothers titles and wealth which their own meagre attainments would never have earned.

John Villiers suffered from periods of insanity, but this did not prevent his being married to Frances, daughter of Sir Edward Coke, and created Viscount Purbeck. Christopher – known as Kit – Villiers flouted more ambitious plans for his marriage by making a love-match with his cousin Elizabeth Sheldon. Though he was not affected by the strain of insanity in his family, he was regarded as little more than an amiable fool; nevertheless, in 1623, the King created him Earl of Anglesey for Buckingham's sake. Buckingham's sister, Susan Villiers, was married to Sir William Feilding, who was created Earl of Denbigh, and their daughter, Lady Margaret Feilding, was married at the age of seven to the Marquis of Hamilton. Anne Brett, a cousin of the Villiers family, was married to

Lionel Cranfield, who was to become Lord Treasurer and Earl of Middlesex.

Buckingham's mother, who enthusiastically acted as a marriage broker, was herself a recipient of a remarkable honour. In 1618 she was created Countess of Buckingham for life. She had been twice married after the death of Sir George Villiers, first to Sir Thomas Rayner and then to Sir William Compton, who survived to witness, though not to share, her good fortune. On her becoming a Countess, Sir William remained a knight; though his step-son's title may have presented a complication, nonetheless his position was humiliating. Sir William was an alcoholic and a nonentity, but as insanity did not debar Purbeck from the peerage, and simplicity did not debar Anglesey, it seems that Sir William was deliberately slighted.

The ennobling of the nucleus of the Villiers family, and the numerous marriages with members of the aristocracy and gentry arranged for all the available single male and female cousins, contributed to securing the position of Buckingham in English society, irrespective of the King's favour. His marriage in 1620 to Lady Katherine Manners, daughter of the Earl of Rutland, completed the process. This effect was quite contrary to that anticipated by the Florentine resident in England, who wrote that it was 'very dangerous for such a powerful courtier to marry at all; in fact a marriage will be taken as evidence of approaching disgrace.'[14] He was obviously thinking of how the fall of Somerset had followed his marriage; but the situation was not analogous. Buckingham's chosen bride was irreproachable, and the only drawback to his choice was the Catholicism of the Manners family. The King required Katherine's conversion, which was achieved by the eloquent arguments of his Welsh chaplain, Dr John Williams, a brilliant and ambitious cleric, whom the King would in due course appoint Lord Keeper and Bishop of Lincoln (he became Archbishop of York in the next reign). No doubt Williams's great abilities would have secured his advancement in any event, but the conversion of Buckingham's future wife was a useful stepping-stone in his career.

Buckingham may have chosen Lady Katherine Manners because the Manners had been the greatest local family in his boyhood, and marriage with one of them would provide him with the most satisfying proof of his success. Or his reasoning may have been that as she was reputedly the richest heiress in England her great wealth would give him the security and independence which he sought. But, whatever his motive, he chose well. Katherine was a rather simple girl, who adored him uncritically, forgave his many infidelities, and wrote to him from the heart when he was absent from her, '... there was never woman loved man as I do you.'[15] In his marriage, as in so many other matters, Buckingham was both wiser and luckier than Somerset.

A further contrast between them was that Buckingham was much more actively ambitious than his predecessor in the King's favour. He wanted to learn the political lessons which the King desired to impart, and he wanted to enjoy the exercise of power. This he achieved, with James's encouragement, until, in the words of Clarendon, he '... entirely disposed of all the offices of the three Kingdoms, without a rival; in dispensing whereof, he was guided more by the rules of appetite than of judgement....'[16]

So complete a control of patronage made Buckingham many enemies, whose harsh verdict is probably echoed in Clarendon's statement; but, though no office ever changed hands without a financial transaction, Buckingham was not devoid of judgement, for he showed a genuine concern to select the right man for the job. His desire to exercise power was infused by a sincere wish to serve the King who was the source of all his fortunes. Undoubtedly his most praiseworthy effort to do so was his attempt to free the King from his perpetual bondage to his debts by urging him to appoint Lionel Cranfield, who since 1613 had been Surveyor General of the Customs, to head a commission to make a full investigation of Government expenditure. Although Cranfield owed his initial appointment to the late Earl of Northampton, and had lately enjoyed the patronage of Bacon, James gave Buckingham full credit for having insisted on his advancement. 'This man', James told the Parliament of 1624, '... made so many projects for my profit that Buckingham fell in liking with him ... and brought him to my service.... I never saw a young courtier that was so careful for the King's profit without any respect as Buckingham was. He found this man so studious for my profit that he backed him against great personages and mean without sparing any man.'[17]

The great personages who suffered from the effects of Cranfield's scrutiny of expenditure were, of course, the Howards. The Lord Treasurer Suffolk, it was discovered, incited by his notoriously avaricious wife, had systematically milked the Treasury of vast sums of money. The Earl and Countess of Suffolk were tried before the Court of Star Chamber, the closing speech for the prosecution being made by Bacon, who had been advanced to the late Lord Ellesmere's office of Lord Chancellor, and raised to the peerage as Baron Verulam. He would rise yet higher to become Viscount St Alban before his own financial misdoings were brought to light, and he to consequent ruin. His prosecution of the Countess of Suffolk was particularly trenchant: he compared her to an exchange woman who kept shop, while her creature Sir J. Bingley cried 'What d'ye lack?' (Sir John was the venal Sub-Treasurer.)

Lord and Lady Suffolk were sentenced to be imprisoned in the Tower during the King's pleasure, and to pay a fine of £30,000. This fine was eventually commuted to a mere £7,000, which showed the King more inclined to mercy than to taking what steps were available to him to recoup his Treasury from the effects of the Suffolks' embezzlement.

Suffolk's son-in-law, Lord Wallingford, was at the same time deprived of his office as Master of the Court of Wards, partly in the course of a general spring-cleaning from office of all Howards and Howard connections, and partly because his wife had been circulating lampoons against Buckingham. James told Lord Wallingford in so many words that this was the principal cause of his dismissal, when he remarked that 'he [Wallingford] had one fault common to him with divers others of his friends and fellows, which could not stand with his service nor [that] of the state, that he was altogether guided and over-ruled by an arch-wife.'[18] Indeed, Lady Suffolk and her daughters Lady Wallingford and Lady Somerset had proved as disastrous a trio of arch-wives as three unfortunate men could have chosen to marry.

Cranfield himself was appointed Master of the Court of Wards, and he replaced the extravagant James Hay as Master of the Wardrobe. Hay had been spending approximately £42,000 a year; Cranfield promised to keep expenditure down to £20,000.[19] In consequence of the many economies which he was able to effect in the Royal Household and other Government departments, in

1620, for the first time in the reign, Government expenditure did not exceed income. However, this achievement was a long way from making the King solvent, for while Suffolk was at the Treasury the King's debts had risen to £900,000.[20]

One member of the Howard family had grown old in office with unimpeachable respectability. Thomas Howard, Earl of Nottingham, the Lord High Admiral and the hero of the Armada, had 'maintained a great calm of dignity unmarred by much intelligence',[21] while the navy had slowly rotted. He resigned without disgrace, and Buckingham was appointed in his place. From 1618 until his death in 1628 the favourite filled the office of Lord High Admiral with enthusiasm and diligence.

Buckingham, according to Dr Lockyer, 'hoped to make some repayment' for the King's favour. 'More than this, by showing his aptitude for the unique position he held, he intended to demonstrate that whatever the means by which he had risen to power, he had, in James's own words, "a brain capable to receive and a bosom trusty to lay up and a person capable to execute any great design of a King".'[22]

CHAPTER FIFTEEN

'Great Combustions'

And surely actions of peace (whatever debauched people say to the contrary) set out a Prince in more orient colours than those of war, and great combustions.

Bishop Williams,
Great Britain's Salomon,
1625

THE KING'S RELATIONSHIP with Buckingham grew ever closer, as the many letters which they exchanged bear witness. When they were apart Buckingham wrote him letters which almost invariably begin 'Dear Dad and Gossip' [i.e. Godfather], and end 'Your Majesty's humble slave and dog'. He signed them with the nick-name which James had bestowed on him: 'Steenie', a diminutive of Stephen, because his face, like Saint Stephen's, resembled the face of an angel.

On one of the many occasions when the King was troubled by lameness, Buckingham wrote to him:

My dear Dad, Gossip and Steward,*
I do not know whether first to express my thanks for your innumerable favours and cares of me, or grief I have to hear you keep your bed, but my comfort is that no other indisposition of health accompanies your lameness, and the time of the year serves so luckily in our absence that by the next [letter] I hope to receive this news, that you are marching upon your well shaped legs again.[1]

His letters were full of private jokes, and sometimes serious reassurances of love, which, always when Buckingham was absent, James must have craved.

All and the least I can say is this: that I naturally so love your person,

* 'Steward' is a pun on the King's surname, and the fact that like a good steward he looked after Buckingham's material interests.

and upon so good experience and knowledge adore all your other parts, which are more than ever one man had, that were not only all your people but all the world besides set together on one side, and you alone on the other, I should to obey and please you, displease, nay despise all [of] them....[2]

The King, Buckingham declared, wrote to him in a style 'of more tenderness than fathers have of children, of more friendship than between equals, and more affection than between lovers in the best kind, man and wife'. On his side, James frequently began his letters to Buckingham 'My only sweet and dear child' and addressed him as 'Sweet Heart' and 'Sweet child and wife'.[3] It was a correspondence in which the languages of familial and sexual love were unself-consciously blended.

While Buckingham became a substitute son and an object of intense love to James, it was a matter of anxiety to him that Prince Charles held himself aloof from the favourite, and on occasion quarrelled with him in public. Charles, who had been created Prince of Wales in 1616, was obviously of increasing importance in Court and kingdom as the King declined in health. He was intensely shy and reserved, and undoubtedly jealous of Buckingham's intimacy with his father, even if he was unsuspecting concerning the nature of it. James had no wish to witness a repetition of the enmity which Prince Henry had shown towards Robert Carr. He adopted a very simple device to make his son and his favourite become friends: he held a feast to inaugurate an era of friendship between them. Rather surprisingly, it was successful. Buckingham displayed his usual skill in falling in with the King's wishes, and Charles was anxious to show himself a dutiful son. But a relationship which began in obedience soon ripened in sincerity. Presently, Charles started to use the nickname 'Steenie' in his communications with Buckingham, and when on one occasion he offended his father, he did not hesitate to write to Buckingham imploring him to put matters right:

... I pray you commend my most humble service to his Majesty, and tell him that I am very sorry that I have done any thing [which] may offend him, and that I will be content to have any penance inflicted upon me, so he may forgive me, although I had never a thought nor never shall have to displease him, yet I deserve to be punished for my ill-

fortune. So hoping never to have occasion to write to you of so ill a subject again, but of many better, I rest, your true, constant, loving friend,
Charles P[4]

It is evident, as Dr Lockyer has observed, that Charles 'accepted Buckingham as a member of the royal family, and found in him not only the company he had hitherto lacked but also a replacement for his lost elder brother'.[5]

By 1620, when Charles was twenty years old and Buckingham was twenty-eight, the age difference between them was less apparent than it would have been when Buckingham was first introduced at Court. Then Charles had been a miserably shy boy and the favourite a dazzling and self-confident youth; thereafter, when they were both adult young men, the friendship between them became a strong bond. It became, as has been previously stated, the strongest friendship which Charles ever experienced; and for Buckingham it was certainly a more congenial type of relationship than the emotional bond which he successfully sustained with King James. However, Buckingham was wise enough to remember that if he had not been the old King's favourite, he would never have been in a position to become the friend of the Prince of Wales.

James had spent his early life in striving to impose order upon his turbulent inheritance, and his middle years in attempting to respond intelligently to the challenge of an unknown kingdom. By 1618 he was tiring, and it would have been an appropriate reward, at the conclusion of a long reign, which stretched back beyond the beginning of his memory, if he could have been allowed to yield to the inertia which he was now beginning to experience, and to live his last years in peace. This reward was not to be permitted him.

The dragons' teeth which had been sown before the marriage of the Princess Elizabeth to the Elector Palatine had been growing quietly during the intervening years, and their crop of armed men began to appear on the battlefields of Europe during the last years of James's reign. A King who had chosen the personal motto '*Beati Pacifici*' had no choice but to attempt to play the part which that motto indicated; but the greatest of James's difficulties arose from the fact that the marriage alliances which he had designed for peace had been made or were being sought with families which furnished the protagonists in the Thirty Years' War. His diplomacy as a peacemaker would be severely hampered by his involvement.

In 1617 the childless Holy Roman Emperor, Matthias, who also held the electoral throne of Bohemia, instructed the Bohemian Estates to nominate his cousin, the Archduke Ferdinand of Styria, as his successor on the Bohemian throne. The very disunity of Bohemian interests, and the existence of an imperial 'Letter of Majesty' guaranteeing toleration to various forms of Protestantism within the country, enabled Matthias to impose his will on the Estates. Lutherans, Calvinists and Utraquists[6] relied on the 'Letter of Majesty' to secure their rights of worship against the known militant Catholicism of the Archduke Ferdinand. A year later all but the Catholic element in the country had thought better of the nomination, the Bohemian opinion of the Imperial vice-regency was shown when the Emperor's deputies, Count Martinitz and Count Slavata, with their secretary, were thrown out of a window of the Hardschin Palace in Prague. Though they survived, as a result of their fortunate landing on a pile of rotting filth, the so-called 'Defenestration of Prague' had long-term results which contrasted savagely with the farcical character of the incident.

The Protestant rebels in Bohemia appealed to Protestant rulers all over Europe to come to their aid. The Lutheran Electors of Saxony and Brandenburg declined to interfere. They were not dissatisfied with the *status quo* within the Empire, according to which a fairly lightly imposed Imperial authority allowed the individual Princes of the Empire to decide the official religion within their principalities. If they aided the Bohemian Protestants against the Emperor, they would risk the disruption of a system which worked to their own advantage. However, the Elector Palatine, influenced by the large ambitions of his adviser Christian of Anhalt, sent an army into Bohemia, commanded by an able *condottiere*, Ernst von Mansfeld, who captured the Catholic stronghold of Pilsen, and for the time being saved Bohemia from Imperial reconquest.

The Spanish Crown was in the long run bound to assist Imperial interests, for the Imperial and Spanish Hapsburgs were closely intermarried and traditionally interdependent. But at this juncture Spain did not desire to become involved in a war in Bohemia, because in 1621 the truce with the United Provinces would expire, bringing the renewal of war in the Netherlands. The crumbling Spanish economy made war on two fronts a perilous eventuality. An unofficial Spanish suggestion that English arbitration would be welcome between the Emperor and the Bohemian rebels was thankfully accepted by James, who appointed James Hay, now Lord Doncaster, to head a peace-making mission. It has been customary to deprecate this appointment, on the grounds of Doncaster's notorious extravagance and his taste for personal ostentation; yet, in a period when ostentation was not considered a fault in a nobleman, Doncaster, whose shrewdness had been proved by his capacity to survive all the scandals and crises of the Jacobean Court, may have been a better choice than the failure of his efforts suggests. The unhappy truth was that the European problem was already too widespread and too profound to be amenable to the good offices of a single peace-making mission.

On 18 August 1619 the Emperor Matthias died, and Ferdinand of Styria was elected as the Emperor Ferdinand II. His election demonstrates how strong was the influence of tradition, and also how disorganized was opposition to the continuance of the Hapsburg rule.

A few days before the Imperial election, the Estates of Bohemia offered the crown of their country to the Elector Palatine. Their hope was that he would be able to defend Bohemia from the expected Imperial counter-attack by the combined strength of the allies who could be expected to come to his aid: the Princes of the Evangelical Union, and the King of Great Britain.

Central European politicians were as ignorant of James's views in 1619 as James had been of the situation which would lead to the present crisis when he had arranged his daughter's marriage in 1613. James's presupposition that the marriage would assist in preserving the peace of Europe had proved mistaken; equally mistaken was the belief of the Bohemian Protestants that James would show more dedication to the maintenance of their religion in Bohemia if his son-in-law were on the throne than he would show to the preservation of international peace.

Frederick suffered agonies of indecision over the Bohemian offer. He sent his Ambassador, Baron Dohna, to London to consult King

James. But, probably over-persuaded by Christian of Anhalt and by Elizabeth, who is said to have encouraged him with the assertion that she would rather eat sauerkraut with a king than roast meat with an Elector, Frederick did not wait for James's answer to his request for advice. In September he secretly informed the Bohemian Estates that he would accept the crown.

James would have advised Frederick to refuse it. He had had time to observe how precarious a matter the maintenance of European peace would be, and every conviction which was most dear to him committed him to an attempt to preserve it. Furthermore, he believed that Ferdinand was the rightful King of Bohemia, as the acknowledged successor of Matthias, and as the representative of the dynasty which held the Empire and the Bohemian throne in conjunction. He had more respect for the principles of lawful monarchy than for considerations of co-religionism, if the latter implied rebellion and usurpation.

When James received the news of Frederick's acceptance he was justifiably incensed that his advice had been sought and not awaited. He condemned the folly of Frederick's decision, and told Baron Dohna that if trouble followed, Frederick must expect no assistance from England. His subjects, he said, were as dear to him as his children, and therefore he would not 'embark them in an unjust and needless quarrel'.[7]

On 2 March 1619, Anne of Denmark died. For some time she had been suffering from dropsy, and her death was not unexpected. She died too early in the year to know that her son-in-law, whose rank had been so great a disappointment to her, would, after all, make her daughter a Queen. Regardless of James's disapproval, Anne would have rejoiced.

Though Anne had been converted to Catholicism long ago in Scotland, and had been sufficiently constant in her newly professed religion to refuse the Anglican Holy Communion at her English coronation in 1603, her religious enthusiasm had waned during the ensuing years. It appears that she died without the last rites of the Catholic Church. The day before her death she was visited by Archbishop Abbott, who was later reported to have requested her to disavow certain specifically Catholic beliefs with the words:

'Madam, we hope your Majesty does not trust to your own merits, nor to the merits of the saints, but only to the blood and merits of Our Saviour.'

The Queen is reported to have replied: 'I renounce the mediation of saints and my own merits, and only rely on my Saviour Christ, who has redeemed my soul by His blood.'[8]

This sounds more like a fictitious account of the Queen's end, written for the edification of Protestants, than a genuine report of a death-bed recantation of Catholicism. It seems far more likely to be true that Anne refused to believe that she was dying, and though Prince Charles asked her to make a will, which she had never done, put off the task until a tomorrow which brought her end. Certainly she died intestate, and her jewels and an unspecified sum of money were stolen by two of her servants. Prince Charles was with his mother when she died; but James himself was ill, at Theobalds.

Shortly after Anne's death he entered his most dangerous illness, later described by Mayerne, during which his life was in danger for eight days.[9] After his recovery James, who seldom wrote poetry during his later years, was moved to compose an epitaph for Anne, inspired by the fact that a comet was visible at the time, a sign which was commonly believed to presage the death of princes:

> Thee to invite, the great God sent His star,
> Whose friends and nearest kin good princes are,
> Who, though they run the race of men and die,
> Death serves but to refine their majesty.
> So did my Queen from hence her court remove,
> And left off earth* to be enthroned above.
> She's changed, not dead, for sure no good prince dies,
> But, as the sun, sets only for to rise.[10]

Anne's body lay in state for ten weeks, while money was found to pay for a fittingly lavish funeral. On 13 May she was buried in Westminster Abbey, with Charles attending as chief mourner.

On 1 June King James returned to London, and rode through the city clad in a suit of pale blue satin, and wearing a hat with blue and white feathers. He was received with great enthusiasm,

* earth i.e. flesh.

and the whole scene perplexed and embarrassed an embassy of condolence which arrived at the same time, sent by the Duke of Lorraine. It was explained to the twenty-four members of the embassy, who were clad in unrelieved black, that England had thrown off mourning for the late Queen, to celebrate the King's recovery of his health.

This episode suggests a mood of callousness which James was probably far from feeling. He and his wife had grown apart, and consequently his epitaph for her does not express an intense experience of grief; it conveys a natural sadness, tempered by a philosophical acceptance of her mortality. Yet, though the statement 'she's changed, not dead' was grounded in faith, the kind of change which implied physical dissolution was not one which James could contemplate with equanimity. Perhaps he celebrated his return to health in an attempt to banish the sombre realization that sooner or later he would have to keep the one appointment which no-one can avoid.

However, with his elder son gone, his wife gone, and the ministers who had served him since the beginning of the reign leaving the world one after another, James was probably led to experience a new sense of urgency in the matter of Prince Charles's marriage. It was important that the succession should be assured in the children of Charles, for if James himself should die, as it had recently been feared that he might, or if Charles should succumb to some sickness or injury before he begot an heir, then the succession would go to Elizabeth and her children, and England would be engulfed in the storm which was about to overwhelm Europe.

The outbreak of the Thirty Years' War is customarily dated from the Bohemian gesture of defiance against the Hapsburg rule, the 'Defenestration of Prague'; but the change from local revolt to general war only became irrevocable with the acceptance by the Elector Palatine of the Bohemian crown.

Frederick, with his pregnant wife, reached Prague in the autumn of 1619, to be received with scenes of wild rejoicing. The streets were vivid with hangings of blue and silver; red and white wine danced in the fountains, and refreshed the throats of a populace parched with cheering; Frederick and Elizabeth scattered new-minted coins bearing the legend 'God and the Estates gave me the Crown'.[11] In December Elizabeth gave birth to a son, who was immediately given the title of Duke of Lusatia, one of the provinces of the kingdom. In later years, when the source of that title was lost, he became famous as Prince Rupert of the Rhine.

The rejoicing in Prague was echoed in England. Frederick was seen as 'the Protestant David going forth to attack the Catholic Goliath',[12] and it was a further cause for enthusiasm that his venture was making the Princess of Great Britain Queen of Bohemia. James, with his wiser view of the situation, did not share the general rejoicing, and he refused to accord his son-in-law the title of King, lest he should seem to be giving his approval to an act of usurpation.

In the meantime the Emperor Ferdinand had not been inactive. By skilful diplomacy with Spain, the Spanish Netherlands and Bavaria, he organized simultaneous invasions of Bohemia and the Palatinate. Maximilian of Bavaria, to whom Ferdinand secretly promised the transfer of Frederick's electorship in return for his co-operation, invaded Bohemia; and Ambrogio Spinola, who had begun to amass forces as soon as he knew of Frederick's acceptance of the Bohemian crown, invaded the Palatinate, acting 'in the knowledge that if he conquered Frederick's lands on the Rhine, a share of them would fall to Spain, and that the Protestant barrier between the source of his military power [northern Italy] and his objective [access to the United Provinces] would be obliterated'.[13] In this way Ferdinand's orchestration of Imperial, Spanish and Bavarian interests vastly enlarged the scope of the war.

During August and September Spinola over-ran the Palatinate, and as autumn drew on Maximilian of Bavaria, with his own army commanded by a renowned general, Count Tilly, and with a supporting force of Imperialist troops, entered Bohemia. On 8 November, four days after the anniversary of Frederick's coronation, they routed the Bohemian forces at the Battle of the White Hill, outside Prague. Frederick and Elizabeth were obliged to flee from their capital under cover of darkness, and from that disastrous night they remained a crownless royal pair, 'the Winter King and Queen' whose reign had extended only from one winter to the next. Frederick found his refuge in pious resignation: 'I commended all to God,' he told his wife. 'He gave it me, He has taken it away, He can give it me again, blessed be His name.'[14]

Frederick's father-in-law did not share this view. Much as James had disapproved of Frederick's acquisition of the Crown of Bohemia, he did not regard Ferdinand's method of retaliation as any more justified. In the summer of 1620, when Spinola first threatened the Palatinate, James had permitted a force of English volunteers under the general command of Sir Horace Vere to go to the defence of Frederick's hereditary lands. On arrival in Germany, Vere divided his force, which was little more than two thousand strong, into three parts, to defend three key strongholds: Vere himself occupied Mannheim, Sir John Burroughs occupied Frankenthal, and Sir Gerard Herbert went to Frederick's capital of Heidelberg.

James had held back from sending Frederick the help for which the Bohemian estates had hoped, and the German princes, from whom support had also been expected had proved no more eager to provide it. But once the Bohemian catastrophe had occurred, the situation appeared to James to be more straightforward: Frederick was no longer occupying an usurped throne, and his own usurped possessions ought to be restored to him. The presence of the English volunteers in the Palatinate provided James with a toe-hold there, should war on Frederick's behalf become desirable, necessary, or unavoidable. But, since they were volunteers, their presence did not commit James to war: they could be disavowed or reinforced as advantage served.

In the autumn of 1620 James decided to summon a Parliament for the New Year. It would be seven years since the Addled Parliament had been dissolved, and James might not have summoned another had he not needed the money to finance a possible war. He was again in poor health when Parliament met on 30 January 1621. He was carried into the House in a portative chair, and some who saw him doubted that he would walk again.

In his opening speech to the assembled Parliament James acknowledged both the threat of war and the need for money, and in speaking of his own efforts to keep the peace, he made a gracious reference to the achievements of Elizabeth I:

I will not say that I have governed as well as she did, but I may say we have had as much peace in our time as in hers. I have laboured as a woman in travail, not ten months but ten years, for within that time I have not had a Parliament nor subsidy [this was to dismiss the existence of the Addled Parliament, which had neither passed legislation nor granted taxation], and, I dare say I have been as sparing to trouble you not with monopolies or in subsidies as ever King before me, considering the greatness of my occasions and charges.[15]

Here, unfortunately, James was at odds with the opinion represented in Parliament, for the session was characterized by a violent attack on monopolies led by Sir Edward Coke. In view of the fact that Coke had recently made assiduous efforts to recover the royal favour – to the extent of forcing his very unwilling daughter to marry John Villiers – had regained his place on the Privy Council in 1617, and had subsequently been appointed to the reforming Treasury commission, his role as an opponent of monopolies in this Parliament is difficult to explain.

He may have had a real detestation of monopolies, on principle disapproving of the granting to individuals of exclusive rights of manufacture or trade in specific commodities. Or he may have realized that the House of Commons was excited by a violent resentment of the Government's profiting from the granting of monopolies, and that it might become out of control unless he himself assumed it. In the event, the Commons expended its fury on two comparatively minor offenders, Sir Francis Mitchell and Sir Giles Mompesson, without directly attacking Buckingham.

Buckingham indeed required shielding from parliamentary wrath, for 'while he thought of himself – with some reason – as a champion of reform, the majority of people regarded him as the principal obstacle in the way of its achievement'.[16] He had undoubtedly profited through the arranging of grants of monopolies to his kinsmen, and this knowledge proved very combustible fuel for the fires of his enemies' resentment.

However, the campaign against the monopolists, manipulated by Coke, by-passed Buckingham and was next directed against the 'referees', whose function was to authorize the granting of patents of monopoly. One of them was Francis Bacon, who was accused, not in this connection but in his judicial capacity, of taking bribes.

He pleaded guilty to the charge of corruption, and on 3 May, without standing trial, he was sentenced to be fined £40,000, to be imprisoned in the Tower during the King's pleasure, and there after to be debarred from office, and to be banished from the Court.

The fall of Bacon has led to much controversy concerning his moral character. That so great a man should have fallen in so squalid a fashion has distressed admirers of his brilliant intellect. However, he was an Elizabethan and Jacobean courtier and high officer of state, besides being a Renaissance philosopher. He had the faults of the public men of his day. The parts that he had played in the trials of Essex and Somerset illustrated that he was not high-minded in the pursuit of his own ambition: he would seek advancement through the downfall of men to whom he had paid court in their time of glory. He was, despite the brilliance of his mind, a time-server in his official career.

S.R. Gardiner's comment on his sentence is a chantable apologia: 'He laid himself open to the criticism of the moralist by fancying that integrity of heart might be left to its own guidance',[17] by which is meant, presumably, that he accepted bribes but did not permit them to affect his decisions. The famous comment of John Aubrey is probably nearer to the opinion of Bacon's own contemporaries: 'He was a *παιδεραστής* [pederast]. His Ganymedes and favourites took bribes; but his lordship always gave judgment *secundum aequum et bonum* [according as was just and good]. His decrees in Chancery stand firm.'[18]

King James, in this as in so many other instances, mitigated the penalties. No doubt he understood the temptations to which Bacon had been subjected, for he said of himself, 'In giving pardons, I do always suppose myself in the offender, and then judge how far the like occasion might have tempted me.'[19]

Parliament was adjourned in June 1621, after it had voted the King two subsidies, which brought in £145,000, and the Commons had made a declaration of their willingness to fight for the Elector Palatine, if the King's diplomacy on his behalf did not regain him his lands. But two subsidies would not finance much fighting, as Sir Edwin Sandys was aware when he remarked, 'If we go to the Palatinate, a million will not discharge the army.'

James recalled Parliament on 20 November, in the hope of receiving further grants of taxation, in case military measures should be required, and also to illustrate that, if he were forced to make war, he would only be doing so as a result of Parliamentary pressure. His reputation as a *rex pacificus* would require such pressure to be publicly apparent. Not all who were in favour of war wanted that war to be fought in Europe; some desired to influence European events by fighting the Spaniards at sea in the Elizabethan manner, financed by privateering and not taxation. They shared the opinion of John Chamberlain, that 'a war of diversion' would be best, 'and not to stand pottering and pelting in the Palatinate only to consume both our men and means'.[20] However, Parliament granted James one more subsidy, at the same time petitioning him for war with Spain and for the marriage of Prince Charles to a Princess of his own religion.

The King, constant in his determination to retain diplomacy and marriage negotiations as his personal responsibility, accused the Commons of encroaching on 'matters far beyond their reach and capacity'. The Commons declared that freedom of speech was their 'ancient and undoubted right'; to which James replied that they enjoyed it not by right but through his grace. This collision led to the Commons drawing up a protestation of their rights on 18 December. James thereupon prorogued Parliament, and tore the protestation out of the Commons' Journal with his own hands, before ordering the dissolution of Parliament.

> James had shown astonishing violence, but, perhaps because such violence was not typical of the man, it had no marked long-term effects, and to regard any of these events as tending towards revolution is teleological. In the next Parliament they were forgotten.... Parliament had done good reformist work on monopolies and had voted taxation; the stalemate that had persisted since 1610 was broken....[21]

While the English Parliament was occupied in the pursuit of monopolists, King Philip III of Spain lay on his deathbed. He sent for his son and daughter. To the latter he said: 'Maria, I am sorry that I must die before I have married you; but your brother will take care of that.' To his son, who was about to become Philip IV, he said: 'Prince, do not forsake her till you have made her an empress.'[22]

His dying command was eventually obeyed, when the Infanta Maria was married to the Emperor's son, the future Ferdinand III. In the meantime, her marriage to Prince Charles continued to be the subject of negotiation. In Spain it was always regarded as an undesirable alternative to the customary union of a Spanish Princess with a member of the House of Austria. In England, though the prospect of a Spanish Queen was unpopular, and the religious difficulties were very great, King James had strong reasons for his pertinacity in attempting to conclude the Spanish match. He was eager to see the English succession assured as swiftly as possible, and though his debts had continued to grow despite Cranfield's recent efforts, the Infanta's dowry would still repay a large proportion of them.

In 1620 James's hopes received new encouragement when Count Gondomar arrived in England for his second period as resident Ambassador. His ambition to see Prince Charles and the Infanta married complemented that of the King, though his reasons were different. He hoped to gain glory through the conversion of the Prince of Wales as a concomitant of the marriage, and through the repeal of the penal laws against the English Catholics. If these two purposes were achieved, with the accession of Charles to his father's throne the conversion of England would follow. While there is very little evidence that these views were held at the Spanish Court, it was from Gondomar that the suggestion first came that Prince Charles should visit Spain to conclude the marriage alliance in person. In Spain he might succumb to the conversion which he would resist in England.

Before the death of Philip III James had told Gondomar, 'I give you my word, as a King, as a gentleman, as a Christian, and as an honest man, that I have no wish to marry my son to anyone except your master's daughter and that I desire no alliance but that of Spain.'[23] This resolution was fortified when James conceived the idea that through a Spanish alliance he might make use of Spanish influence to secure the restoration of the Elector Palatine to his hereditary lands. His hope was that Spain would exert pressure on the Emperor to relinquish his hold upon the Palatinate, and restore both the territory and the electorship to Frederick.

The proposals were not unacceptable in Spain, though the pawn in this diplomacy which Spain preferred was a malleable child, Frederick's eldest son, Prince Frederick Henry, who, it was suggested, should be sent to Vienna for his education, and later married to an Austrian Archduchess. Upon his marriage, the Palatinate should be restored to him, and, after the death of Maximilian of Bavaria, the electorship. The conversion of Frederick Henry was tacitly considered to be an integral part of this scheme.

While James apparently did not recognize that the Spaniards hoped to achieve the conversion of his own son, he was quick to perceive that the conversion of Frederick Henry was intended. He proposed that if the young Prince were sent to Vienna, he should be accompanied by Protestant tutors, to safeguard his faith.[24] This proposal could not be attractive to either Spanish or Imperial interests, but Spain attempted to gild the pill of Frederick Henry's change of religion with the suggestion that Frederick himself, while his son resided in Vienna, should be permitted to administer his former lands in Frederick Henry's name, and that should Maximilian of Bavaria predecease him, the electorship should be restored to him.

These proposals and counter-proposals were brushed away like the cobwebs which they possibly resembled when Frederick signified his inflexible determination not to recover anything which he had lost through compromise. Once again, he was probably inspired by Elizabeth, in whom the spirit of compromise had never found a habitation, and who, in consequence, throughout a long life, was to find herself playing the role of a loser.

While Europe was gradually engulfed in a conflict which would last for a generation, James still sought to be an international peacemaker. Perhaps it is the greatest memorial of his genuine desire for peace that he sought to enlist the aid of Pope Gregory XV, to whom he wrote on the last day of September 1622:

Most Holy Father,

Your holiness will perhaps marvel that we, differing from you in point of religion, should now first salute you with our letters. Howbeit, such is the trouble of our minds for these calamitous discords and bloodsheds, which for these years bypast have so miserably rent the Christian world; and so great is our care and daily solicitude to stop the course of these growing evils betimes (so much as in us lies) as we could no longer abstain, considering that we all worship the same most blessed Trinity, nor hope for salvation by any other means than by the blood and merits of our Lord and Saviour, Jesus Christ. But we break this silence to move your holiness, by these our letters, friendly and seriously, that you would be pleased, together with us, to put your hand to so pious a work, and so worthy of a Christian prince....[25]

This letter, ineffective though the appeal proved to be, was an action of peace which, to borrow Bishop Williams's words, sets out James's reputation 'in more orient colours' than those of his fellow potentates, who were responsible for the 'great combustions'.

CHAPTER SIXTEEN

The Dormition of Solomon

Dormivit Salomon – Solomon slept

Bishop Williams,
Great Britain's Salomon,
1625

WITH A SENSE of liberation, and in a mood of high adventure, the brothers Jack and Tom Smith rode towards Dover on 18 February 1623. In the distance they saw a stately cavalcade approaching. The Ambassador of the Spanish Netherlands was riding to London, escorted by King James's Master of Ceremonies, Sir Lewis Lewkenor, and by the Lieutenant of Dover Castle, Sir Henry Mainwaring. The brothers Smith swerved off the road, and galloped across country to avoid encountering the procession. Sir Henry Mainwaring sent a message back to Canterbury, ordering the arrest of two horsemen who had been seen behaving suspiciously. When Jack and Tom Smith reached Canterbury they ran into the arms of the law. Tom Smith thereupon took off his false beard, and told the Mayor of Canterbury that he was the Marquis of Buckingham, and that he was on his way incognito to inspect the navy. Jack Smith, who allowed his brother to do the talking, was the Prince of Wales. Ill concealed by their absurdly unimaginative false names and equally unrealistic false beards, the King's son and favourite were on their way to Spain.

King James celebrated their adventure in a pastoral poem, in which Britain was Arcadia, and himself the presiding deity, Pan:

What sudden change hath darked of late
The glory of the Arcadian state?
The fleecy flocks refuse to feed,
The lambs to play, the ewes to breed;
  The altars smoke, the offerings burn,
  Till Jack and Tom do safe return.

The Spring neglects her course to keep
The air with mighty storms doth weep;
The pretty birds disdain to sing,
The meads to swell, the woods to spring;
  The mountains droop, the fountains mourn,
  Till Jack and Tom do safe return.

What may it be that moves this woe?
Whose want affects Arcadia so?
The hope of Greece, the prop of arts,
Was Princely Jack, the joy of hearts!
  And Tom was to our royal Pan
  The chiefest swain, and truest man.

The lofty trees of Menalus
Did shake with wind from Hesperus,
Whose sweet delicious air did fly
Through all the bounds of Arcadie.
  Which moved a vein in Jack and Tom
  To see the coast it issued from.

The wind was love, which princes stout
To pages turn[s]; but who can doubt,
Where equal fortune love procures
And equal love success assures,
  But venturous Jack will bring to Greece
  The best of prize, the Golden Fleece.*

Love is a world of many Spains,
Where coldest hills and hottest plains,
With barren rocks and fertile fields
By turns despair and comfort yields;
  But who can doubt of prosperous luck
  Where love and fortune doth conduct?

Thy grandsire, go[o]dsire, father too,
Were thine examples so to do;
Their brave attempts in heat of love
France, Scotland, Denmark, did approve;
  So Jack and Tom do nothing new
  When love and fortune they pursue.

* The mythological golden fleece represents the Order of the Golden Fleece, the highest honour bestowed by the King of Spain, and so, by analogy, the Infanta herself.

Kind shepherds that have loved them long,
Be not too rash in censuring wrong;
Correct your fears, leave off to mourn,
The heavens shall favour their return!
Commit the care to royal Pan
Of Jack his son, and Tom his man.[1]

This light verse does not conceal the King's underlying anxiety. Indeed, he had experienced the greatest reluctance in yielding to the Prince's desire to go to Spain. Buckingham, who was resolved to accompany Charles, pressed the King determinedly for his consent, and suggested that they should take with them Sir Francis Cottington, who had served as an envoy in Spain and therefore had knowledge of the country. James, forced into reluctant agreement, sent for Cottington and asked his opinion of the projected journey, in Charles's and Buckingham's presence.

'Cottington,' he said, 'here is Baby Charles and Steenie, who have a great mind to go by post into Spain to fetch home the Infanta, and will have but two more in their company, and have chosen you for one. What think you of the journey?'

Cottington was placed in a very difficult position, for he did not want to offend the Prince or Buckingham, and yet he did not want to give the King a false impression of the situation as he saw it. Courageously, he gave his true opinion, which was that once the Spaniards had the Prince in their hands, they would use his almost hostage-like position at the Spanish Court to make new and exorbitant demands on behalf of the English Catholics. At this, King James flung himself on his bed, and cried out in an agony of apprehension: 'I told you this before!'

Buckingham turned savagely on Cottington, and accused him of having given the King a presumptuous answer, for all that the King had desired to know from him was the condition of the roads.

'Nay, by God, Steenie, you are much to blame to use him so!' exclaimed James, angered by Buckingham's deliberate perversion of his words. 'He answered me directly to the question I asked him, and very honestly and wisely....'[2]

However, the King was persuaded, much against his better judgement, to let them go; and Cottington, who was to be proved right by events in Spain, met the Prince and the favourite at Dover. They were also accompanied by Endymion Porter, later a favoured courtier of Charles I, who at this time was Buckingham's secretary for Spanish correspondence. He was a quarter Spanish, and would be useful as an interpreter not only of the language but also of Spanish mentality and customs.

Charles and Buckingham intended to travel incognito all the way to Spain, which was why they took only the two companions. Their departure from England was supposed to be secret, but it was very speedily known as a result of the incident on the Dover road, as a letter written by the King on 26 February makes plain:

> My Sweet Boys, and dear venturous knights, worthy to be put in a new romance,
>
> I thank you for your comfortable letters, but, alas, think it not possible that you can be many hours undiscovered, for your parting was so blown abroad that day ye came to Dover....
>
> I sent Doncaster to the French King, with a short letter of my own hand to ... acquaint him with my son's passing, unknown, through his country; and this I have done for fear that, upon the first rumour of your passing, he should take a pretext to stop you; and therefore, Baby Charles, ye shall do well how soon ye come to ... Spain, to write a courteous excuse of your hasty passage to the French King, and send a gentleman with it, if by any means ye may spare any....
>
> Your poor old dad is lamer than ever he was, and writes all this out of his naked bed. God Almighty bless you both, my sweet boys, and send you a safe happy return....
>
> James R.[3]

James was bravely making the best of a situation which in reality worried him very much indeed. The journey would be full of natural hazards, besides the dangers of the political situation which would arise through the presence of the Prince of Wales in Spain. James could extract some comfort from the fact that he himself had insisted on sailing secretly from Scotland in 1589, to bring home his bride from Denmark; that his father, Lord Darnley, had gone to Scotland from England to pay court to his mother, Mary, Queen of Scots, when she was a young widow; and that his grandfather, King James V of Scotland, had travelled incognito to France and had induced a very reluctant King François I to allow him to marry his daughter Madeleine.

None of these situations was perfectly analogous, for James himself had been already married to Anne of Denmark by proxy; Darnley had wooed a sovereign Queen who was free to make her own choice of whom she would marry; and James v had won the French King's daughter before the Reformation, so that the religious issue had not existed to complicate the conditions of marriage. However, his marriage provided the nearest parallel to Charles's adventure, and the most encouraging, in that it showed that personal contact could succeed where formal diplomacy had failed.

Charles was not acting in a wholly impetuous and foolish manner in insisting upon going to Spain. Had there been no precedents, no persuasions would have made James amenable to the proposition that he should go. But in northern Europe the convention that an impassioned suitor should present himself before his bride with every appearance of impetuous informality was a well-established ritual of royal wooing, which made it occasionally possible to cut a Gordian knot in diplomacy. However, neither the ritual nor its underlying purpose had a counterpart at the Spanish Court, which was unparalleled for the rigidity of its protocol. This, Charles would discover during his months in Spain.

When King James lay in bed writing the first of many letters to the son whom he still called by his childhood nickname, he was complaining of a condition which was not likely to improve, although, after his illness of 1621, when he had been carried to the opening of Parliament, he had at least regained the use of his legs, contrary to the expectations of some spectators.

In 1621 Daniel Mytens painted the last official portrait of the King, which shows him seated, wearing his Garter robes. It is an informal portrait, in that the King is shown bare-headed, sitting relaxed in his chair, with his plumed hat on the table beside him, and without the symbols of regality. But it is an impressive portrayal of worn-out authority. James's hands hang over the arms of his chair, their drooping posture eloquent of the weariness of his spirit. His face is devoid of the vigour which animates the portraits painted of him in middle age. His expression is sombre, his gaze detached, and his tired eyes beneath their heavy lids are sunk far back in the sockets. He has the face of a man who has suffered a great deal, and who could be much older than his fifty-five years.

Some people thought that James himself was at least partly to blame for his ill-health. According to the medical opinion of the time his diet was very ill-advised. He ate too much and too fast when he came in hungry from hunting, and he suffered from consequential indigestion. Also, as the uncharitable Sir Anthony Weldon recorded: 'It is true, he drank very often, which was rather out of a custom than any delight, and his drink was of that kind of strength as Frontinack, Canary, High Country wine, Tent wine, and Scottish ale, that had he not had a very strong brain, might have been daily overtaken. . . .'[4] Of his drinking habits Dr Maurice Ashley has more kindly remarked: 'He could not bear pain – who can? – and for that reason he drank more than before, no doubt in the hope that it was a soporific. This accelerated the decline of his health.'[5]

Bishop Goodman draws attention to the fact that King James ate a great deal of soft fruit, which would probably have worsened the diarrhoea from which he so frequently suffered:

> I think that King James every autumn (of his last years) did feed a little more than moderately upon fruits; he had his grapes, his nectarines and other fruits in his own keeping, besides we did see that he fed very plentifully on them from abroad. I remember that Mr French of the Spicery, who sometimes did present him with the first strawberries, cherries and other fruits and kneeling to the King had some speech to use to him . . . but the King never had patience to hear him one word, but his hand was in the basket.[6]

Sir John Oglander, who was only slightly acquainted with him, had heard that 'a sheep's head, well boiled, and the flesh taken off and broiled, with butter for the sauce . . . was King James's dish'.[7] This, if truly reported, was a simple and harmless taste; perhaps the ordinariness of it might have made it appeal to the King, in contrast to the exotic dishes served at the Court banquets, such as that cold pie containing 'ambergris, magisterial of pearl, musk, etc.', which was so unpleasant in its effects.*

The ailing King, especially during the absence of Charles and Buckingham, was cosseted by the ladies of the Villiers family. Buckingham's mother, who, in Archbishop Mathew's judgement, 'would

* *vide supra*, p. 85.

hardly have come into the King's life had the Queen been still alive ... fulfilled a double function as a middle-aged gossip and as a nurse'.[8] Surprisingly, James, who had shown so little taste for feminine company throughout his life, became warmly attached to the Countess of Buckingham, and to Buckingham's wife, whom he called his daughter. He also grew touchingly fond of Buckingham's daughter Mary, who was known as Mall, and who obviously took the place in his affections of the grandchildren whom he had never seen.

However, despite the comforting attentions of his surrogate family, James's thoughts turned constantly to his absent son and favourite, to whom he had written seven times within their first month away.

My Sweet Boys, [he wrote on 17 March] I write this now my seventh letter ... sent in my ship called the *Adventure*, to my two boy-adventurers, whom God ever bless.

And now to begin with *Jove principium*, I have sent you, my Baby, two of your chaplains fittest for this purpose ... with all stuff and adornment fit for the service of God. I have fully instructed them, so as all their behaviour and service shall, I hope, prove decent, and agreeable to the purity of the primitive church, and yet as near the Roman form as can lawfully be done, for it hath ever been my way to go with the church of Rome *usque ad aras*....

I send you also the jewels as I promised, some of mine and such of yours, I mean both of you, as are worthy the sending, aye, or my Baby's presenting his mistress. I send him ... a good looking-glass with my picture in it, to be hung at her girdle, which ye must tell her ye have caused it to be so enchanted by art magic, that whensoever she shall be pleased to look in it, she shall see the fairest lady that either her brother or your father's dominions can afford.... Ye shall give her a goodly rope of pearls, ye shall give her a carquanet or collar, thirteen great balas rubies, thirteen knots or conques of pearls, and ye shall give her a head-dressing of two and twenty great pear pearls....

I send you for your wearing the three brethren, that ye know full well, but newly set, and the Mirror of France, the fellow of the Portugal diamond, which I would wish you to wear alone in your hat*.... As for thee, my sweet gossip, I send thee a fair table diamond, which I would

*These jewels were mentioned previously, as those which James himself had worn at the wedding of his daughter in 1613. *Vide supra* p. 117.

once have given thee before, if thou would have taken it, for wearing in thy hat, or where thou pleases....

And now for the form of my Baby's presenting of his jewels to his mistress, I leave that to himself... only I would not have them presented all at once, but at the more sundry times the better, and I would have the rarest and richest kept hindmost....

Thus you see how, as long as I want [i.e. lack] the comfort of my sweet boys' conversation, I am forced, yea, and delight, to converse with them by long letters. God bless you both, my sweet boys, and send you after a successful journey, a joyful happy return in the arms of your dear dad,

James R.[9]

What happened in Spain was very different from what James imagined as he wrote this generous and loving letter.

Charles and Buckingham had reached Madrid on 7 March, and presented themselves at the house of the anxious and embarrassed English Ambassador, Digby, who had recently been created Earl of Bristol. 'I must confess,' wrote Bristol to the King, '... that if your Majesty had been pleased to ask my advice concerning the Prince his coming in this manner, I should rather have dissuaded than given any such counsel, especially before the coming of the dispensation.'[10]

Without a dispensation from the Pope, a marriage between a Catholic Princess and a Protestant Prince could not take place at all. Should the Pope refuse a dispensation, Charles's journey would have been to no purpose, and the damage to English prestige would be considerable. But neither Bristol nor Charles himself knew that the King of Spain had sent the Duke of Pastrana to Rome with an urgent message to the Pope, asking him not to grant a dispensation; and this he had done because when Charles had first arrived in Spain, the Spanish Court had assumed that he had come to announce his willingness to adopt Catholicism, and upon the rapid discovery that he had not, King Philip had turned against the marriage altogether.

By the time Pastrana reached Rome, however, the dispensation was already on its way to Spain; though even had he arrived before it was issued, it is unlikely that the Pope would have listened favourably to Philip's request.

For the Pope the interests of the Catholic Church were of

supreme importance. He knew that, if he declined to grant a dispensation, he would provoke the anger of King James and risk his retaliation upon the English Catholics. Since their condition was already alleviated, and the proposed treaty would bring them considerable further relief, Pope Gregory felt obliged to issue the dispensation while imposing harsher conditions.

The dispensation arrived in Madrid on 24 April, and the provisions were harsh indeed. They were considerably harsher than they had been when the marriage had been first discussed.* As before, it was required that the religious education of the children of the marriage should be in the hands of the Infanta. But now, it was further required that all the members of her household should be Spanish, and nominated by her brother King Philip. The religious life of this household was to be directed by a bishop, assisted by twenty-four priests, who, though resident in England, were not to be subject to English law. The Infanta's chapel was to be a public place of worship for the English Catholics. These were the public articles of the marriage treaty, to which King James gained the reluctant consent of the English Privy Council.

There were further secret clauses. The King was required to assure perpetual toleration for the Catholics in all his kingdoms, and to permit them to practise their religion freely within their own houses. No law was to be passed against the Catholics which did not affect their fellow subjects, and the King was to ask Parliament for the repeal of the penal laws, and to undertake not to give the royal assent to any anti-Catholic legislation which might be proposed in the future.

It seems probable that Pope Gregory was influenced, in framing these conditions, by the supposition that Prince Charles would embrace Catholicism. In the seventeenth century, toleration of religious minorities was seldom officially guaranteed, and never so fully provided for as in these proposed conditions. It would have been unrealistic even for the most sanguine of popes or Catholic rulers to have expected them to be accepted, except upon the expectation of Charles's conversion to Catholicism either on his marriage or on his accession.

When Charles remained both constant in his Anglicanism and

* *Vide supra* p. 153.

enthusiastic for the marriage, Philip, in consternation, sought another way of escape. He appointed a commission of theologians to advise him upon what conditions he should require as guarantees that the Pope's conditions would be honoured, before he could in conscience allow the marriage to go forward. The commission recommended that the betrothal of the Prince of Wales and the Infanta be permitted to take place at once, and the marriage be solemnized and consummated a year later. The intervening period would give King James the opportunity to show his good faith by relieving the English Catholics of their disabilities.

Cottington returned to England and presented the conditions to King James, who was appalled. On 14 June he wrote to Charles and Buckingham:

My Sweet Boys,

Your letter by Cottington hath stricken me dead; I fear it shall very much shorten my days, and I am the more perplexed that I know not how to satisfy the people's expectation here, neither know I what to say to the Council....

But as for my advice and directions that ye crave, in case they will not alter their decree, it is, in a word, to come speedily away, and if ye can get leave, give over all treaty. And this I speak without respect of any security they can offer you, except ye never look to see your old dad again, whom I fear ye shall never see, if you see him not before winter. Alas, I now repent me sore, that ever I suffered you to go away. I care not for match nor nothing, so I may once have you in my arms again. God grant it, God grant it, God grant it; amen, amen, amen! I protest ye shall be as heartily welcome as if ye had done all things ye went for, so that I may once have you in my arms again; and God bless you both, my only sweet son, and my only best, sweet servant, and let me hear from you quickly, with all speed, as ye love my life; and so God send you a happy and joyful meeting in the arms of your dear dad,

James R.[11]

Yet, after his initial shock, James decided to accept the terms of the treaty. At first he feared that the period of probation demanded before the consummation of the marriage was in fact being demanded precisely as Cottington had prophesied, so that Charles would be in effect a hostage at the Spanish Court until his father had rescinded the anti-Catholic legislation. However, both Charles and his father were determined to salvage the marriage if they could, because upon it so many aspects of the King's policy depended.

On 7 July Charles paid a formal visit to the King of Spain, ostensibly to take his leave; instead he announced his capitulation to the Papal terms and to the Spanish amendments. Philip IV could do nothing but appear to be delighted, and order the celebration of the betrothal. As a gesture of goodwill, he shortened the probation period to eight months.

With great solemnity, on 20 July, James ratified the marriage treaty in the Chapel Royal at Whitehall. Later, in private, he swore to abide by the secret clauses, in the presence of the Resident Spanish Ambassador, the Marquis of Inojosa, who had succeeded Gondomar, and of a special envoy, Don Carlos de Coloma. In the new Banqueting House, which Inigo Jones had built for the wedding of the Prince of Wales, the King and the Ambassadors dined off plates 'all of pure and perfect gold', but the rejoicings of the English Court were noticeably unspontaneous.

Prince Charles, in Spain, was persuaded to swear to one more secret condition, in addition to those presented to his father, which made it appear that, though his capitulation had forced the hand of Philip IV, still his conversion was desired, and not despaired of, in the end. He swore: 'That as often as the most illustrious Lady Infanta shall require that I should give ear to Divines or others whom her Highness shall be pleased to employ in matter of the Roman Catholic religion, I will hearken to them willingly without all difficulty, and laying aside all excuse.'[12]

Both King James and his son were at this time equally determined to conclude the Spanish marriage, though not for the same reasons. The Infanta's dowry probably occupied a smaller place in Charles's mind than in his father's. At this period of the Prince's life, finance was not the serious problem for him that it would become when he entered into his inheritance. But both James and Charles were equally concerned with the question of the Palatinate, and equally determined to make the treaty with Spain the occasion for the recovery of Frederick's hereditary lands. Charles's attachment to his sister Elizabeth was strong, and his sense of loyalty to her influenced him both while he was in Spain and after his return to England.

Then, Charles had a third reason for his eagerness for the marriage, and that was desire for the Infanta herself.

As James had long ago imagined himself to be in love with Anne of Denmark even before he had met her, so Charles had become romantically infatuated with the idea of the Infanta. When at last he saw her, kept maddeningly distant from him by the rigid etiquette of the Spanish Court, he conceived a grand passion for her. Her fair hair, white skin, and remote, rather childlike expression, made her seem the personification of unattainable beauty. Charles was permitted to gaze his fill at her from a distance, and later to speak to her, but only in the presence of a defensive phalanx of attendants. He loved and longed, and he did not discover that the Infanta had a violent distaste for the prospect of marriage to a heretic. He did not then know that she had declared that she would sooner become a nun.

Once Charles and his father had sworn a treaty there was no further attempt to detain the Prince in Spain. He could return to England to wait the agreed eight months for his bride. So long as King James's goodwill to the English Catholics was satisfactorily displayed, there would be no complications. Charles took his leave of the Infanta on 28 August; two days later King James wrote her a formal letter of welcome:

> Madam,
> The celebrity of your virtues has not only attracted, in the capacity of a lover, my very dear son to come from afar to see you, but has inspired me also with an ardent desire of having the happiness of your presence, and of enjoying the pleasure of embracing such a Princess in the quality of a daughter, an unequalled comfort to
>
> Your very affectionate father,
> J.R.[13]

Charles left Madrid on 30 August, and rode as far as the Escorial, where he stayed three days; before his departure he empowered King Philip, or his brother Don Carlos, to act as his proxy, upon the signification of the English Ambassador, when the marriage was solemnized. On 2 September he took the road to Santander. But at some time during the past month Charles had undergone a change of heart. His capacity for masking his feelings was such that none had had the least suspicion of it. His reasons for turning against the marriage were as strong as his previous determination to insist upon it. His efforts to gain a firm undertaking with regard to the Palatinate had failed. Philip IV's all-powerful favourite and chief minister, the Count-Duke of Olivares, had thought of a sensible plan, backed by the Imperial Ambassador, that Charles should marry not the Infanta but the daughter of the Emperor Ferdinand, and the Elector Palatine's son should marry another Austrian Archduchess, so that Ferdinand 'would be personally committed to finding a satisfactory solution to the Palatinate question'.[14] However, by the time Charles had reached Spain, the negotiations for his marriage to the Infanta had progressed so far that it was difficult to go back to the beginning.

The English proposal that if the King of Spain failed to persuade Ferdinand and his allies to yield up the Palatinate, then, as part of the marriage treaty, Spanish troops should join with an English force to expel them, was met by a categorical statement from Olvares: 'We have a maxim of state that the King of Spain must never fight against the Emperor. We cannot employ our forces against the House of Austria.'[15]

Once Charles had realized that his efforts to gain anything for his sister and brother-in-law through the Spanish marriage were doomed to be brushed aside with polite words, he also became disabused concerning the object of his romantic passion. As soon as he was the Infant's affianced bridegroom, it was no longer possible to confine their contact to a few words exchanged in the presence of many witnesses. At first, he informed his father with delight, 'she sits publicly with me at the plays'; but his initial joy in her proximity quickly wore off when he discovered that her virginal modesty was not occasioned by regal Spanish reserve, but by cold detestation of the person of a heretic. The Infanta possessed the inflexible will-power which is often disguised by an ultra-feminine exterior, and Charles had neither the charm nor the sexual magnetism which might have overcome it.

Once he was safely on the road to Santander he wrote to Lord Bristol:

You know that I told you, I feared when I came away, the Infanta might go to a monastery, after I was contracted by virtue of a dispensation granted from Rome, and so the marriage might be broken, and the King my father and all the world might condemn me, and account me a rash-headed fool not to have prevented it. And therefore do not dispose of my proxy, until you hear more from me ...[16]

In effect, Charles had cancelled his proxy before he sailed from Spain. On 5 October the Prince and Buckingham landed at Portsmouth. Late the next day they reached Royston, and embraced King James as he descended the stair to meet them: the 'happy and comfortable return in the arms of your dear dad' which James had so many times wished for was for the moment enjoyed. The King had yet to learn that Charles and Buckingham had brought with them the ruin of his peace policy.

1624, the last full year of the King's life, was also probably the loneliest, for he became alienated from the two beings whom he loved above all others, his son and his favourite.

Both the young men had returned changed and matured from their Spanish journey. Buckingham had received his dukedom from the King, during his absence, not only as a particular mark of love and favour, but also, in all probability, to give him equality with the Count-Duke of Olivares. Buckingham's developing arrogance, his assertive Protestantism, and his contempt for Spanish protocol had made him intensely unpopular in Spain. But he had learnt an important lesson from his contact with the Spanish Court: he had learnt what immense power a ministerial favourite could wield. He came home less content than before to play the part of James's 'humble slave and dog'; he had a new role waiting for him, as the next King's *alter ego*.

Charles, too, came home a more confident and self-sufficient young man than he had been when he went away. 'He seemed to shed his fear of his father along with his love of the Infanta, and at the end of January he told James categorically that he would not hear of either friendship or alliance with Spain.'[17]

James had been extremely ill during the autumn of 1623; with the coming of the new year he was very frail. The determination with which he defended his peace policy is all the more remarkable in these circumstances. There is no appearance of the senility from which it is frequently said that he suffered. The last Parliament of the reign assembled in 1624, and James fought a sustained and resolute rearguard action to assert his peace policy against the national bellicosity which Charles and Buckingham sought to arouse.

> Never soldiers [said the King, in his opening speech on 19 February] marching the deserts and dry sands of Arabia where there is no water, could more thirst in hot weather for drink, than I do now for a happy end of this our meeting. And now I hope that after the miscarriage of three Parliaments this will prove happy.... The proper use of a Parliament is ... to confer with the King, as governor of the kingdom, and to give their [*sic*] advice in matters of greatest importance concerning the state and defence of the King, with the church and kingdom....
>
> Consider with yourselves the state of Christendom, my children, and this my own kingdom. Consider of these, and upon all give me your advice ... you that are the representative body of this kingdom ... [be] ... my true glasses to show me the hearts of my people.[18]

Remarkably, James was now inviting Parliament to discuss those very areas of policy of which, in 1621, he had forbidden discussion. In so doing, he was persuaded that

> Parliament could be used as a weapon in diplomatic negotiations, and it was for this reason that questions of foreign policy were submitted to it. Unlike his son and favourite who wanted to engage Parliament to finance a war against Spain, James wished to use its aggressive designs to extort better conditions for the peaceful restitution of the Palatinate. And if, in the last resort, negotiations proved impossible, he felt confident of his power to direct the war to the ultimate realization of his longtime ambition, the restoration of the Palatinate.... He insisted that the recovery of the Palatinate was the only justifiable reason for the commencement of hostilities, and when the Commons refused his request to have this specifically included in the subsidy bill, he asserted his right to 'alter it and set his marginal note upon it'.[19]

Unfortunately, James failed to control the war-fever which Charles and Buckingham were eager to encourage. It was easy for Buckingham to make the Commons 'drunk with imagined Elizabethan splendours', and to encourage them to suppose that a sea-war against Spain could be 'self-financing, if not profitable'.[20] Parliament granted three subsidies, which it wished to be employed principally to strengthen the navy for the envisaged war at sea, and to aid the Dutch against Spain, both of which causes owed their inspiration to the ideas of the last reign. The three subsidies yielded £253,139. 12s. 2¾d. After the prorogation of Parliament, this relatively modest sum was spent over and over again by Charles and Buckingham, who allotted £720,000 to war preparations, which did not include expenditure on the Navy; £360,000 to the King of Denmark, to finance his intervention in the Thirty Years' War; and £240,000 to Ernst von Mansfeld, to pay for the conscription of an army in England, to fight in the Protestant cause. The opportunity provided by the English volunteers in the Palatinate had by now ceased to exist; the last of them had surrendered the previous year, and Sir Gerard Herbert had been killed.

When Parliament was for the first time let loose upon the discussion of foreign affairs, Lionel Cranfield, Earl of Middlesex, who, if only for reasons of economy, supported the King's policy of recovering the Palatinate through diplomacy, fell victim to the consequences of his resistance to Buckingham. He was too clear-sighted to be tied to Buckingham's interests merely because he was married to his cousin, Anne Brett; indeed, Buckingham suspected that Middlesex had tried to advance his attractive young brother-in-law, Arthur Brett, as a rival favourite. In April 1624 Middlesex was impeached in the House of Commons on charges of financial corruption. He was tried and found guilty by the Lords, and sentenced to loss of office, imprisonment in the Tower during the King's pleasure, and to a fine of £50,000. James made a speech in his defence, which did not save him.

The fall of Middlesex deeply offended the King. With reference to the revival of the mediaeval process of impeachment, with which Buckingham would be threatened in his turn, James said to him prophetically, 'You are a fool, you are making a rod with which you will be scourged yourself.' And to Charles he said, 'You will live to have your bellyful of Parliaments.'[21] But if James felt, like Shakespeare's John of Gaunt,

> Methinks I am a prophet new inspir'd,
> And thus expiring do foretell of him ...

Charles had as little inclination as Richard II to listen.

On 29 May 1624 James prorogued Parliament, and promised to

recall it 'towards the winter'. He did not do so, and this speech was his public leavetaking of his kingdom.

James was obliged to submit to the repudiation of the treaty with Spain, and to allow his son to negotiate a marriage with the sister of Louis XIII of France. The Catholic Henrietta Maria was scarcely more popular as Queen of England than the Spanish Infanta would have been.

After James had put his signature on the French treaty with a stamp because his arthritic fingers could not move a pen, Prince Charles promised that he would at his accession grant 'to all the Roman Catholic subjects of the Crown of Great Britain the utmost of liberty and franchise in everything regarding their religion which they would have had in virtue of any articles which were agreed upon by the treaty of marriage with Spain'.[22]

The French alliance had purchased nothing, for while France had entered the Thirty Years' War for the purpose of resisting and reducing the Hapsburg power, French interests were not engaged in the restitution of the Palatinate. Where James's policy might have gained some concessions at last, its reversal by his son and favourite caused the same price to be paid for nothing at all. As the reign drew to its end England was at war with Spain, although no action had been taken.

James was ill again at Christmas 1624. He kept to his bed and could attend neither the religious observances nor the entertainments of the season. Perhaps sensible of his coming end, he wrote a touching letter to Buckingham, seeking the comfort of a final reconciliation:

My only sweet and dear child,

Notwithstanding of your desiring me to write yesterday yet had I written in the evening, if at my coming in out of the park such a drowsiness had not comed [*sic*] upon me, as I was forced to sit and sleep in my chair half an hour. And yet I cannot content myself without sending you this billet, praying God that I may have a joyful and comfortable meeting with you, and that we may make at this Christenmass a new marriage, ever to be kept hereafter; for God so love me, as I desire only to live in this world for your sake, and that I had rather live banished in any part of the earth with you, than live a sorrowful widow-life without you. And so God bless you, my sweet child and wife, and grant that ye may ever be a comfort to your dear dad and husband,

James R.[23]

It cost Buckingham nothing to be kind, for his role in the new reign was already assured by the closeness of his friendship with Charles, which the Spanish journey had cemented. But Buckingham's solicitous attendance at the King's deathbed, and the efforts of both the Duke and his mother to restore the King by the application of herbal remedies of which the royal physicians disapproved, led inevitably to the accusation that James had been poisoned by his favourite, who was turning impatiently to the rising sun. The fact that James was dying swiftly enough to make such impatience unnecessary should be sufficient answer. Despite the frictions of the past year, 'Buckingham loved James – not perhaps in the same way, or with the same physical intensity that James loved him, but with a depth of affection that created a firm bond between them.... The Duke felt bereft by the King's death, and could not hide his grief.'[24]

King James's final illness took place at Theobalds in March 1625. He was attended on his deathbed by Bishop Williams, who heard his confession, give him absolution and Holy Communion, and reported that his last audible words were '*Veni, Jesu Domine*', from the penultimate verse of the *Book of Revelation*.

'As he lived like a King, so he died like a Saint,' said Williams, 'without any pangs or convulsion at all, *Dormivit Salomon*, Solomon slept.'

On 24 March James suffered a stroke, which he survived, speechless but conscious, for three days; on 27 March he died.

EPILOGUE

The King's Reputation

I am glad to see the world so tenderly affected toward him, for I assure you all men apprehend what a loss we should have, if God should take him from us....

John Chamberlain, 1619

ON 7 MAY 1625, the embalmed body of King James VI of Scotland and I of England was buried in Westminster Abbey. The funeral sermon was preached by Bishop Williams, who took as his theme the comparison between King James, whom he called 'Great Britain's Salomon', and his Biblical namesake.

I dare presume to say [the Bishop declared] you never read in your lives of two Kings more fully paralleled amongst themselves, and better distinguished from all other Kings besides themselves. King Solomon is said to be *unigenitus coram matre sua*, the only son of his mother. So was King James. King Solomon was of a complexion white and ruddy. So was King James. Solomon was an infant King, *puer parvulus*, a little child. So was King James, a King at the age of thirteen months. Solomon began his reign in the life of his predecessor. So by the force and compulsion of that state [i.e. Scotland] did our late Sovereign King James. Solomon was twice crowned and anointed a King. So was King James. Solomon's minority was rough through the quarrels of the former sovereign; so was that of King James. Solomon was learned above all the Princes of the East. So was King James above all the Princes of the universal world. Solomon was a writer in prose and verse. So in a very pure and exquisite manner was our sweet sovereign King James. Solomon was the greatest patron we ever read of to Church and Churchmen; and yet no greater (let the House of Aaron [i.e. the Clergy] now confess) than King James. Solomon was honoured with Ambassadors from all the Kings of the earth. And so as you know was King James. Solomon was a main improver of his home commodities as you may see in his trading with Hiram. And God knows it was the daily study of King James. Solomon was a great maintainer of shipping and navigation; a most proper attribute to King James. Solomon beautified very much his capital city with buildings and waterworks. So did King James. Every man lived in peace under his vine and his fig-tree in the days of Solomon. And so they did in the blessed days of King James. And yet towards his end, King Solomon had secret enemies, Razan, Hadad and Jeroboam, and prepared for a war upon his going to his grave.... So had, and so did, King James. Lastly, before any hostile act we read of in history, King Solomon died in peace, when he had lived about sixty years ... and so you know did King James....[1]

In part this oration may be dismissed as a fine example of baroque prose, in which the comparison between the complexions of King Solomon and King James serves only a rhetorical purpose; but it is also a succinct summary of King James's life, and some of Williams's statements concerning him are worth considering for the bearing that they have on his personal achievements and his posthumous reputation.

Williams's eulogy of James as a patron of churchmen deserves particular attention since it comes from a churchman. Williams, admittedly, was the type of bishop which James most favoured: a servant of the State as well as of the Church. Williams held the office of Lord Keeper concurrently with the bishopric of Lincoln, and if he saw in the two aspects of his power a reflection of the days of 'splendian Wolsey', as he himself described the great Cardinal, James probably and more justifiably saw in them an extension to England of the Scottish usage, which he had introduced, of the employment of bishops to buttress the royal authority.

James favoured Williams and other English divines who shared his own Calvinism, including Archbishop Abbott, whose appointment as Primate was a wise accommodation with Puritan opinion. Abbott, even if he was not an outstandingly saintly churchman, or an exceptionally able administrator, 'did .. . maintain the peace of the Church and that is not an unworthy attainment'.[2]

Other of James's dealings with the Church, calculated to appeal to Puritan opinion in England and to be approved in Scotland, were likewise worthy of recognition as making no contribution to the religio-political troubles which beset both kingdoms in the next reign. James gave strong approbation to the proceedings of the Synod of Dort in 1618, and officially endorsed the Calvinist doctrines which it expounded. He also appointed a number of bishops who were known to hold Calvinist beliefs, among them Carleton, Davenant, Downhame, Ussher, Hall, and Williams himself.[3]

The Calvinist bishops had good cause to praise King James, and would have found greater cause after Charles I had appointed William Laud to the archbishopric of Canterbury in 1633, and the peace of the Church in both England and Scotland was broken.

Williams's praise of King James's 'daily study' for the improvement of trade was less justified, or less grounded in knowledge of the King's actions. Of economics James understood nothing. His most notorious attempt to benefit English trade resulted in disaster, when he accepted the advice of Alderman Cockayne that the English wool trade was suffering from the fact that English woollen cloth was exported in an intermediate state, to be cleaned, dyed and finished in the Netherlands, and that these processes could be performed successfully by the Flemish and Dutch refugees who had settled in East Anglia, and the cloth exported at greater profit. In 1614 James attempted to implement Cockayne's project by cancelling the Merchant Adventurers' charter, and forbidding the export of unfinished cloth. The immediate result was that the Dutch placed an embargo on the English export in its new form, while the East Anglian dyeing and finishing industry could not handle the greater volume of work which was suddenly required of it. The resultant recession in the wool trade was exacerbated by the effects of the outbreak of the European war, which in turn led to general economic depression. The King was blamed because the immediate harm caused by his well-intentioned though inexpert interference was obvious; but the larger causes of the general depression lay beyond his control, or that of anyone else.

James's economic fallibility showed itself principally in his uncontrolled extravagance, which throughout the reign added steadily to the mountainous accumulation of his debts. Yet surprisingly, one of his harshest critics did not find this unfortunate trait blameworthy. Sir Anthony Weldon wrote: '... his bounty was not discommendable, for his raising of favourites was the worst; rewarding old servants and relieving his native countrymen was infinitely more to be commended in him than condemned.'[4]

Williams's claim that James, like Solomon, 'beautified very much his capital city with buildings ...' was considerably exaggerated, though the bishop probably did not exaggerate the King's intention. The greatest architectural monument to King James's patronage is Inigo Jones's Banqueting House in Whitehall, which is now the only surviving building of Whitehall Palace as King James knew it, and happily so, for it is one of the most beautiful buildings in London. James imagined a new palace of which the Banqueting House was only a beginning; neither he nor his successors could afford to give reality to their vision. The Queen's House at Greenwich, which Inigo Jones began to build for Anne of Denmark, was completed in the next reign for Henrietta Maria.

Peace was the most undoubted benefit which King James gave to his subjects, among those benefits for which Bishop Williams praised him, and towards the end of his reign he even endeavoured to maintain it for them against their will. It is the fate of most rulers who live long and maintain peace that a new and bellicose generation grows up, which, never having known the horrors of war, sees in some burning issue an excellent reason to 'cry havoc'.

Weldon wrote of King James's peace-keeping diplomacy: 'He had rather spend £100,0000 on embassies, to keep or procure peace with dishonour, than £10,000 on an army that would have forced peace with honour.'[5] The doubtful value of that argument may be appreciated by readers who have witnessed the repeated wars of the bloodiest century in history. They may consider that the prices which James was prepared to pay for settlements which might have maintained or restored the peace of Europe were small and not dishonourable prices, by comparison with the great price in human suffering which Europe paid between 1618 and 1648.

Arthur Wilson linked James's dedication to peace with the decline of his reputation during the next generation:

Peace was maintained by him as in the time of Augustus; and peace begot plenty, and plenty begot ease and wantonness, and ease and wantonness begot poetry, and poetry swelled to that bulk in his time, that it begot strange monstrous satires against the King's own person, that haunted both court and country, which expressed, would be too bitter to leave a sweet perfume behind him. And though bitter ingredients are good to embalm and preserve dead bodies, yet these were such as might endanger to kill a living name.... And the tongues of those times, more fluent than my pen, made every little miscarriage (being not able to discover their true operations, like small seeds hid in earthy darkness) grow up, and spread into such exuberant branches, that evil report did often perch upon them.[6]

Wilson's fancifully expressed hypothesis enshrines a simpler truth:

> The evil that men do lives after them,
> The good is oft interred with their bones.

The reason why this truth should be particularly apparent in the case of King James is not far to seek. All kings have enemies, and during the Interregnum the scurrilous or vindictive writings of King James's enemies were given a new lease of life by the temporarily victorious enemies of the monarchy. When monarchists had risked their lives and possessions for King Charles I in the Civil War, their thoughts were of him and not of his father; if they could excuse his failures by laying the blame for them upon the character and policy of his father, they were willing to do so.

Bishop Goodman and Sir William Sanderson, who held James's memory in respect, wrote favourable accounts of his reign, and Sanderson prefaced his with an elegy on the late King which included the lines:

> Kings are as gods; o do not then
> Rake in their graves to prove them men.

But the process of raking in the grave, which is now known by the less graphic term of 'character assassination', had already taken place.

The view of King James promulgated during the Interregnum had a natural appeal to the eighteenth century, which saw the establishment of constitutional monarchy. The friction between James and his Parliament took on a different significance when it was viewed from the other side of the Hanoverian Settlement. The Jacobean House of Commons then appeared to be defending, and the King attacking, a style of government of which neither would have appproved.

During the nineteenth century scholarly interpretation of the reign of James I began to undergo a change, but the popular image of him was fixed by Scott and Macaulay. Even S.R. Gardiner, who was too judicious to accept a view of James which had manifestly undergone distortion, was not bold enough to discard it and follow the indications which are clearly present in the pages of his great work.

Only in the present century has a more confident change of view brought with it a gradual rehabilitation of King James's reputation, at least among scholars. Reassessment of reputations has recently enjoyed an academic vogue, but in many instances, including that of James, a revisionist campaign has a more profound value than that of an academic exercise. The purpose of such a campaign is to re-establish in the minds of scholars, students and general readers the almost forgotten fact that King James VI and I was a generally respected, if not a popular, King; and to make once more explicable the reason why, when he had had a close encounter with death in 1619, John Chamberlain could write: 'All men apprehend what a loss we should have, if God should take him from us.'

He was a king who deeply respected the institution of monarchy, as an institution ordained by God, and not as a vehicle of self-aggrandizement. His occasional disregard for his personal dignity serves to illustrate how little he was concerned with self-aggrandizement. He was a king who believed profoundly in the responsible nature of his office. A sense of responsibility, he believed, was the touchstone which served to differentiate a king from a tyrant. A true king, he had long ago written in *Basilikon Doron*, 'acknowledgeth himself ordained for his people, having received from God the burden of government whereof he must be countable', whereas 'a tyrant thinketh his people ordained for him, a prey to his passions and inordinate appetites'.

Though the inherent faults of human nature make it impossible for any man to live up to the best of his aspirations, King James VI and I did so with sufficient success to deserve the best of his epitaphs:

King James the Peaceful and the Just.

Bibliographies

(All works listed are published in Scotland or England unless otherwise detailed.)

A. WRITINGS BY KING JAMES VI AND I

1 *The Essayes of a Prentise in the Divine Art of Poesie* (1584)
2 *Ane Fruitfull Meditatioun* ... (1588)
3 *Ane Meditatioun upon the First Buke of the Chronicles of Kings* (1589)
4 *His Maiesties Poeticall Exercises* ... (1591)
5 *Daemonologie* (1597)
6 *The Trew Law of Free Monarchies* (1598)
7 *Basilikon Doron* (1599)
8 *A Counterblaste to Tobacco* (1604)
9 *Triplici Nodo, Triplex Cuneus: or An Apologie for the Oath of Allegiance* (1607)
10 *Declaration du Roy Jacques I pour le Droit des Rois* (1615); English Edition, *A Remonstrance for the Rights of Kings* (1616)
The Works of James King of Great Britain, etc., Collected by Bishop James Montague (1616)
11 *A Meditation upon the Lord's Prayer* (1619)
12 *A Meditation upon the 27, 28, 29 Verses of the XXVII Chapter of S. Matthew: or A Pattern for a King's Inauguration* (1620)

B. LATER EDITIONS OF WRITINGS BY KING JAMES

Arber, Edward, *A Counterblaste to Tobacco* (English Reprints series No 19, 1869)
Craigie, J., *The Poems of King James VI of Scotland* (Scottish Text Society, 2 vols, 1948, 1952)
McIlwain, C.H., *The Political Works of James I* (Harvard, 1918) [also contains some of the King's major speeches]
Rait, Robert S., *Lusus Regius* (1901) [A Selection of the King's poems]
Westcott, Allan F., *New Poems by James I of England* (Columbia University Press, 1911)

C. CONTEMPORARY AND NEAR-CONTEMPORARY SOURCES: RECORDS, LETTERS, MEMOIRS, HISTORIES, LITERATURE

Abbotsford Miscellany
A[gar], B[en], *King James His Apothegmes* (1643)
Ashton, Robert (ed.), *James I by His Contemporaries* (1969) [A Selection of

contemporary writings about the King, grouped in thematic chapters, each with an introductory essay by the editor]
Aubrey, John, (ed. O. Lawson Dick), *Brief Lives* (1949)
Barlow, William, *The Summe and Substance of the Conference ... at Hampton Court* (1604)
Birch, Thomas, *The Court and Times of James the First* (2 vols, 1849) [Contemporary Letters]
Calendar of Salisbury Manuscripts (Historical Manuscripts Commission, 1883, etc.)
Calendar of State Papers, Venetian
Chamberlain, John, *The Letters of John Chamberlain* (ed. N.E. McClure, Philadelphia, 1939)
Clarendon, Edward, Earl of, *The History of the Rebellion and Civil Wars in England* (ed. W.D. Mackray, 1888)
Coke, Roger, *A Detection of the Court and State of England. ...* (1694)
Cornwallis, Sir Charles, *A Discourse of the Most Illustrious Prince Henry* (written 1626, pub. 1641, collected in *Somers' Tracts*; *see* Somers)
Cornwallis, Sir Charles, *The Life and Death of Henry, Prince of Wales* (1641, in *Somers' Tracts; see* Somers)
Goodman, Bishop Godfrey, *The Court of King James* (ed. J.S. Brewer, 2 vols, 1839)
Hacket, John, *Scrinia Reserata: A Memorial Offer'd to the Great Deservings of John Williams, D.D.* (1692)
Harington, Sir John, *Nugae Antiquae* (ed. T. Park, 1804)
Harleian Miscellany IX
Hutchinson, Lucy, *Memoirs of Colonel Hutchinson* (ed. Rev. Julius Hutchinson, 1908)
Jonson, Ben, *Masques and Entertainments* (ed. H. Morley, 1889)
Letters of the Kings of England (ed. J.O. Halliwell, 2 vols, 1846) [contains a generous selection of the King's letters, from the later years of the reign]
Masques, A Book of: in Honour of Allardyce Nicoll (1967. *See* Bentley, Bibliography D)
Nicols, J., *The Progresses ... of King James I* (4 vols, 1828)
Oglander, Sir John, *A Royalist's Notebook: The Commonplace Book of Sir John Oglander* (ed. F. Bamford, 1936)
Osborne, Francis, 'Traditionall Memoyres on the Raigne of King James the First' in *Secret History of the Court of James the First* (1811)
Rushworth, John, *Historical Collections ... Beginning the Sixteenth Year of King James, Anno 1618 ...* (1682)
Sanderson, Sir William, *A Compleat History of the Lives and Reigns of Mary, Queen of Scotland, and of her Son and Successor, James* (1656)
Somers' Tracts (2nd ed., 1809)
State Trials (ed. William Cobbett, 1809)
Tanner, J.R. (ed), *Constitutional Documents of the Reign of James I* (1930)
Weldon, Sir Anthony, *The Court and Character of King James ...* (1651)
Wilson, Arthur, *The History of Great Britain, Being the Life and Reign of King James the First ...* (1653)

Winwood, Sir Ralph, *Memorials of Affairs of State ...* (ed. E. Sawyer, 1725)
Wodrow, Robert, *Collections upon the Lives of the Reformers ... of the Church of Scotland* (Maitland Club, 1844)

D. LATER WRITINGS: BOOKS, ESSAYS AND PUBLICATIONS IN PERIODICALS

Akrigg, G.P.V., *Jacobean Pageant, or the Court of King James I* (1962)
Ashley, Maurice, *Life in Stuart England* (1964)
Ashley, Maurice, *The House of Stuart: Its Rise and Fall* (1980)
Ashley, Maurice, *The Stuarts in Love* (1963)
Bentley, Gerald Eades, General Introduction to *A Book of Masques* (1967)
Bingham, Caroline, *James VI of Scotland* (1979)
Bingham, Caroline, *The Making of a King: the Early Years of James VI and I* (1968)
Bossy, John, 'The English Catholic Community 1603–25' in *The Reign of James VI and I* (ed. Alan G.R. Smith, *see* Smith)
Carter, Charles H., 'The Ambassadors of Early Modern Europe: Patterns of Diplomatic Representation in the Early Seventeenth Century in *From the Renaissance to the Counter-Reformation* (*see below*)
Carter, Charles H. (ed.), *From the Renaissance to the Counter-Reformation: Essays in Honour of Garrett Mattingly* (1968)
Carter, Charles H., *The Secret Diplomacy of the Hapsburgs, 1598–1625* (Columbia University Press, 1964)
Cecil, Algernon, *A Life of Robert Cecil, First Earl of Salisbury* (1915)
Coakley, Thomas M., 'Robert Cecil in Power: Elizabethan Politics in Two Reigns', in *Early Stuart Studies* (ed. Howard S. Reinmuth, *see* Reinmuth)
Cunnington, C. Willott, and Phyllis, *A Handbook of English Costume in the Seventeenth Century* (1963)
Curtis, Mark H., 'Hampton Court Conference and its Aftermath', in *History* XLVI (Feb. 1961)
Davies, Godfrey, *The Early Stuarts 1603–60* (1937)
Dictionary of National Biography
Dietz, Frederick Charles, *English Public Finance, 1558–1641* (American Historical Association, 1932)
Donaldson, Gordon, *Scotland: James V to James VII* (1965)
Elton G.R., 'A Highroad to Civil War?' in *From the Renaissance to the Counter-Reformation* (ed. Charles H. Carter, 1968)
Fergusson, Sir James, *The White Hind and Other Discoveries* (1963) [historical essays]
Fraser, Lady Antonia, *King James VI of Scotland, I of England* (1974)
Gardiner, S.R., *The History of England, 1603–42* (1864) [the first five volumes]
George, Charles, *The Stuarts: A Century of Experiment, 1603–1714* (1973)
Handover, P.M., *Arbella Stuart: Royal Lady of Hardwick and Cousin to King James* (1957)
Henderson, T.F., *James VI* and *I* (1904)
Henderson, T.F., *The Royal Stewarts* (1914)
Hunter, *see* Macalpine and Hunter

Hurstfied, Joel, 'Gunpowder Plot and the Politics of Dissent' in *Early Stuart Studies* (ed. Howard S. Reinmuth, *see* Reinmuth)

Jones, W.J., 'Ellesmere and Politics, 1603–17', in *Early Stuart Studies* (ed. Howard S. Reinmuth, *see* Reinmuth)

Joseph, B.L., *Shakespeare's Eden: The Commonwealth of England, 1558–1629* (1971)

Kautz, Arthur P., 'The Selection of Jacobean Bishops' in *Early Stuart Studies* (ed. Howard S. Reinmuth, *see* Reinmuth)

Kenyon, J.P., *The Stuarts: A Study in English Kingship* (3rd ed., 1966)

Kenyon, J.P., *Stuart England* (1978)

Lockyer, Roger, *Buckingham: The Life of George Villiers, Duke of Buckingham 1592–1628* (forthcoming)

Macalpine, Ida, and Hunter, Richard, *Porphyria – A Royal Malady* (1968)

Mathew, David, *The Jacobean Age* (1938)

Mathew, David, *James I* (1967)

Mattingly, Garrett, *Renaissance Diplomacy* (1955)

McElwee, William, *The Wisest Fool in Christendom* (1958)

Moir, Thomas L., *The Addled Parliament of 1614* (1958)

Oxford Book of Seventeenth Century Verse

Prestwich, Menna, *Cranfield, Politics and Profits under the Early Stuarts* (1966)

Prestwich, Menna, 'English Politics and Administration, 1603–25' in *The Reign of James VI* and *I* (ed. Alan G.R. Smith, *see* Smith)

Reinmuth, Howard S. Jr, *Early Stuart Studies: Essays in Honour of David Harris Willson* (University of Minnesota Press, 1970)

Ruigh, Robert E., *The Parliament of 1624, Politics and Foreign Policy* (Harvard University Press, 1971)

Russell, Conrad, 'Parliamentary History in Perspective, 1604–20' in *History 61* (1976)

Sackville-West, V., *Knowle and the Sackvilles*

Schwarz, Marc L., *James I and the Historians: Toward a Reconsideration* (XIII Journal of British Studies, 2 May 1974)

Smith, Alan G.R. (ed.), *The Reign of James VI and I* ('Problems in Focus', 1973)

Smith, Logan Pearsall, *The Life and Letters of Sir Henry Wotton* (1907)

Stone, Laurence, *The Crisis of the Aristocracy, 1558–1641* (1963)

Strong, Roy, *The English Icon: Elizabethan and Jacobean Portraiture* (1969)

Tanner, J.R., *English Constitutional Conflicts of the Seventeenth Century, 1603–89* (reprint 1962)

Trevelyan, G.M., *England under the Stuarts* (1904)

Trevor-Roper, Hugh, *Historical Essays* (1957)

Usher, R.G., *The Reconstruction of the English Church* (1910)

Wedgwood, C.V., *Poetry and Politics under the Stuarts* (University of Michigan, 1964)

Wedgwood, C.V., *The Thirty Years War* (1938)

Wedgwood, C.V., *Truth and Opinion: Historical Essays* (1960)

White, Beatrice, *Cast of Ravens: The Strange Case of Sir Thomas Overbury* (1965)

Williams, Charles, *James I* (1934)
Williams, Ethel Carleton, *Anne of Denmark* (1970)
Willson, D.H., *King James VI and I* (1956)
Willson, D.H., 'King James I and Anglo-Scottish Unity' in *Conflict in Stuart England* (ed. W.A. Aiken and B.D. Henning, 1960)

Notes and References

CHAPTER ONE: 'THE AUGMENTATION'

1 'Il Ré è di faccia bella, nobile e gioviale, di color bianco, pelo assai biondo, barba quadra e lungetta, bocca piccola, naso asciutto e profilato, huomo allegro, nè grasso nè magro, di vita ben fatta, pun tosto grande che piccolo.' Degli Effeti to Del Bufalo, June 1603, *cit.* Gardiner, vol. I, p. 87 f.n.
2 Arthur Wilson, *The History of Great Britain, being the Life and Reign of King James the First*, etc. (1653), p. 289.
3 Millington's 'True Naration ...' in Nichols, *Progresses of James I*, vol. I, pp 58–9.
4 B.M. Harl. MSS 6986, *cit.* Nichols, vol. I, pp 147–8 (spelling anglicized by author).
5 *Journal of Sir Roger Wilbraham*, *cit.* Ashton, *James I by His Contemporaries*, p. 8.
6 Cecil to Elizabeth, 1592, *cit.* Algernon Cecil, *A Life of Robert Cecil*, p. 60.
7 John Savile, *A Salutative Poem to the Majestie of King James*, 1603.
8 Wilbraham, in Ashton, *op. cit.*, p. 62.
9 Millington, in Nichols, vol. I, pp 79–80.
10 Cecil to Master of Gray, c. 25 April 1603, *cit.* Algernon Cecil, *op. cit.*, pp 194–5.
11 Cecil to Lord Burghley, 16 February 1588, *ibid.*, p. 24.
12 Millington, in Nichols, vol. I, p. 84.
13 *Ibid.*, p. 89.
14 *Ibid.*, p. 96. The 'Imperial' status of England had been declared by Henry VIII, who in his struggles with the Papacy could not allow himself to be technically subordinate to Charles V, the Holy Roman Emperor. James V, Henry VIII's nephew and James VI and I's grandfather, had likewise claimed 'imperium' for the Crown of Scots.
15 Nichols, vol. I, p 99 f.n.
16 Bingham, *James VI of Scotland*, pp 77–9.
17 Some lovely examples of Scottish architecture and interior decoration dating from James VI's reign are illustrated in *Painted Ceilings of Scotland*, M.R. Apted (H.M.S.O. Edinburgh, 1966).
18 Mathew, *James I*, p. 161.
19 Akrigg, *Jacobean Pageant*, p. 19.
20 *Ibid.*, p. 20.
21 Wilbraham, in Ashton, p. 62.
22 Chamberlain to Carleton, 30 March 1603, Birch, *Court and Times of James I* vol. I, p. 3.

23 Wilbraham, *ibid.*
24 These figures are given by Ashton, *James I by His Contemporaries*, p. 105. Many of Elizabeth's knight's were dubbed by her military commanders – notably by Essex in Ireland – and these were the creations which did not enjoy the Queen's approval.
25 Wilbraham, *ibid.*
26 Nichols, vol. I, pp 153–4 (Letter undated, spelling modernized by author).

CHAPTER TWO: 'HELLISH SPIDERS'

1 Mathew, *James I*, pp 135–6.
2 Edward Bruce is referred to as 'Commendator of Kinloss' in Bingham, *James VI of Scotland*, p. 159. He was the possessor of a 'commendam' or secularized ecclesiastical title, which was converted into an hereditary peerage. These peerages were known as 'Lordships of Erection'.
3 Mathew, *ibid.*, p. 135.
4 *Ibid.* Archbishop Mathew adds the footnote: 'The period of S.R. Gardiner was the heyday of concern for these complexities. In the last three-quarters of a century the interest of historians has turned to broader channels.'
5 Kenyon, *Stuart England*, p. 28.
6 *State Trials*, vol. II, p. 6.
7 Goodman, vol. I, p. 209.
8 *The Secret Correspondence of Sir Robert Cecil with James VI, King of Scotland* (Edinburgh, 1766), p. 118.
9 *State Trials*, vol. II, pp. 19–20.
10 *Ibid.*, p. 20.
11 Mathew, *op. cit.*, p. 137. This hypothesis is sustained in the following paragraph: 'It may be thought that this is going too far, but let us now examine the only possible alternative. Raleigh's own outlook was glorious and Elizabethan. He had fought the Spaniards, he neither liked nor respected them. He had the ordinary west country gentleman's hearty dislike for the Church of Rome. Is it possible that he could have changed so suddenly in these essentials?'

CHAPTER THREE: 'NO NOVEL DEVICE'

1 *Essays of a Prentise in the Divine Art of Poesie* (1584); *His Maiesties Poeticall Exercises* (1591); *Ane Fruitfull Meditatioun* ... [on Revelation xx, vv. 7–10] (1588); *Ane Meditatioun upon the First Buke of the Chronicles of the Kings* ... (1589).
2 *Basilikon Doron*, in McIlwain, *Political Works of James I*, p. 52.
3 Preface to the Authorized Version of the Bible, 1611.
4 The apt phrase 'a regal Calvinist' was coined by Archbishop Mathew, *James I*, p. 127. It remains the best definition of James's religious standpoint.
5 *State Trials*, vol. I, p. 83.
6 *Ibid.*, vol. II, pp 71–2.
7 *Ibid.*, p. 73.
8 *Ibid.*, pp 73–4.

9 Kenyon, *Stuart England*, p. 49.
10 *State Trials*, vol. II, p. 75.
11 Mathew, *op. cit.*, p. 127.
12 'Millenery Petition' in Tanner, *Constitutional Documents of the Reign of James I*, p. 57.
13 *State Trials*, vol. II, p. 75.
14 *Ibid.*, p. 76.
15 *Ibid.*, p. 80.
16 Kenyon, *op. cit.*, p. 61.
17 *State Trials*, vol. II, p. 84.
18 *Ibid.*, pp 85–6.

CHAPTER FOUR: PRINCE AND STATE

1 St John Fisher, St Thomas More, Queen Anne Boleyn and Queen Catherine Howard had all been imprisoned in the Tower before their executions under Henry VIII. The Plantagenet heir, Edward, Earl of Warwick, and the pretender Perkin Warbeck had been imprisoned in the Tower and executed by Henry VII. The two sons of Edward IV, the 'Princes in the Tower', were believed to have been murdered there by Richard III, and King Henry VI had undoubtedly been murdered in the Tower to secure Edward IV's tenure of the throne. King James I might well have echoed the sentiment which Shakespeare credited to the elder of the two doomed Princes: 'I do not like the Tower, of any place'. (*Richard III*, Act 3, Scene i)
2 The orator's original words were: 'Christus ... comminatur: "Ne homo separet quod Deus conjunxit". Paries intergerius inter haec duo regna, te reguante, Dei digito recessit ... non duo regna amplius, nec duos reges; non duos pastores, nec duos greges ... non duas regiones, nec duas religiones. Unus Rex, unus grex, una lex, et, ubi erat ab initio, una Albion. Omnia in uno Deo coelesti unum, omnia in uno Deo terrestri ("dixi vos deos" ait Scriptura) unum.' Nichols, vol. I, p. 331.
3 *Ibid.*, p. 320.
4 *Ibid.*, p. 321.
5 Arthur Wilson, *op. cit.*, p. 13.
6 *Basilikon Doron*, in McIlwain, *Political Works of James I*, p. 52.
7 Nichols, vol. I, pp. 358–9. The poetic name of Troynovant for London is thought to have been a corruption of 'Trinovant', the pre-Roman city of the Trinovantes. The form 'Troynovant', which suggests 'New Troy', may have been the origin of the English myth that London was founded by descendants of refugees from fallen Troy.
8 *Cit.*, Akrigg, p. 363.
9 'He loves the chase above all the pleasures of this world, living in the saddle for six hours on end....' M. de Fontenay's description of James VI of Scotland, 1585. *Cit.* Bingham, *James VI of Scotland*, p. 75.
10 The First Parliament of James I met on 19 March 1604 and was dissolved on 9 February 1611. The Second (or 'Addled') Parliament sat from 5 April to 7 June 1614. The third Parliament lasted from 30 January 1621 to 6 January

1622. The Fourth Parliament met on 19 February 1624, and was prorogued on 29 May 1624. It was dissolved by the King's death, on 27 March 1625.

11 Kenyon, *Stuart England*, p. 57.
12 The King's Speech, 19 March 1604, in McIlwain, *op. cit.*, p. 269.
13 *Ibid.*, pp 271–2.
14 *Ibid.*, p. 272.
15 *Ibid.*
16 Burns's re-working of an old song is the most familiar form of this sentiment:

What force or guile could not subdue,
  Thro' many warlike ages,
Is wrought now by a coward few,
  For hireling traitor's wages.
The English steel we could disdain,
  Secure in valour's station;
But English gold has been our bane
  Such a parcel of rogues in a nation.

However, if patriots believed that venal politicians had allowed their nation to be devoured by its neighbour, they would have been unjust in supposing that such a result had ever been the intention of King James VI and I. As Professor Gordon Donaldson has written in *Scotland: The Shaping of a Nation* (1974): 'The events of 1603 and 1707 were only two incidents in a long process, a process of which it is not easy to discern the beginning, and a process of which we have not yet seen the end.' (*op. cit.*, p. 59)

17 Bingham, *James VI of Scotland*, p. 140.
18 G.M. Trevelyan, *England under the Stuarts*, pp 96–7.
19 Akrigg, *op. cit.*, p. 367.
20 Tanner, *Constitutional Conflicts of the Reign of James I*, p. 30.
21 G.R. Elton, 'A High Road to Civil War?' in *From Renaissance to Counter-Reformation: Essays in honour of Garrett Mattingly*, pp 336–7.
22 *Ibid.*, p. 340.

CHAPTER FIVE: A TRAIN OF GUNPOWDER

1 Sir James Fergusson, 'The Last Monks at Crossraguel' in *The White Hind*, pp 54–66.
2 Bingham, *James VI of Scotland*, p. 82.
3 McIlwain, *Political Works of James I*, pp 275–6.
4 John Buxton, *Elizabethan Taste*, p. 28.
5 *His Majesties Speach in This Last Session of Parliament, etc.* (London, 1605) *cit.* Akrigg, pp 72–3.
6 Joel Hurstfield, *Gunpowder Plot and the Politics of Dissent*, in *Early Stuart Studies*, p. 98: 'Tresham is widely and I think correctly believed to have been the Writer of the Monteagle letter.'
7 Akrigg, *op. cit.*, p. 73.
8 Mathew, *James I*, p. 158.
9 The murder of David Riccio, for example, was carried out by Douglases, and

men connected with that family by marriage, *see* Bingham, *James VI of Scotland*, p. 15.

10 Mathew, *op. cit.*, p. 148.
11 Akrigg, *op. cit.*, p. 70.
12 McIlwain, *op. cit.*, pp 281ff.
13 Goodman, *Court of King James I*, vol. I, pp 106–7. On this matter, see also Hurstfield, *op. cit.*, pp 106–8.
14 There was a 'celebrated debate' (Hurstfield's phrase) between Father John Gerard (not to be confused with his seventeenth-century namesake) who wrote *What was the Gunpowder Plot?* (1897), and S.R. Gardiner, who replied with *What Gunpowder Plot Was.*
15 Mathew, *op. cit.*, p. 149.
16 Hurstfield, *op. cit.*, pp 109–10.

CHAPTER SIX: THE KING AND THE JESUITS

1 *State Trials*, vol. II, pp 233–4.
2 *Ibid.*, p. 247.
3 Akrigg, *op. cit.*, p. 76.
4 Bingham, *op. cit.*, pp 73, 113, 134, 136, 147–8.
5 Hurstfield, *op. cit.*, p. 103: Guy Fawkes 'had from the beginning prayed that he might perform that which might be for the advancement of the Catholic faith and saving of his own soul.' *cit.* H.M.C. Cal. Salisbury MSS, XVII, p. 479.
6 Bossy, 'The English Catholic Community, 1603–24' in *The Reign of James VI and I*, p. 93. The author of *A Theological Disputation Concerning the Oath of Allegiance* (1613) was the Benedictine Thomas Preston. He used the pseudonym 'Roger Widdrington', which was the name of a prominent Northumbrian Catholic gentleman.
7 James I, *A Premonition* ... in McIlwain, *op. cit.*, pp 122–4.
8 *Ibid.*, pp 124, 125.
9 Akrigg, *op. cit.*, pp 310–11.
10 James I, *An Apologie* ... in McIlwain, *op. cit.*, p. 76.
11 *Ibid.*
12 Mathew, *Jacobean England*, p. 11.

CHAPTER SEVEN: THE POISONED FOUNTAIN

1 Giovanni Carlo Scaramelli, Venetian Secretary in England, to the Doge and Senate, 23 May 1603, *CSP Venetian*, vol. X, p. 39.
2 James I, *A Counterblaste to Tobacco*, in Arber's *English Reprints*, No 19, p. 112.
3 *Ibid.*, p. 97.
4 *Cit.* Bingham, *op. cit.*, pp 150–1.
5 Stone, *The Crisis of the Aristocracy*, p. 665.
6 Westcott, *New Poems by James I of England*: 'A Complaint of his Mistressis Absense from Court' (Amatoria XVI), 'A Dreame on his Mistris My Ladie

Glammes' (Amatoria XVII) and possibly 'Constant Love in all Conditions' (Amatoria XIII), pp 10–12, 12–19 and 7.

7 *Ibid.* Miscellanea XLIX, p. 39.

8 *Ibid.* Note on poem classified as Miscellanea XLIX, p. 98. Westcott was enabled to make the identification by way of a 'Sonnet on the death of the Lady Cicely Weems, Lady of Tillebarne' by Sir David Murray of Gorty, published with his *Tragicall Death of Sophonisba*, in 1611. This poem made use of James's Cicely/Sicily conceit. Westcott supposed that James had borrowed it from Sir David Murray, but it seems to me that the reverse is the truth, because Murray's poem is a lament for the lady's death, and James's is not.

9 Birch, *Court and Times of James I*, vol. I, p. 92.

10 Harington, *Nugae Antiquae*, vol. I, p. 395.

11 Weldon, *Court and Character of King James*, (1651), pp 57–8.

12 *Ibid.*, pp 58–9.

13 Oglander, *A Royalist's Notebook*, p. 196.

14 Halliwell, *Letters of the Kings of England*, vol. I, p. 133.

15 Arthur Wilson, *op. cit.*, pp 76–7.

16 Akrigg, *op. cit.*, p. 173; *Cit.* Dietz, *Exchequer Receipts and Issues*, p. 168.

17 Osborn, *Traditional Memoirs*, p. 533.

18 *Ibid.*

19 Chamberlain to Carleton, *Chamberlain's Letters*, vol. I, p. 253.

20 Stone, *op. cit.*, provides the following interesting comments on this matter: 'Once rooted in the public mind, this association of sexual depravity with the court took a long time to wear off. At the trial of Stephen Colledge in 1681 the accused was charged that "Speaking of the King [Charles II], he said that he came of a race of buggerers, for his grandfather King James, buggered the old Duke of Buckingham [George Villiers]"', p. 668. And 'Some of the most characteristic features of the Puritan ethic, austerity in sex and drink, frugality in clothes and expenditure ... were responsible for exacerbating relations between Court and Country and thus dividing the peerage against itself.... This explains the increasingly obsessive, indeed at times pathological, character of the Country's attitude towards the immorality ... and extravagance of the Court.' p. 742

CHAPTER EIGHT: 'THIS EATING CANKER OF WANT'

1 Dietz, *English Public Finance 1558–1641*, p. 101.

2 Bingham, *op. cit.*, ch. II, note 12.

3 McIlwain, *op. cit.*, p. 46.

4 Dietz, *op. cit.*, p. 100; Kenyon, *Stuart England*, p. 54.

5 Akrigg, *op. cit.*, p. 87.

6 *Ibid.*, p. 156.

7 *Ibid.*, p. 89.

8 Goodman, *op. cit.*, vol. I, pp 308–9.

9 Osborn, *op. cit.*, p. 537.

10 Salisbury to Dirleton, 6 February 1606, *cit.* Mathew, *James I*, p. 162.

11 H.M.C. Cal. Salisbury MSS, vol. XVII, pp 122–3.

12 Osborn, *op. cit.*, p. 512.
13 *A Declaration, etc.*, (London, 1610), *cit.* Akrigg, *op. cit.*, p. 92.
14 Dietz, *op. cit.*, p. 121; Akrigg, *op. cit.*, p. 94.
15 Kenyon, *op. cit.*, p. 65.
16 *Ibid.*, p. 66.
17 Akrigg, *op. cit.*, p. 235.
18 *Ibid.*, p. 236.

CHAPTER NINE: 'THE EXPECTANCY AND ROSE OF THE FAIR STATE'

1 Cornwallis, 'The Life and Death of Prince Henry' in *Somers Tracts*, vol. II, p. 249.
2 *Ibid.*, pp 250–1.
3 *Ibid.*, p. 228.
4 Cornwallis, 'A Discourse of the Most Illustrious Prince Henry' in *Somers' Tracts*, vol. II, p. 224.
5 Cornwallis, 'Life and Death, etc.', *op. cit.*, p. 230.
6 Akrigg, *op. cit.*, p. 132.
7 Cornwallis, 'Discourse, etc.,' *op. cit.*, p. 220.
8 Jonson, 'An Exposultation with Inigo Jones' in *A Book of Masques*, p. 5.
9 Jonson, 'Oberon, The Fairy Prince', ll 253–60, in *ibid.*, p. 60.
10 Jonson, 'Oberon', ll 233–46, *ibid.*, pp 59–60.
11 Jonson, *Epigrammes XXXVI To the Ghost of Martial.*
12 Jonson, 'Oberon', ll 274–9, *ibid.*, pp 60–61.
13 '*Masque of Flowers*', ll 234–41, in *A Book of Masques*, p. 166.
14 B.M. Harl, MSS 642 ff 246–8, *cit.* Akrigg, *op. cit.*, p. 133.
15 Cornwallis, 'Life and Death', *op. cit.*, p. 231.
16 *Ibid.*, p. 232.
17 *Ibid.*, p. 233.
18 *Ibid.*, p. 234.
19 *Ibid.*, p. 235.
20 *Ibid.*, p. 251.

CHAPTER TEN: THE KING'S DAUGHTER

1 Wedgwood, *The Thirty Years' War*, p. 52.
2 Mathew, *op. cit.*, p. 193.
3 Wodrow, *Collections upon the Lives of the Reformers ... of the Church of Scotland*, vol. II, p. 27.
4 Wedgwood, *ibid.*
5 Mathew, *op. cit.*, p. 196.
6 Roger Coke, *A Detection of the Court and State of England*, vol. I, p. 64.
7 Wedgwood, *op. cit.*, p. 91.
8 Winwood, *Memorials*, vol. III, p. 404.
9 Mathew, *ibid.*
10 *Ibid.*
11 B.M. Harl, MSS 7003 f. 59, *cit.* Akrigg, *op. cit.*, p. 118.

CHAPTER ELEVEN: 'THE HEARTS OF KINGS ARE DEEP'

1 Gerald Eades Bentley in General Introduction to *A Book of Masques*, p. 3.
2 *Cit.* Akrigg, *op. cit.*, p. 182.
3 White, *Cast of Ravens*, p. 8.
4 B.M. Add. MSS 35832, *Cit.* White, *op. cit.*, p. 51.
5 Akrigg, *op. cit.*, p. 187.
6 Halliwell, *Letters of the Kings of England*, vol. II, pp 126–33.
7 *Cit.* Akrigg, *op. cit.*, p. 189.
8 Goodman, *op. cit.*, vol. I, pp 224–6.

CHAPTER TWELVE: POISON IN THE TOWER

1 Nichols, *Progresses*, vol. III, pp 81–2.
2 Lockyer, *Buckingham*, MS, p. 16.
3 There are several versions of this satirical poem: *Vide* Akrigg, *op. cit.*, pp 200–1; White, *Cast of Ravens*, p. 227. White gives further references: B.M. Add. MS 15476; B.M. Add. MSS 15227, f. 42v; and M.S. Rawlinson D 1048, f. 64. While the Earl of Somerset was unkindly treated by satirists, his wife could not have expected to avoid similar treatment. The following anonymous verse is but one example of the cruel mockery which her misdoings inspired:

On the Countess of Somerset
From Katherine's dock was launched a pink
Which sprung a leak, but did not sink.
From thence she drove to Essex shore,
Expecting rigging, yard, and store.
The like disaster to prevent,
With wind in poop, she sailed to Kent.
At Rochester she anchor cast,
Which Canterbury did distast[e].
But Winchester, with Ely's help,
Did hale on shore this lion's whelp.
She was crank-sided and did reel
To Somerset to mend her keel,
To stop her leak and scale her fort,
And make her fit for sea and port.

(MS Ashmole 38, f. 136).
4 *State Trials*, vol. I, p. 305.
5 White, *op. cit.*, pp 32–3.
6 Mathew, *op. cit.*, p. 214.
7 White, *op. cit.*, pp 132, 135.
8 B.M. MS Cott. Titus. C. VII, f. 108v, *cit.*, White, *op. cit.*, p. 77.
9 Akrigg, *op. cit.*, p. 200.
10 Weldon, *op. cit.*, p. 110.
11 *Cit.* White, *op. cit.*, p. 169.

12 *Ibid.*, p. 171.
13 *Ibid.*
14 *Ibid.*, p. 173.
15 Wilson, *op. cit.*, p. 83.
16 *Ibid.*
17 *Harleian Miscellany IX*, p. 560.

CHAPTER THIRTEEN: GOLDEN MIRAGES

1 *Anonymous Journal* in *Commons' Debates*, ed. Notestein, vol. II, p. 2.
2 Tanner, *Constitutional Documents*, p. 17.
3 Russell, 'Parliamentary History in Perspective, 1604–1629' in *History*, vol. 61 (1976), p. 9.
4 *Commons Journals*, vol. I, p. 506.
5 *Cit.* Kenyon, *Stuart England*, p. 37.
6 Carter, *Secret Diplomacy of the Hapsburgs 1598–1625*, p. 122.
7 Notably by Carter in *op. cit.*, and by Garrett Mattingly in *Renaissance Diplomacy*.
8 Middleton, *A Game at Chess*, Act V, Scene III.
9 Bingham, *op. cit.*, p. 101.
10 Carter, *op. cit.*, p. 123.
11 *Ibid.*, p. 133.
12 *Cit.* Ernest A. Stratmann, 'Ralegh [*sic*] Plans his Last Voyage' in *The Mariner's Mirror* (1964), pp 261–70.
13 Akrigg, *op. cit.*, p. 330.
14 Mathew, *op. cit.*, p. 263.

CHAPTER FOURTEEN: THE LAST FAVOURITE

1 *CSP Venetian*, 1617–19, pp 113–14.
2 Clarendon, *The History of the Rebellion*, ed. Macray, vol. I, p. 10.
3 Lucy Hutchinson, *Memoirs of Colonel Hutchinson*, p. 67.
4 Sir John Oglander's comment on James's demonstrative love of his favourites was quoted, in part, in chapter seven, *see* note 13. But Archbishop Mathew makes the point that 'the widespread knowledge of the King's weakness ... was not seen in these explicit terms in the court circle', *op. cit.*, p. 314. However, this point is arguable on the grounds that people do not comment upon what they see every day. Oglander, who was only slightly acquainted with King James, would be far more likely to express surprise at the King's 'great dalliance' with his favourites, than would a courtier who saw evidence of the King's loves more frequently.
5 Lockyer, *Buckingham*, MS p. 16.
6 Nichols, *Progresses*, vol. III, p. 309.
7 Chamberlain, *Letters*, vol. I, p. 649.
8 Nichols, *op. cit.*, vol. III, p. 373.
9 Mathew, *op. cit.*, p. 258.
10 Nichols, *ibid.*, pp 338–43.

11 Weldon, 'The Character of King James' in *op. cit.*, pp 164–75.
12 B.M. MS Sloane 1679, ff 42v–51v, *cit.* and trans. from original Latin by Macalpine and Hunter, *Porphyria: A Royal Malady*, pp 27–8.
13 *Ibid.*
14 *Cit.* Lockyer, MS p. 48.
15 Goodman, *op. cit.*, vol. II, p. 312.
16 Clarendon, *op. cit.*, vol. I, p. 12.
17 *Cit.* Lockyer, MS p. 42a.
18 Chamberlain, *op. cit.*, vol. II, p. 207.
19 Menna Prestwich, 'English Politics and Administration, 1603–25' in *The Reign of James I*, p. 154.
20 Kenyon, *op. cit.*, p. 77.
21 Mathew, *op. cit.*, p. 268.
22 Lockyer, MS p. 63.

CHAPTER FIFTEEN: 'GREAT COMBUSTIONS'

1 *Cit.* Akrigg, *op. cit.*, p. 225.
2 Halliwell, *Letters of the Kings of England*, vol. II, p. 246.
3 *Ibid.*, *passim.*
4 Nichols, *op. cit.*, vol. III, pp 484–5.
5 Lockyer, MS p. 28.
6 Wedgwood, *The Thirty Years War*, p. 66: 'The distinguishing mark of Utraquism ... was that the laity might receive the Communion in both kinds; otherwise it differed only in detail from Catholicism.'
7 Akrigg, *op. cit.*, p. 335.
8 Sir James Balfour's MSS: *Madam the Queen's Death and the Manner therof*, in *Abbotsford Miscellany*, p. 81.
9 *Vide supra*, p. 167.
10 *Cit.* D.H. Willson, *King James VI and I*, pp 403–4. In this verse the King was expressing an idea which was commonly accepted at this period. It is still familiar through Shakespeare's succinct expression of it in *Julius Caesar*, Act II, scene 2:

> When beggars die, there are no comets seen,
> The heavens themselves blaze forth the death of princes.

11 Wedgwood, *op. cit.*, p. 96.
12 Lockyer, MS p. 69.
13 Wedgwood, *op. cit.*, p. 104.
14 *Ibid.*, p. 112.
15 *Anonymous Journal*, in *Commons Debates*, vol. II, p. 2.
16 Lockyer, MS p. 75.
17 Gardiner, *op. cit.*, vol. IV, p. 105.
18 Aubrey, *Brief Lives*, ed. Lawson Dick, p. 120.
19 *Crumbs Fall'n from King James's Table* in *The Miscellaneous Works of Sir Thomas Overbury*, ed. E.F. Rimbault, p. 272.
20 *Cit.* Lockyer, MS p. 93.

21 Kenyon, *op. cit.*, p. 87.
22 Gardiner, *op. cit.*, vol. IV, p. 190.
23 *Ibid.*, vol. III, p. 338.
24 Mathew, *op. cit.*, p. 303.
25 Halliwell, *op. cit.*, vol. II, pp 159–60.

CHAPTER SIXTEEN: THE DORMITION OF SOLOMON

1 Halliwell, *op. cit.*, vol. II, pp 171–2.
2 Clarendon, *op. cit.*, vol. I, pp 21–2.
3 Halliwell, *op. cit.*, vol. II, pp 166–8.
4 Weldon, 'The Character of King James' in *op. cit.*, p. 166.
5 Maurice Ashley, *The House of Stuart*, p. 128.
6 Goodman, *op. cit.*, vol. I, pp 409–10.
7 Oglander, *A Royalist's Notebook*, p. 215.
8 Mathew, *op. cit.*, p. 296.
9 Halliwell, *op. cit.*, vol. II, pp 179–82.
10 *Cit.* Akrigg, *op. cit.*, p. 348.
11 Halliwell, *op. cit.*, vol. II, pp 207–8.
12 Rushworth, *Historical Collections*, p. 86.
13 Halliwell, *op. cit.*, vol. II, p. 227.
14 Lockyer, MS p. 113.
15 Gardiner, *op. cit.*, vol. V, p. 106.
16 Halliwell, *op. cit.*, vol. II, p. 229.
17 Lockyer, MS p. 168.
18 B.M. Harl. MSS 159, ff 10–12, *Cit.* Ruigh, *The Parliament of 1624*, pp 154–6.
19 Ruigh, *op. cit.*, pp 384–5.
20 Kenyon, *op. cit.*, p. 90.
21 Clarendon, *op. cit.*, vol. I, p. 28.
22 Gardiner, *op. cit.*, vol. V, pp 227–8.
23 Halliwell, *op. cit.*, vol. II, p. 236.
24 Lockyer, MS p. 249.

EPILOGUE: THE KING'S REPUTATION

1 Williams, *Great Britain's Salomon*, *cit.* Ashton, *James I by his Contemporaries*, pp 19–20. (The quotation *supra* omits the Biblical references which were inserted in the original text.)
2 Marc L. Schwarz, citing Russell, *The Crisis of Parliaments: English History 1509–1660*, p. 280.
3 Marc L. Schwarz, 'James I and the Historians', XIII, *Journal of British Studies* 2 (May 1974), p. 123.
4 Weldon, 'The Character of King James' in *op. cit.*, p. 171.
5 *Ibid.*
6 Wilson, *op. cit.*, pp 289–90.

Index